Enterprise Web 2.0
with EGL

Enterprise Web 2.0
with EGL

Ben Margolis

with Danny Allan

MC PRESS

MC Press Online, LP
Lewisville, TX 75077

Enterprise Web 2.0 with EGL
Ben Margolis with Danny Allan

First Edition

First Printing—May 2009

© 2009 Ben Margolis, All rights reserved

MC Press offers excellent discounts on this book when orderd in quantity for bulk purchases or special sales, which may include custom covers and content particular to your business, training goals, marketing focus, and branding interest.

For information regarding permissions or special orders, please contact:
MC Press
Corporate offices
125 N. Woodland Trail
Lewisville, TX 75077 USA

For information regarding sales and/or customer service, please contact:
MC Press
P.O. Box 4300
Big Sandy, TX 75755-4300 USA

ISBN: 978-158347-091-6

To Jeri Petersen

Contents

Preface ix
Our Presentation x
Acknowledgements xi

Part I. Overview

Chapter 1:   **Introduction** 3
Modes of Reliance on IT 3
    Support Mode 4
    Factory Mode 5
    Turnaround Mode 5
    Strategic Mode 6
IT as a Commodity 6
Software that Fulfills Its Role 7
Software that Enables a Competitive Advantage 8
    Web 2.0 8
    Service-Oriented Architecture 12
Grow Your Software 15
    Agile Development 16
    The Importance of Abstraction
        in a Computer Language 18
    The Importance of Wide Coverage
        by a Computer Language 25
Accentuate the Negative 25
    Are Enterprise Languages Disruptive? 26
    Do Enterprise Languages Inhibit Innovation? 26
    Do Enterprise Languages Have Flaws
        Caused by Higher Abstraction? 27
    Are Enterprise Languages Old News? 28

Chapter 2: **Web 2.0** **29**
Interactive Web Sites 29
 Networks 29
 Collaboration 35
 Brand Image 36
 Revenue 37
 Owning and Extending Data 39
Rich Internet Applications 39

Chapter 3: **Introduction to Web Security** **45**
Security Trends 45
Threats by Type 46
Security by Location 47
 Data in Transit 47
 Server-Side Security 55
 Client-Side Security 58
Use of an LDAP-Compliant Server 60
Security for a Rich Internet Application 60
 Web Servers and Application Servers 61
 Container-Managed Authentication 62
 Security Options 63
Risk 65
 Assessing Risk 65
 Responding to Risk 66

Chapter 4: **Service-Oriented Architecture** **69**
Structure of a Service-Oriented Application 69
Aspects of a Service 70
 Service Implementation 70
 Elementary Access Details 71
 Contract 71
Loose Coupling 72
Service Registry 74
Service Level Agreement 74
Web and Binary-Exchange Services 75
Architectural Styles in Web Services 76

Traditional RPC-Style SOAP Services 77
REST Services 78
REST-RPC Services 79

Part II. Web 2.0 Solutions with EGL

Chapter 5:   **EGL Scope** **83**
Uses of EGL 83
Supported Technologies 85
Runtime Environment 85
Persistent Data Storage 87
User Interface 89
Support for Service-Oriented Architecture 91
Network Communication 93
Report Production 93
Integration with Existing Code 94
Integrating Multiple Products that Support EGL 95

Chapter 6:   **EGL Rich UI in Context** **97**
Multiple Tiers 97
Support for Old and New Programming Models 98
The DOM Tree 99
Rich UI Handler 104
Rich UI Editor 107
Embedded Handlers 109
Service access 110
Use of Libraries 112
Model, View, Controller 112
MVC in EGL Rich UI 113
Validating Form 116
Validators 117
Form Validation, Commit, and Publish 118
Defining Displayable Text in an External File 119
Simulating Page Flow 120

Switching Pages in the Simplest Case 123
Switching Pages and Updating the Address Bar 124
Handler Communication with Infobus 127

Chapter 7:   **Services and EGL Rich UI** **131**
CICS Web Services 131
Access of IBM i Programs as Web Services 133
End-to-End Processing 133
EGL Projects and Deployment 134
Example of End-to-End Processing 135
EGL Deployment Descriptor 136
Service Client Bindings 137
Web Service Deployment 137
How Do You Set the Location Data for Service Access? . . 137
Access of SOAP Services 138
Access of EGL REST Services 139
Access of Third-Party REST Services 139
What is the Location for an EGL-Generated Service? 141

Part III. Programming with EGL

Chapter 8:   **Overview of Generation** **145**
EGL Compilation 146
EGL Build 147
EGL Generation 147

Chapter 9:   **Language Organization** **149**
Data Types 149
Categories of EGL Data Types 151
Data Item 152
Record Part 153
Dictionary Part 156
Data table 158

Logic Parts 159
   Categories of EGL Logic Parts 161
   Program Within a Run Unit 161
   Library 162
   Service 163
   Handler 165
Prototype Parts 165
   Categories of EGL Prototype Parts 165
   Interface Part 166
   ExternalType Part 167
   Delegate Part 167
User Interface Parts 169
   Form Part 169
   FormGroup part 170
Annotations 170
Stereotypes 173
Set-Value Blocks 174
Packages 176
Use Statement 179

Chapter 10: **Runtime Values** **181**
Constants 181
Variables 182
   Using the New Operator 184
   Using a Set-Value Block with a Reference Variable . . . 185
Arrays 186
   Array Literals 186
   Dynamic Arrays 186
   Structure-Field Arrays 188
Assigning One Variable to Another 189
   Value Variable to a Value Variable 189
   Value Variable to a Reference Variable 189
   Reference Variable to a Reference Variable 191
   Reference Variable to a Value Variable 194
   Assigning a Record that Includes a Reference Field . . . 196
   Adding a Record to an Array of Records 197
Expressions 199

Name Resolution in Expressions 200
Assignment and Reference Compatibility 202
Static and Dynamic Access 202

Chapter 11:   **EGL System Resources** **207**
EGL Statements 207
Code Documentation 208
Data Assignment 209
Conditional Processing 211
Loop Control 213
Transfer of Control Within a Program 214
Transfer of Control Out of a Program 216
System Libraries 217
Exception Handling 218
Propagation 221
Exception Fields 222

Chapter 12:   **Files and Relational Databases** **225**
Logical Unit of Work 225
Data-Access Statements 226
File Access 227
File Names and Resource Associations 228
Resource Associations Part 228
ResourceAssociation Field 229
Escape Character 229
Support for Relational Databases 230
Insertion and Retrieval 230
Implicit and Explicit SQL Statements 231
Open and ForEach 233
Dynamic Arrays of SQL Records 235
Exception Handling 237

Chapter 13:   **Reporting** **239**
Support for BIRT Reports 239
Initial Access of the BIRT Report Engine 240

BIRT Handler 241
Support for EGL Text Reporting 243

Chapter 14: **JavaServer Faces** **249**
Introduction to JSF 249
EGL JSF and EGL Rich UI 251
EGL JSF Handler 251
Development Example 253
Generation Outputs 258
Binding a Web-Page Field to a Variable or Function . . 259
EGL JSF in Context 260
Frameworks 261
View 262
JSF Life Cycle 265

Appendix A: **Sources of Information** **271**
EGL and Rich UI 271
MC Press 271
Eclipse and BIRT 272
JavaServer Faces 272

Appendix B: **EGL Rich UI Widgets** **273**
Styles 273
Widget Types by Category 276
Container Widgets 277
Common Fields 278
Box 278
Div 279
FloatLeft 280
FloatRight 281
Grouping 283
Information Widgets 284
Grid 284
HTML 287
Image 288

Shadow 289
Span 290
TextLabel 291
Tree 291
Interactive Widgets 293
BidiTextArea 293
BidiTextField 293
Button 293
CheckBox 294
Combo 295
Hyperlink 296
List 297
ListMulti 297
Menu 299
PasswordTextField 302
RadioGroup 302
TextArea 303
TextField 304
Hover Widgets 305
GridTooltip 305
Tooltip 307
TreeTooltip 309
Fields available in most widgets 310

Endnotes **313**

Preface

Sometimes, you need a subtle insight to see the way forward. For instance, when electricity became available in the mid-1800s, many companies saw the technology simply as a way to support the business processes that had been in use for generations.[1]

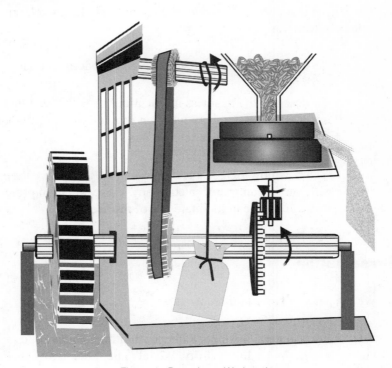

Figure 1: Powering a Workstation

These companies used a central power source to run the plant's equipment. In earlier times, the source was a water wheel; in later times, an electric generator. In both periods, the transfer of power occurred by way of physical motion, "by an elaborate system of pulleys and gears."[2] (Figure 1.)

The way forward required an insight into how to use electricity to maximum effect. "By wiring their plants and installing electric motors in their machines, [smart manufacturers] were able to dispense with the cumbersome, inflexible, and costly gearing systems, gaining an important efficiency advantage over their slower-moving competitors."[3]

The introduction of software in the last half-century has been similar to the introduction of electricity. Both technologies were able to support a company's older processes and made possible new ways to respond to the marketplace. Both technologies benefited early adopters and were later required by companies in general. Both were most effective when they helped a company to fulfill its mission flexibly.

The aim of this book is to show a way forward in the development of enterprise software:

- To explore the place of software in a modern company

- To describe the business implications of *Web 2.0*, which is a set of innovative techniques that provide for the collaborative use of the Internet

- To show how EGL—a technology used to create enterprise software—can protect a company's investment in pre-existing software and can facilitate use of the Web

Our Presentation

We present our story in three parts.

Part I is for a general business audience and focuses on issues of software, business economics, and security. We talk about the use of abstraction in software and why the issue matters, but we don't bore you. Okay, we don't bore you *much*. And if you've ever wondered why social Web sites like Facebook and Twitter accommodate users without charge, or what a digital signature is, you'll be glad to have given us a little time. The later chapters have more technical detail than do the earlier ones, but we give the non-technical reader a sense of the issues addressed.

Part II is primarily for software professionals. We tell the scope of EGL. We also show how the language lets you develop software that can access data from decades-old applications *and* from the latest sources on the Web.

Part III is for developers and students. We assume only a semester of computer science as we describe the main constructs of EGL, from data types to array processing, from database access to reporting. Most of this material was first published in *IBM Rational Business Developer with EGL*, which is replaced with the current work.

Our intent throughout is to tell a story as if speaking to a friend who's in a hurry.

Acknowledgements

Many people came through. Ralph Earle continues to be an insightful editor, and Orly Margolis's illustrations and day-to-day assistance were essential.

Thanks to Brian Svihovec, Chris Laffra, and Alex Schaffer for sharing their knowledge of Internet technology; and to Joe Vincens, Mark Evans, and Dan Bruce for clarifying the ways of services. Paul Hoffman and Alice Connors are gracious and precise, as is Jing Qian. And thanks to those who provided a new direction: Todd Britton, Jonathan Sayles, Tim Wilson, and Albert Ho, with a nod to Will Smythe and Michael Connor and a grin to Scott Pecnik.

Special mentions go to the consultants from afar: Scott Ambler, Jack Mason, Luis Suarez, Marc van Zadelhoff, Marie Wieck, Nicholas Carr, W. Brian Arthur, Paul A. David, Dean Paizis, and the folks at IBM business partner Morpheus Limited.

Cheers as always to Hayden Lindsey, Susan LaFera, and Bob Cancilla.

And thanks to fellow gremlins: Debra Taylor, Lewis Shiner, Susan Peich, Laura Willey, Brenda Roy, Jane Revak, Tim McMackin, Gary Makely, and Michael B. Schwartz.

Understand this: Annette Taylor is a fine rewriter; and Mike, a fine reviewer.

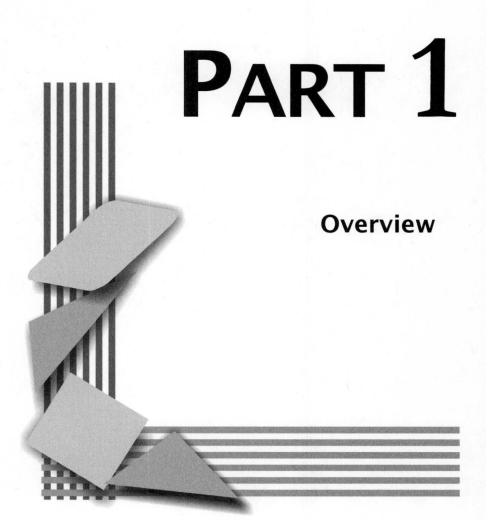

PART 1

Overview

CHAPTER 1

Introduction

If you are overseeing a budget for information technology (IT), you are probably being cautious, and for good reason. At this writing, the economic downturn is global and severe, the worst since the Great Depression. When you review your company's need for software in light of financial constraint, you'll likely ask, "How do we minimize change, and how do we better handle the change that is unavoidable?"

Your answer depends on the importance of new software in your company's operation. For example, a firm that uses only long-standing applications might place a moratorium on new software development. In the opposite case, a firm that differentiates itself by adding new function might upgrade systems immediately. The use of software for differentiation might involve any of several benefits such as improved internal processes, better exchange of data with suppliers, or a more compelling outreach to potential customers.

We'll review the extent to which different companies rely on software. We use a set of categories—*modes of reliance*—to suggest how your company might respond to the current situation.[1]

Modes of Reliance on IT

To categorize the different ways that a company uses IT, analysts Nolan and McFarlan suggest a grid whose axes represent first, "how much [a] company relies on ... smoothly operating technology systems" and second, "how much

[a] company relies on IT for its competitive edge."[2] We illustrate the four modes of reliance and describe them in relation to software (Figure 1.1).

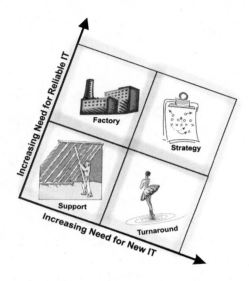

Figure 1.1: Modes of Reliance on IT

Support Mode

A company in support mode uses software defensively to help employees fulfill activities that are internal to the company. The company accepts relatively poor online performance and uses manual processes as needed to make up for deficiencies in automated systems. The systems are not for customers or suppliers.

A clothing manufacturer that handles its own design, production, and distribution might be in support mode. In this case, developers focus on maintainence, and the guiding principle for IT personnel is "Don't waste money."[3]

If your company is in support mode, consider incremental changes that add value, along with pilot projects that give your company experience in software technologies that might be of interest in the future.

Factory Mode

A company in factory mode also uses software defensively, but in this case the software is fast and reliable and is central to operational success, much as a set of conveyor belts is central to a manufacturing plant. "If the ... belts fail, production stops."[4]

For example, an airline that has a sophisticated reservation system is in factory mode. Customers and suppliers access the system, and the guiding principle for IT is "Don't cut corners."[5]

If your company is in factory mode, consider adopting innovations that are proven and that respond to a specific need. "Typically, factory-mode organizations are not interested in being the first to implement a new technology, but their top management... monitor[s] the competitive landscape for any change that would require a more aggressive use of IT."[6]

Turnaround Mode

A company in turnaround mode is on offense, retaining old systems for a time, but upgrading to a considerably new level of software for "major process and service improvements, cost reductions, and a competitive edge."[7]

An insurance firm might be in turnaround mode when implementing an online system to address customers directly. The new effort is an expensive gamble, and the guiding principle is "Don't fail."

Almost any company must consider how to protect its current investment in software. However, if your company is in turnaround mode, you need to be particularly concerned with limiting the company's vulnerability. *Enterprise modernization* implies both technological upgrades and the integration of pre-existing systems.

A firm in turnaround mode often makes changes so profound that even temporary reversion to manual systems is not possible. The firm moves either to factory mode or to a state of continual upgrade, as described next.

Strategic Mode

A company in strategic mode is nearly always on offense and requires that systems be highly reliable even during innovation.

An example company is a defense contractor that receives components for ever-changing equipment from multiple locations and then assembles the product within days. The component-integration software requires continual upgrade, and the project-management software requires attention, too.

The guiding principle is "Spend as needed, and monitor results intently." If your company is in strategic mode, you'll want to retain the option of using the full range of capabilities provided by a given technology, and you want to have the flexibility of using additional technologies in the future.

IT as a Commodity

Our educated guess is that the majority of large- and medium-size companies in the industrial world are—or soon will be—in factory mode. Our guess is educated by the likes of analyst Nicholas Carr, who writes as follows: "By now, the core functions of IT—data storage, data processing, and data transport—have become available and affordable.... They are becoming costs of doing business that must be paid by all but provide distinctions to no one."[8]

Carr argues that IT is following the lead of other infrastructure technologies such as railroad transport and electric generation, which provide economic value by virtue of being shared rather than being wholly proprietary. For example, little wealth would have been created by miles of one-company track laid only to transport material to specific suppliers and customers. The greater wealth came from miles of shared and standardized track.

The later equivalent of either transit on a rail or electricity on a grid is data on a network.

For Carr, IT is becoming a commodity like the older technologies. Even a short-term lack of electric power can weaken a company, yet the presence of electricity gives no one firm a competitive advantage. Similarly, even a short-term need for manual processes can weaken a company in factory or strategic mode, yet traditional types of automation do not offer a competitive advantage to any one firm.

Whether IT is best seen as a commodity, companies will continue to spend much on information technology. In relation to business logic, a prudent manager asks

- How do we gain access to inexpensive software that fulfills its role?

- Is it still possible to gain a competitive advantage even as we defend ourselves against disruption?

Software that Fulfills Its Role

A company seeks software that has three characteristics: high quality; sufficient longevity; and reasonable cost:

- Software is of high quality if it fulfills the business need well. Measurement of quality includes minimal errors, an appropriately quick response to a single invocation, and (as necessary) an appropriately quick response to simultaneous invocations.

  Interactive software additionally requires ease of use; attractiveness; and increasingly, some of the user-centered function available in Web 2.0.

- Software is of sufficient longevity if it can remain in service despite external changes of at least three kinds: business-process change, as may result (for example) from a merger or from new government regulation; business-data change, as may result from a social development like the need to store email addresses; and technical change—for example, change in operating systems, databases, connectivity software, and interface devices.

- Software is of reasonable cost if it is inexpensive to purchase, to license, or to develop and maintain, in comparison to the cost of fulfilling the automated task in some other way.

If a company writes software, the development effort must contribute to the company's long-term success rather than draining resources. The test of economic viability is always present, perhaps now more than ever.

Software that Enables a Competitive Advantage

Strategists John Seely Brown and John Hagel respond to Carr's statement that IT offers less competitive advantage than in previous years: "Significant opportunities for innovation continue to occur because advances in IT create possibilities not previously economically available.... Companies have tended to think too narrowly. In particular, many companies have become locked into the view that IT can reduce transaction costs but then think of transaction costs as encompassing only the transfer of... data from one place to another. Viewed more broadly, transaction costs encompass such challenging business issues as the creation of meaning, the building of trust, and the development and dissemination of knowledge. These dimensions of transaction costs often represent significant bottlenecks to performance improvements and competitive advantage."[10]

In the next sections, we introduce two areas (perhaps familiar ones) that enable competitive advantage: Web 2.0 and service-oriented architecture.

Web 2.0

The World Wide Web is an Internet subsystem that provides access to more than "a trillion unique" pages.[13] The Web also provides access to software services that offer data and functionality for many purposes, as described later.

The public-domain Web dates from 1993, when pages were already viewable.[14] From the mid-1990s, people have been responding to input forms, but early users didn't collaborate with one another online.

The essential Web technology is largely unchanged, but changes in practice and in related technologies now let users update pages, build and access services that provide enterprise data, and run browser-based software that has the look and feel of desktop applications.

The phrase *Web 2.0* became popular in 2004.[15] We use it to mean the sum of Web capabilities that are available to companies in 2009.

Web 2.0 has two aspects outside of services: interactive Web sites and Rich Internet Applications.

Interactive Web Sites. In general, a *Web site* is a collection of pages retrievable from an Internet domain—for example, www.ibm.com—or is a defined subset of those pages such as the IBM Rational Cafés (www.ibm.com/rational/cafe). The pages are *served*—that is, transmitted—from a *Web server*, which is specialized software that, in most cases, runs on a machine remote from the user.

Here is a list of Web site features that are new in Web 2.0:

- *Blog*—a journal for expressing opinions or experiences and for displaying responses that are entered online. The word *blog* is derived from from the phrase *Web log*.

- *Wiki*—a page set where users can edit a large percentage of the content.

- *Social site*—a multiperson journal with access rules that allow a given user to share text and possibly multimedia content with a subset of other users.

- *Virtual world*—an imagined location (or simulation of a real one) that in most cases is shared in real time with other users. A given user controls the behavior of an *avatar*, which is a graphical representation of the user. A virtual world is used for social interaction and for multiperson games.

Web site facilities can include:

- *Instant messaging*—a stream of text shared between two or more users.

- *Really Simple Syndication (RSS) feed*—a mechanism for providing content updates on an ongoing basis so that users can retrieve those updates according to the users' schedules. Some users aggregate the input with feeds from other sources for re-display at another Web site.

- *Tagging*—a means of assigning keywords to units of information such as articles, photos, and videos so as to categorize those units for later retrieval, including retrieval by other users and by software.

- *Social bookmarking*—a means of saving a Web address for future use. Users can now tag Web addresses as they tag other units of information, for retrieval by other users and by software.

- *Profiles*—biographies for Web site contributors, including people represented on social sites.

- *Cross-site integration*—a relationship between Web sites such that an input at one can affect another. For example, a user at a blog may click an icon to indicate that a given article is worthy. The user's keystroke affects a ranking of articles at a second Web site, where units of information are organized by subject and relative popularity.

Here are benefits of interactive Web sites:

- Faster collaboration in pursuit of a business goal

- Improved brand image

- Increased revenue

We describe these benefits in Chapter 2.

Rich Internet Applications. A Rich Internet Application (RIA) is a Web-based application that runs in a browser. The RIA has greater function than a traditional Web site, providing the visual and interactive characteristics of a desktop application.

An RIA allows for a user experience that goes beyond simply receiving a page and submitting a form. For example, after a user clicks a radio button, the code might respond by changing the content of a textbox (Figure 1.2).

Figure 1.2: Client-Side Processing

The change occurs quickly because the logic runs locally. This client-side processing is in contrast to server-side processing, which involves forming a page on the Web server and transmitting that page to the browser (Figure 1.3).

Figure 1.3: Server-Side Processing

Server-side processing often involves the download of multiple pages. The client-side approach lessens the load on the server-side machine and reduces the need for hardware.

The RIA technology described in this book relies on Asynchronous JavaScript and XML (AJAX). AJAX permits the runtime invocation of remote code and the subsequent update of all of a Web page or a section of the page. For example, after the user selects a purchase order from a list box, the RIA might request transmission of order-item details from the remote Web server and then place those details in a table displayed to the user (Figure 1.4).

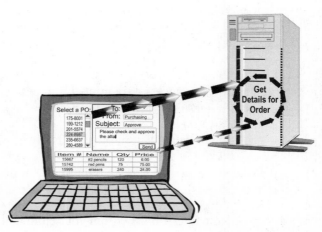

Figure 1.4: Use of AJAX in a Rich Internet Application

As shown, the user can continue working elsewhere on the page. However, a further aspect of data-transfer technology is that the user may not even notice that time elapsed between specifying one detail—in this case, an order number—and receiving a response.

Here are economic benefits of Rich Internet Applications:

- Increased user efficiency

- Faster application development from multiple sources on the Web

- Easier software distribution

- Reduced need for server-side hardware

- Increased responsiveness on an intranet

We further describe the benefits of RIAs in Chapter 2.

Service-Oriented Architecture

A second area that enables competitive advantage is service-oriented architecture (SOA).[16] SOA is a way of organizing software and involves the deployment of more-or-less independent logical units called *services*, each of which

- Handles a business process such as calculating an insurance quote or distributing email, or handles a relatively technical task such as accessing a database, or provides business data and the technical details needed to construct a graphical interface.

- Can access another service and, with the appropriate runtime technology, can access a traditional program and respond to different kinds of requesters—for example, to a Web application.

- Is relatively independent of other software so that changes to a requester require few or no changes to the service, while changes to the internal logic of a service require few or no changes to the requester. This relative independence is called *loose coupling*.

A service can handle interactions within your company, as well as between your company and its suppliers and customers.

SOA implies a style of development, with concern for the business as a whole and with an increased focus on modularity and reuse. SOA isn't only for new code, though. Migration of existing applications is especially appropriate in the following cases:

- The applications are monolithic, combining the logic of user interface, business processing, and data access, with update of one kind of logic requiring your company to test multiple kinds of behavior.

- The applications are hard to understand—first, because the logic is monolithic, but second, because logic was repeatedly patched rather than rewritten as requirements changed. Updates take extra time as developers try to decipher the logic, and as the complexity grows, additional errors accompany updates.

- The application inventory has duplicate logic. Requests for change are unnecessarily disruptive, requiring changes in several places.

From the developer's point of view, a change to a service orientation is primarily a change in emphasis, and many aspects of the development task are unaffected.

Business Implications of SOA

SOA has several important implications for business. First, when each component is a relatively standalone unit, your company can respond to business or technological changes more quickly and with less expense and confusion.

In general, a company's ability to respond quickly and well to change is known as *agility*. The main promise of service-oriented architecture is that a well-crafted SOA will increase agility over time.

SOA also has an important effect on how people work together. Aside from the most technical services, a well-written service is *coarse-grained*, meaning that the area of concern is broad enough so that business people can understand the purpose of the service even if they know little about software. To the extent that a collection of coarse-grained services handles your company's business procedures, the firm's business analysts and software professionals can share information knowledgeably, can include end users in early deliberations about the purpose and scope of each service, and can understand all the implications of changing a business procedure. Ease of human communication is an important benefit of SOA and suggests that the architecture will become the primary organizing principle for business processing.

Also, well-designed services are more likely to be reusable. Your company benefits from reuse in at least two ways: first, by avoiding the expense of developing new software, and second, by increasing the reliability of the software inventory over time. The firm can do less extensive testing if an existing service is placed in a new application, in comparison to the testing required to deploy software that was written from scratch.

Last, SOA lets companies make business processes and data more widely available. For example, imagine agents at an insurance company sitting at workstations and invoking a mainframe process to quote insurance prices for specific customers. In response to competitive pressure, the company now wants customers to request quotes on the Web, which traditionally has no direct link to a mainframe. What is necessary before the company can accept personal data from a browser, run the data through analytic software on the mainframe, and respond to the customer? The solution includes developing new services to handle the interaction of browser and analytic software. The business implication is a more modern process, with expanded markets.

The State of SOA

In February 2009, InformationWeek reported on "the state of SOA," saying that "many companies are moving forward with SOA implementations," and that a far larger number of implementers were satisfied with the results than were unsatisfied. Of interest is that the surveyed companies tended to use a technology called Representational State Transfer (REST), which requires less administration than do the technologies that were popular in the early years of SOA.[17] Chapter 4 gives further details on the technical issues.

A month earlier, Computer Economics reported a "surge" in SOA deployments in 2008, with 58% of surveyed organizations reporting at least some service orientation. Also, "organizations are reporting very positive returns on their SOA investments." The overall message was that SOA really *is* becoming the primary organizing principle for business processing.[18]

SOA and Cloud Computing

Cloud computing is an emerging business model for acquiring or delivering IT capabilities from a *cloud*, which is a term that can refer either to the Internet or to whatever computers are available from a user's access device.[19]

A cloud can comprise hundreds of thousands of machines, along with the software that makes complex processing possible across machine boundaries. The machines sometimes fulfill the requirements of *grid computing*: they work together as a smaller set of virtual machines or perhaps even as one machine. In light of the quantity of data now available, scientists are using clouds to answer questions that require enormous processing power.[20]

For general uses, a single machine in the cloud often runs software that simulates the presence of multiple, virtual machines, each assigned to a different application or customer. Cloud computing in this sense involves IT capabilities that are offered remotely on a flexible, as-needed basis; for example, resource capacity such as data storage, platform function such as that needed to test software, and business services such as those needed to manage sales-contact data. The user is not aware of the source of a given capability.

An industry focus is on developing power-management technology to minimize energy use in the data centers where the physical machines are located.[21]

The movement to cloud computing does not diminish a service orientation; instead, a service orientation enables an easier migration of business software to whatever machine configurations will be in effect.

Grow Your Software

We've introduced two areas that enable competitive advantage: Web 2.0 and SOA. We'll now return to the question of how to develop inexpensive software that fulfills the need of a modern enterprise.

In 1987, Frederick Brooks advised use of an organic approach to software development. "Grow, don't build," he said. The details of a modern system "are too complicated to be specified accurately in advance, and too complex to be built faultlessly." He also noted that an iterative process increased developer productivity: "Enthusiasm jumps when there is a running system, even a simple one. Efforts redouble when the first picture from a new graphics software system appears on the screen, even if it is only a rectangle. One always has, at every stage in the process, a working system.... Teams can *grow* much more complex entities in four months than they can build."[22]

Let's consider how best to grow software (Figure 1.5).

Figure 1.5: Botany

Agile Development

Agile development is a philosophy of software creation that addresses the need for fast completion of work in the face of changing requirements. The basic idea is as follows:

- Rely on the active participation of managers, developers, and users to ensure that the work fulfills business requirements and technical best practices.

- Establish milestones at which interested parties review a growing application, analyze past experience, and make changes to the design. The emphasis is on developing working code at each stage.

- Use extensive code tests to ensure quality.

- Improve the allocation of personnel resources by minimizing the following three factors: specialization among developers, organizational hierarchy, and documentation.

- Use a collegial approach to project governance; that is, for establishing rules, standards, and measurements and for enforcing those rules. "For example, the traditional approach to coding guidelines [is] to create them and then enforce their usage through formal inspections. [The agile way is] to write the guidelines collaboratively with your programmers, explain why it is important for everyone to adopt the guidelines, and then provide tooling and support to make it as easy as possible for developers to follow those guidelines."[23]

Surveys indicate that, in many cases, agile development provides better results in comparison to traditional methodologies.[24]

We should also note the value of *prototyping*—creating code that demonstrates intended functionality but that lacks required features such as error handling or database access. "The hardest single part of building a software system is deciding precisely what to build..... For the truth is, the client does not know what he wants."[25]

Prototyping has value, even in a time of agile development, because making fundamental changes to deliverable software increases errors and hinders performance, requiring work that might be avoided by use of a prototype.[26]

Last, we want to emphasize the importance of thinking about software development in relation to the business process being supported. John Brown and John Hagel III advise "short-term (often 6- to 12-month) operating initiatives designed to test and refine specific innovations in business practices." A long-term vision is required in that the work must be consistent with a strategic view of the firm's long-term capabilities and markets. However, the short-term operational focus protects the company. "If done right, these innovations can reduce the financial risks by generating near-term returns that can help fund subsequent waves of operating initiatives."[11]

Agile development helps make these kind of initiatives successful.

The Importance of Abstraction in a Computer Language

We now consider abstraction, which is a word that seems to make eyes glaze over. We hope our overview is useful even for readers who are familiar with the issues raised.

To abstract is to consider a general category rather than the related specific; for example, to think of "a number" rather than "50." The ability to abstract is central to software design, allowing us to create a set of operations—a general process. For example, the operations needed to convert fahrenheit to celsius are as follows: deduct 32, multiply by 5, and divide by 9. Whether the input is 50 or 100 is not important in defining the process, which is independent of any particular input or output. The process named "convert temperature" is a higher-level abstraction because it uses "number," a lower-level one.

To abstract is also to focus on a composition rather than on its elements. The record "employee record" is a higher-level abstraction than any of the constituent data items such as "employee number" or "salary." Similarly, the process "update the employee record" is a higher-level abstraction than any of the constituent steps such as "display the old record" or "store the new data."

A higher-level abstraction lets us hide details. A travel agent who clicks a button to convert 50° fahrenheit to 10° celsius is not focusing on the arithmetic. The agent uses the automated process to do the conversion quickly and without drudgery and—more to the point—to focus on issues related to a business process such as advising a traveler. A clerk who seeks to "update the employee record" is similarly focused on the business implications of the process, not on the technical details.

An abstraction such as "employee record" helps us to think clearly and to comunicate quickly, leading to better decisions, execution, and collaboration.

Let's review the historical trend toward greater abstraction and note the effect of that trend on software quality, longevity, and cost.[27]

Machine-Specific Coding with 1s and 0s

At first, programmers coded statements in 1s and 0s in a form ultimately called *machine language*. A specific series of digits was appropriate only for a specific kind of hardware such as the first UNIVAC computer (1951).

Our review of three factors suggests the economic viability of software development during this period:

- Quality measurements were specific to the machine type and mostly involved memory usage and processing speed. Code development was prone to error, and resolution of those errors was difficult and time-consuming.

- Longevity was limited in the sense that a program worked only as long as the program ran on a particular machine type.

- Cost was high not only because hardware was expensive, but because development was done only by computer scientists, and much work was required to cause even a small change to the logic.

Machine-Specific Coding with Assembly Language

The change to assembly language meant that programmers now wrote statements in a syntax that provided greater abstraction. For example, the following statement copied data from an area named DX to an area named AX.

```
MOV AX, DX
```

The instructions were represented by mnemonics such as MOV and were accompanied by references to named data areas such as AX and DX. The programmer's task was first, to create an assembly-language program, and second, to use that program as input to an *assembler*, which was a new industrial tool: a logical unit that transformed each assembly-language statement into a number of machine-language instructions.

Here are details on economic viability:

- Quality improved. The scheme hid details from the programmer, who was able to think more clearly about the coding task. Errors were fewer and more easily fixed. Companies could now automate business-related tasks such as storing inventory details.

- Longevity improved because a change from one hardware version to the next tended to require little or no change to the assembly language, even when details in the machine language changed.

- Cost was lowered because writing and changing a program took less time than before.

The increase in economic viability gives a first example of an important rule: *increasing abstraction has economic value*.

Machine-Independent Coding with Third-Generation Languages

The emergence of third-generation languages represented a further increase in abstraction. For example, the following COBOL statement converts fahrenheit to celsius and is equivalent to hundreds of assembly-language statements.

```
COMPUTE CELSIUS = (FAHRENHEIT - 32) * 5 / 9.
```

Third-generation language statements began with English-language terms such as COMPUTE and were accompanied by references to data areas whose names—such as CELSIUS—were meaningful in a business context. The programmer used source code as input to a *compiler*, a tool that transformed each statement into thousands of machine-specific instructions; that is, into the 1s and 0s required by the hardware.

Here are details on the three factors:

- Quality continued to improve. Business applications became more sophisticated in relation to computation and storage. User interfaces were integrated into business processes, increasing productivity.

  Coding errors decreased as a result of writing only a few instructions to fulfill a task that previously required far more. A new tool—the *source-code debugger*—helped programmers find errors even as the human focus remained primarily on the business application, with analysis of computer memory of less importance over time.

  The coding task became clearer to the business analysts who were working with programmers. People whose primary credential was business knowledge could now write applications.

  On the negative side, "the early compilers occasionally introduced errors" during compilation.[28] Also, the compiled output fulfilled its task slowly in comparison to the speed of assembled code. When faster processing was required, programmers continued to rely on assembly language.

To some extent, those negatives were handled by improvements in technology. However, the speed issue reminds us of the importance of economic tradeoffs. Use of the third-generation languages made sense even in the face of less-than optimal performance because programmers were expensive—their efficiency mattered greatly— while the cost of machine time was increasingly inexpensive.

•   Longevity improved because business applications could be *ported*— retargeted to a machine of a different type.

Porting is especially easy for programs written in Java. A Java programmer wrote source code and used it as input to an *interpreter*, which created an output that was intermediate between the source code and the compiled code. The interpreted output was then made available to a *virtual machine*, a type of software that itself offered increased abstraction: the internal processing was specific to one or another runtime platform, but the external purpose was everywhere the same. The technology allowed the same Java program to run as is, on a wide variety of platforms.

Object-oriented programs such as Java also offered a new kind of abstraction: a *class*, which was a definition of both data and logic, as used to create specific *objects* at run time. Java classes promoted reuse, as did similar constructs in other object-oriented languages. The ability to reuse classes further increased longevity.

•   The cost of software development decreased, if you consider logic that did calculations equivalent to those performed in an earlier time. However, the overall cost increased to reflect the increase in quality and longevity.

As Frederick P. Brooks wrote in 1987: "Surely the most powerful stroke for software productivity, reliability, and simplicity has been the progressive use of high-level languages for programming. Most observers credit that development with at least a factor of five in productivity, and with concomitant gains in reliability, simplicity, and comprehensibility."[29]

Infrastructure-Independent Coding with an Enterprise Language

In the early twenty-first century, companies that develop software face more than a variety of hardware; they face a variety of *technical domains*—broad categories of technical issues that must be addressed by enterprise applications.

Here are the domains:

- The *runtime platform*, which is software that determines what resources are available to the application and how the user invokes the application

- *Persistent data storage*, which comprises the database, file, and queuing systems from which an application reads data and to which the application writes data

- The *user interface*, which is the interactive mechanism for presenting and receiving user data

- *Network communication*, which is the means for transferring data between machines

- *Report production*, which is the mechanism for formatting business reports and presenting them to a screen or printer

- *Older-code integration*, which is necessary to protect a company's investment in IT

The complexity of those domains has increased in recent years as business requirements became greater; for example, as companies wrote applications for business-to-business processing and for customer access on the Web.

In light of the new complexity, companies can improve the economic viability of software development. Here's how:

- Write new applications in an *enterprise language*, which lets a programmer ignore many specifics of the technical domains; and

- Use tools that are akin to assemblers and compilers, as needed to convert source code to a less abstract form.

The language described in this book is the IBM enterprise language, EGL. The primary conversion tool is the *EGL generator*, and the output format is Java, COBOL, or JavaScript, which can run on a wide range of platforms.

One way to see the increased simplicity of an enterprise language is to consider that, in code written with a third-generation language, the statements that access a database include details that are specific to the kind of database, whether relational or hierarchical.

The EGL approach is more general. For example, the following code stores an order record named **myOrderRecord**, regardless of whether the storage area is a relational database, hierarchical database, message queue, or file.

```
add myOrderRecord;
```

What makes the simplicity possible?

Earlier in the logic, the EGL programmer assigns property-value pairs to define the *kind* of record being added. If the record **myOrderRecord** is meant to provide access to a relational database, the record might be based on the following definition.

```
Record OrderRecordType type sqlRecord {
      tablenames=[["ORDERS"]],
      keyItems=[orderID] }

   orderID INT
      { Column="ID" };
   orderStatus CHAR(1)
      { Column="STATUS" };
end
```

The meaning of this definition is explained in Chapter 12. For our current purpose, we distinguish *imperative programming*, which is the use of procedural logic, from *declarative programming*, which is the use of non-procedural detail, as shown in the definition. The declarative choice increases quality and developer productivity for this reason: "Declarative programming.... is another form of reuse of preprogrammed, prevalidated logic."[30] The preprogrammed logic in this case is the EGL generator and other system code.

Again, the increase in abstraction increases the economic viability of software development:

- Quality increases because the greater simplicity increases the focus on business issues. As before, ease of thought reduces errors and facilitates cooperation among interested parties.

  Quality also increases for a reason that is only indirectly tied to the details we've described. A company that uses an enterprise language can retain developers who are knowledgeable in business processes, even if those developers lack the time needed to stay current with technical change. The retention of those people also means that they can continue to provide an institutional memory, as is useful for any number of reasons, including maintenance of existing applications.

- Longevity of the code increases because developers can write logic in response to current requirements, with most domain-specific details handled by the system code. As technology changes, the source often requires minimal or no update.

  An example of this flexibility is that an EGL program written for one platform can be configured easily for use on another. Developers can create EGL software and be assured that the code will retain its value if their company needs to migrate to another supported platform. Similarly, an EGL program that accesses a database system retains value if the company changes the type of database system in use.

  Last, an enterprise language supports the continued use of existing code. For example, a Web application developed with EGL can access older logic quite easily, sometimes as a result of a few keystrokes.

- Cost decreases. Software development takes less time than before, with less expense for source-code change over time. The costs associated with errors are less, and not only because of the language. The products that offer support for EGL provide several kinds of error protection, including a source-code debugger and other interactive assistance. Last, the ability to integrate existing applications means that pre-existing software can remain in use, providing an additional saving.

The Importance of Wide Coverage by a Computer Language

A good enterprise language can be helpful for developing even a limited range of code; for example, Web applications or the data-access services that provide enterprise data to those applications. However, if a computer language is suitable for many purposes, a company can more easily create what Frederick Brooks called "an organization for change."[31]

Brooks saw the need in the early 1970s, when COBOL and PL/1 provided a technical uniformity: "Each man must be assigned to jobs that broaden him, so that the whole force is technically flexible. On a large project, the manager needs to keep two or three top programmers in a technical cavalry that can gallop to the rescue wherever the battle is thickest."[32]

If all developers are familiar with a single language that is used for multiple purposes, the company is more likely to gain effective cooperation, with lower training costs. And a team of developers using similar tools and constructs is more likely to complete projects on time and within budget.

These project-oriented benefits are additional reasons to consider EGL.

Accentuate the Negative

In 1944, composer Harold Arlen and singer-songwriter Johnny Mercer published "Accentuate the Positive":

> You've got to accentuate the positive
> Eliminate the negative
> And latch on to the affirmative
> Don't mess with Mister In-Between[33]

With due respect to Johnny Mercer, we'll conclude this introduction by accentuating the following questions so as to address the issues directly:

- Are enterprise languages disruptive?

- Do enterprise languages inhibit innovation?

- Do enterprise languages have flaws caused by higher abstraction?

- Are enterprise languages old news?

Are Enterprise Languages Disruptive?

Disruptive? Not very. The technology being described is essentially *conservative*. In many cases, a company uses it for *enterprise modernization*: to integrate old logic with new; and, in particular, to expose pre-existing logic to a new set of users or in new ways.

A technology that offers the best support for enterprise modernization avoids changing business processes that are wholly acceptable to management. In particular, an "enterprise language" that negatively affects customers is not an enterprise language.

Within the company, training is necessary; and later chapters of this book offer a good start for understanding EGL. Our main audience for those chapters is developers, but we ask you to consider that aligning business and technology works best when both parties make an effort.

Developers increasingly add value as they gain insight into the business. Can't line-of-business managers add more value if they gain further insight into the issues being addressed by developers? The use of an enterprise language makes reciprocal understanding easier.

An area of possible disruption within software development is the use of a new integrated development environment (IDE). The products that support EGL are based on *Eclipse*, a publicly available IDE that is described at *http://www.eclipse.org*. The move to Eclipse can increase productivity, but requires training and a period of adjustment.

Do Enterprise Languages Inhibit Innovation?

EGL hides many of the runtime details that would otherwise require your attention. However, you are rarely constrained by this convenience.

For example, you code Rich Internet Applications with the language feature known as *EGL Rich UI*. You are likely to code only in EGL, but you have the ability to write custom JavaScript or to access JavaScript libraries instead of relying on the default behavior of EGL.

The same pattern applies to other supported technology. For example, when you write EGL code to access a relational database from a service or program, you can include Structured Query Language (SQL) statements. Similarly, you can incorporate Java code within an EGL program that is written for Windows, Linux, IBM i, and so forth.

Do Enterprise Languages Have Flaws Caused by Higher Abstraction?

Enterprise languages struggle with issues that affected earlier tries at raising the level of abstraction: the first issue is reliability, and the second is performance in comparison to what is possible with an older technology.

First, consider reliability. Software is inherently complex, and any technology that simplifies application development will be complex. Development-time editors can introduce errors, and the processes that convert source code to a less-abstract form can do the same. Flaws are also possible in the system code that supports runtime processing. The issues exist, but their severity tends to lessen over time.

In regard to performance at application run time, companies will likely be pleased: programmer time is expensive; computer time for *batch programs* (programs that do not interact with users) is less expensive; and interactive code is not significantly affected by a performance difference. Years ago, in the context of computer time-sharing, Frederick Brooks noted that improvements in interactive response time can "pass the human threshold of noticeability, about 100 milliseconds."[35]

A company interested in an enterprise language should begin a trial only after asking many questions. What company stands behind the technology? How long has the technology been in use? What is the customer experience?

EGL is the culmination of more than 25 years of experience in designing syntax for rapid application development. The underlying system code has been the object of extensive testing; yet the language reflects recent innovations in data structure, error handling, and Web access. In the words of IBM Vice President Hayden Lindsey, "EGL is well established—several thousand enterprises use a predecessor language for essential applications— yet the language is current."

To review customer experience, see the following Web site: *http://www.ibm.com/rational/eglcafe/docs/DOC-2701.*

Are Enterprise Languages Old News?

People who are just learning about the IBM enterprise language sometimes assume that it's merely an update to an older technology.

We offer an analogy. In the 1960's, Macy's wanted to build a department store in Queens, New York. The plan was likened to the city's Guggenheim Museum, which was designed by Frank Lloyd Wright. The Macy's building was to be more than functional; it was to be beautiful.

The firm bought most of the land needed, but could not sway Mary Sondek, an elderly homeowner who valued her residence more than she valued the money on offer. The Sondek house stayed. Macy's built a circular structure with an inward notch that broke the circle. The irregularity was there to accommodate someone who had an established right, but the building itself was modern.[36]

EGL is like a circular building with a notch that accommodates those who wrote code with a predecessor language. Some aspects of EGL are there to allow migration of programs written with Cross System Product, VisualAge Generator, or Informix 4GL, but EGL encompasses more than those aspects. The new language was architected for consistency and has an ease-of-use that the predecessor languages never had.

CHAPTER **2**

Web 2.0

We describe the benefits of Web 2.0, including details on network economics.

Interactive Web Sites

According to The Nielsen Company, people worldwide spent almost 10% of their Internet hours on blogs and social sites in 2008, and the percentage increased at a rate three times greater than for overall Internet use.[1] Should your company be either developing a new site or expanding its current one to take advantage of this trend? Before we help answer that question, we'll cover some background information on Web-based social networks.

Networks

In general, a *network* is a set of nodes and the links that connect them[2] (Figure 2.1).

Networks can be real or ideal. For example, a real *technological network* is physical and man-made, providing links and destinations for electricity or transport or (at a higher level) for data. Examples are electric grids, airline routes, and the Internet. In comparison, an ideal technological network is like a map; it's a representation that gives a model of the real world and

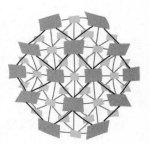

Figure 2.1: Network

excludes some details, as required to think about the economics or logistics of a situation.

A technological network may provide the practical basis for a *social network,* which links individuals or groups and is often composed of many clusters of related nodes (Figure 2.2).

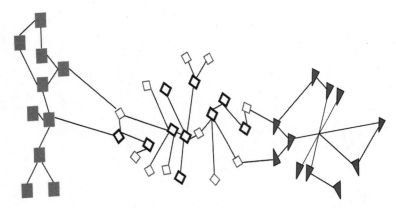

Figure 2.2: Social Network

Our main focus is on a social network of Web site users who are linked to one another and are separately linked to the Web-site provider. This kind of network provides a competitive advantage in part because of network effects, as described next.

Network Effects

A *network effect* is a change in the value of participating in a network as a result of other participants joining or leaving.[3] For example, the first users of a telephone system are able to phone only a few people. As more users participate, the value increases for those first users and for the system's owners.

In relation to Web-site development, we care about network effects because they imply changes in a user's willingness to contribute content, to be present for advertising, and to pay for continued participation.

Consider a Web site whose users can retrieve Web pages but can neither contribute to the site nor read content from other users. The social network is in a hub-and-spoke format, with the hub representing the Web-site provider and each spoke representing a user (Figure 2.3).

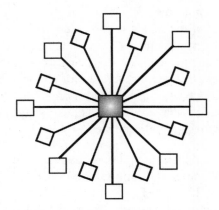

Figure 2.3: Hub-and-Spoke (Radial) Network

Each additional user has relatively little effect on how the earlier participants value the network. If the site becomes slower as the user base grows, the effects are present, and negative. If the presence of additional users causes the site to offer new function, the effects are positive.

Now consider a Web site whose users interact. Here, the social network is more complex (as suggested in Figure 2.2); and the network effects are strong. In general, as the size of the online community increases, even non-paying users are adding value. They contribute content that makes the site more compelling to others. Also, they represent a source of potential direct income to the network provider, as well as an immediate attraction to advertisers.

Value of a Network to the Provider

The specific value of network effects is in dispute. One famous measure— Metcalfe's law—was designed only for small networks and measured the benefit for all viable *hardware* connections: "When you connect computers together, the cost of doing so is n, but the value is n^2, because each of the machines that you hook up gets to talk to all of the other machines on the network." The value of network effects for non-interactive Web sites are substantially lower.[4]

David Reed suggests a three-part valuation. First, the value for non-interactive function on a Web site is represented by n; that is, the value increases in proportion to the number of users. Second, the value for peer-to-peer transactional function such as classified ads and responses to them can be represented by n^2; the value increases in proportion to the square of the number of users. Third, the value for social interaction can be represented by a stunning 2^n; the value increases exponentially as users join. "If you can manage or influence the networks that connect you to suppliers and customers to create more value for all concerned, that extra value can be used as a competitive weapon. So paying attention to network value is a crucial strategic issue, especially as businesses move their customer and supplier relationships into the 'net."[5]

Our final word on the quantitative measurement of network effects comes from James Hendler and Jennifer Goldbeck: "While none of these [measurements] have been validated in practice, it is clear that [network effects are] quite real, and even the most pessimistic view still provides for significant value as the number of connections in the network grows."[6]

And network effects are only part of the story of value. "Accumulation of data [about participants] make it possible for vendors and advertisers to tailor products and services..., thus making the site even more attractive."[7] Last, new users add publicity, requiring less expenditure to attract the next users.[8]

"Of Networks, There Will Be Few"

Given all the potential, why not invest heavily to create a public network under your company's control?

In a 2000 speech, economist W. Brian Arthur expressed the market situation as follows: "Competition in networks will shake out according to what I believe can be almost called a Law: 'Of networks, there will be few.' We currently have 9,500 commercial banking companies in the United States. I believe we will have only a single-digit number of digital-banking virtual networks in the future. Perhaps three, perhaps half-a-dozen. One reason is that digital networks by definition will have global reach, and this will diminish greatly the importance of locality. So a very few networks can cover a full global clientele. A second reason that there will be few networks in any market niche is increasing returns—the tendency of that which gets ahead to stay ahead and go on to lock in a market.... once the shake out of competitors in that niche is complete."[9] Arthur and others contend that the differentiation of one network from another will rarely overcome the forces that tend to create near-monopolies for one network in a given market.

Legg-Mason analyst Michael J. Mauboussin explains those forces in greater detail.[10] He compares the traditional economics of a manufacturing company, where the variable costs are crucial, with the economics of a social network.

"As a manufacturing company increases its output, its marginal and average unit costs decline (to a point)." The benefit of that variable-cost decline begins to reverse "well before dominance: Market shares in the industrial world rarely top 50%."[11] Figure 2.4 illustrates a manufacturer's variable-cost curve.

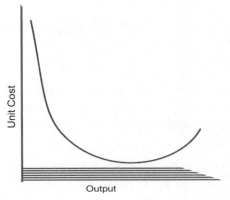

Figure 2.4: Manufacturer's Variable-Cost Curve

The equivalent curve for a social network also falls as services are rendered to an increasing number of users. Moreover, the cost structure suggests a better long-term opportunity. Fixed costs are relatively high, all-but ensuring early losses; but once you've created a network, each additional user costs little to support.

The determining factor for network success is found on the demand side.

The value of the network rises at an increasing rate because of network effects (Figure 2.5).

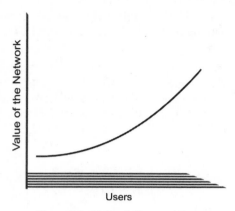

Figure 2.5: Network Demand Curve

A near-monopoly position is possible if the network reaches a tipping point, when people who are not yet in the network require less and less expenditure from the provider before they agree to join[12] (Figure 2.6).

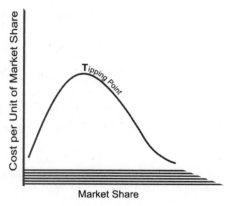

Figure 2.6: Tipping Point

Can a near-monopoly be broken? Yes, competitors have reason to compete. Technology and situations change, and the network provider is forced to make R&D and customer-relations expenditures to maintain its position. But the inertia of users who participate in a given Web site will tend to keep those users locked in. The current users know the site's interface and can quickly find what they want.

The economics of creating social networks are powerful. Many companies are enjoying a benefit, and most companies today need a Web presence if only because their competitors have one. Nevertheless, a vast investment in creating an interactive site is prudent only if a company has a clear idea of how to become the one dominant force in a market.

For many companies, a more careful choice is to access existing social networks to fulfill specific objectives, while using the company's own Web site for collaborative purpose, for brand image, and for revenue. We turn to these issues next.

Collaboration

A company can use Web technology to gain the benefits of faster collaboration, whether for internal tasks or for interacting with customers and suppliers. For example, here are ways you might build a team:[13]

- Search for potential team members more quickly by use of profiles, tags, and bookmarks

- Help validate the potential contribution of those people by reviewing their online posts

- Initiate a direct dialogue with subject-area experts to gain a clearer understanding of issues, with less bureaucracy

- Capture project information easily

- Spread project innovations quickly

- Foster a sense of connectedness and recognition among team members, who may be dispersed geographically

Web technology also helps to enable *crowdsourcing*, which is (in essence) using a large, amorphous group to fulfill a task.[14] In some cases, the main implication is that labor is free or inexpensive, as when a software-testing company pays a piecemeal rate for each error report. However, a second form of crowdsourcing is *open innovation*, which involves a public request for help in solving a complex problem. For example, development of more than 35 percent of new products at Procter & Gamble involves external sources.[15] One such source is Innocentive, which offers prizes from $5000 to $1,000,000 to persons who solve a specified problem.[16]

Science writer John K. Borchardt explains why open innovation makes sense: "Buying or licensing [other people's ideas can free] companies to focus their internal R&D on areas where they have clear competitive advantages. The results include decreased R&D risks and more funds available for the most promising opportunities. This focus also enables organizations to identify innovations to sell or license to other firms."[17]

Brand Image

Presence on the Web is necessary for most companies, to promote a message, to sell product, and to respond to online criticism.

For example, a company Web site can help to define a brand even if the site content includes only mission statements, product details, and contact information. The important point here is a graphically attractive layout and an intuitive way to pass from one Web-page activity to the next.

A robust site might include *wizards*—interactive software that leads a user through a complex decision (in many cases, for product selection); *chat*—instant messaging with a customer-service representative; *internal search*—a means of quick access to the site's data; and an online purchase process that gives existing customers the ability to use contact details from previous orders. Also of interest are order-tracking details; billing history; product videos; and product reviews that accept public comments with minimal or no censorship by the company.[18]

That last item can be discomforting, but analyst Jeremiah Owyang suggests that the "happy marketing speak" on traditional Web sites has a price: "Trusted decisions are being made on other locations on the Internet"; in particular, on sites that allow customers to share opinions and rate products.[19] In general, your company cannot control the conversation on the Web, but can respond to inaccuracies.

Additional efforts are possible. Author Tom Funk suggests that a company create its own blog and participate in blogs that are read by customers and by others in its industry. He also suggests a presence on social sites: not to sell, but to be an interesting and trusted presence.[20]

Revenue

Web applications can generate revenue in various ways. One way is to follow a *freemium* business model: provide some benefit without charge and provide other benefit only if the user agrees to pay a premium.[21] For example, a financial site might offer free report abstracts, with full reports provided only to subscribers. A second variation is found on blogs and social sites, where a non-paying user can fulfill a subset of tasks; for example, reading posts but not writing them, or reviewing details about potential business contacts but accepting the following limitation: email addresses for those contacts are available only to users who pay a monthly fee.

A second way to generate revenue is by making advertising space available on your Web site. You can sell the space directly, whether to companies that have goods to offer or to agencies that serve those companies. In addition, you can participate in a revenue-sharing model, accepting ads from intermediaries such as Google™, which provides third-party ads.[22]

In most cases, the income received from accepting ads is based on a measure of user interaction; for example, cost per click, cost per thousand *impressions* (user views), or cost per *acquisition* (a purchase or signup).[23]

A third way to generate revenue is to act as a broker. Some sites act as intermediaries between comsumers; for example, for automobiles. Other sites handle requests for industrial equipment, for rendering computer-aided design (CAD) files, or for partnerships.[24]

A fourth way to generate revenue is by direct sales; and, in particular, by taking advantage of "The Long Tail," which is how author Chris Anderson explains the importance of niche markets in online commerce.[25]

The Long Tail is the rightmost part of a particular kind of statistical distribution; in this case, a distribution that relates the per-item number of units sold to the per-item sales ranking (Figure 2.7).

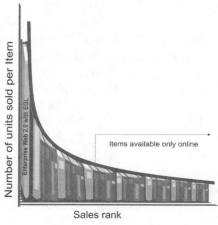

Figure 2.7: The Long Tail

Here's an example. Online books that rank low in sales provide a relatively large percentage of overall sales compared to the equivalent percentage in a brick-and-mortar store. The difference can be large: "The average Barnes & Noble superstore [in the United States] carries around 100,000 titles. Yet more than a quarter of Amazon's book sales come from outside its top 100,000 titles."[26]

What enables the increased sales of lower-ranked products? First, the customer base of an online store is not restricted to people who are in physical proximity; the sheer number of potential customers is much greater. Second, the per-unit cost of overhead is less for an online store, which requires no shelf space and—in the case for downloads—may not require a physical inventory at all. Third, an online store can make targeted suggestions for any visitor—"People who bought this book also bought..."—and in this way lead that visitor to choices that are appropriate but even less mainstream. Fourth, an online store can use an individual's stated preferences, purchase history, or other information to tailor advertisements, mailings, and aspects of the real-time experience.

A company can also share in the Long Tail of an online store such as Amazon, acting as an affiliate whose visitors can click-through to a product-specific page on the retailer. In this case, the affiliate receives a small percentage of the sale.

Owning and Extending Data

Before we move on to Rich Internet Applications, we'd like to emphasize the benefit of a company's owning and extending its Web-site data, to the extent possible. Publisher Tim O'Reilly offers the following history:

- MapQuest® licensed its mapping data from suppliers. The lack of ownership allowed Google and other firms to create competitive offerings that licensed the same data. Google then facilitated programmatic access to the licensed data, becoming the intermediary for companies that used the data and placing itself in a position to capitalize on the usage.

- The original Amazon.com database came from R.R. Bowker, a firm that assigns the International Standard Book Number (ISBN) for each book published in the United States."Amazon relentlessly enhanced the data, adding publisher-supplied data such as cover images, table of contents, index, and sample material" and adding the reviews and rankings provided by Amazon users. As a result, "Amazon, not Bowker, is the primary source for bibliographic data on books," making the site attractive to a wide range of users.

"Failure to understand the importance of owning an application's core data will eventually undercut [a company's] competitive position."[27]

Rich Internet Applications

We've described the use of Web sites for better collaboration, improved branding, and revenue generation. Yet many companies find that highly functional, browser-based applications are the most important Web 2.0 technology.

The next sections describe some of the benefits of those applications.

Mashups

A Rich Internet Application lets your company quickly develop *mashups*, each of which is a combination of software capability from different sources.

Here's one scenario. A hospitality company has a different reservation system for each of several hotel chains that were acquired over time. Each system relies on a different set of software products for storing, accessing, and manipulating data. A member of the reservation staff responds to phone calls by typing details on a personal computer and switching between different windows. One window accesses the system for one of the hotel chains, one window accesses the system for another.

A traveler calls to say, "I need a hotel room for the first week in May." The clerk types the details for one chain and finds that no rooms are available. The clerk then types the same details for a second chain, and the traveler interrupts the search by saying that the intended dates are not in May but in June. The clerk revises the search, finds no rooms, and returns to the first system with the new dates. And so on. The need to repeatedly type the same information slows response time and adds a potentially harsh quality to the conversation.

The way forward is to modernize the software. A Web application that can access data from multiple Web services can display data from all the systems. In this case, the clerk can gain information from several hotel chains and, if the interface is well designed, can respond quickly to the traveler's changing requests.

The kind of Web application we've just described is an *enterprise mashup*—a collection of logic and data that has significant value to the company and is useful over time. Here's a less formal example. Your company develops an application to let travelers reserve rooms in one or another city. With Web 2.0, the application can provide access to a Google map for each hotel and can include, within the map, a weather forecast for the city. Neither the mapping software nor the forecast software was created with the other in mind, yet the two kinds of software are usefully integrated in a creative way.

The ability to access Web services within or outside a company makes a huge amount of data available. The effect is to increase convenience for users and to reduce development expense.

The Web site *programmableWeb.com* provides access to publicly available mashups, which in most cases do not have the business significance of an enterprise mashup but are interesting for what they reveal about modern software. The site categorizes mashups in various ways and indicates the most popular mashups, as well as the most popular sources. The mashups are often licensed under Creative Commons, which is a non-profit organization that "provides free licenses and other legal tools to mark creative work with the freedom the creator wants it to carry, so others can share, remix, use commercially, or any combination thereof."[28]

Quality Interfaces

RIA interfaces are flexible and have a dynamic quality. As always, the developer's job is to create an interaction that gives users a set of choices appropriate to the business need. An additional goal is to let users be productive in their individual ways while protecting them from distractions and from being overwhelmed by unwanted choice.

Consider an interface that lets users find a real-estate property of interest. The user can search for a specific location, price range, type of property, and so on (Figure 2.8).

Figure 2.8: Real-Estate Application, Photo Tab

The user changes entries at the left of the screen to display a set of pictures that reflect the search criteria. The user then uses a mouse to move a cursor over the set of pictures and in this way scrolls the images to the right or left. The bottom area of the screen shows details on whatever house is displayed at the front and center.

The user browses multiple properties and selects a few favorites, dragging one and then another picture from the center of the screen to an area on the right. The user then clicks on the **Results** tab to see details on the selected properties (Figure 2.9).

Figure 2.9: Real-Estate Application, Results Tab

The user accesses the mortgage calculator at the top right to learn the monthly payment needed to pay back a loan of a given size and term for one property and then the next. The user gets the information with a quickness that helps make comparisons easier.

The real-estate application provides many options in one onscreen area. The application lets the user move function from one part of the screen to another and even allows temporary removal of an area, for a more productive user-code interaction.

Could this kind of quickness and flexibility be provided by a Web application that relies *solely* on transferring pages from a server to the browser? Not easily, if at all. The ability to have such flexible behavior in a Web application became feasible only with client-side processing.

In a second example, a cell-phone user at a conference checks meeting availability, schedules events, and interacts with other attendees (Figure 2.10).

Figure 2.10: Conference Scheduler

A well-designed RIA increases user productivity in several ways. First, the application saves time at start-up by downloading only some of the information needed by the user. Second, the time needed for subsequent updates is often not noticed by the user. The downloads are quick because they're limited to the information that is required at a given moment. Third, the downloads are responsive to the business need because they reflect the user's choice. Fourth, the developer can structure the workflow so that the user's time is respected.

In addition, the ability to provide RIAs to hand-held devices implies a potentially close integration of software and usage. A sales representative in the field or a shipping clerk in a warehouse can receive information in real time and in a convenient way.

Enterprise Modernization

RIAs access services that in turn interact with long-standing programs. An important role for an RIA is to provide a new front end for logic that was previously available only to a terminal or workstation. We explore this issue in Chapter 7.

Deployment

A Rich Internet Application is deployed on a Web server such as WebSphere®
Application Server or Apache Tomcat. In response to changing business or
technical needs, the company can quickly re-deploy the RIA by updating that
location, without re-installing the application on multiple workstations. Users
can then access the most recent version of the application by clicking a button
or typing a Web address, whether in a Web browser or mobile device.

Introduction to Web Security

S ecurity is essential when your company is using the Web. We offer a modest overview, with details specific to EGL.

Security Trends

An attacker no longer needs to be near a company to steal critical data or otherwise do harm. A Web site provides an entry point for malicious activity from almost anywhere in the world.

In January 2009, researchers at IBM Internet Security Systems reported that the number and severity of system vulnerabilities increased during the previous year. The majority of problems were found in Web server applications, which are "increasingly vulnerable and highly profitable" to criminals.[1] Earlier studies by the Gartner Group and by the Mitre Corporation (in partnership with the U.S. Department of Homeland Security) also found a growing problem. The authors of the Mitre study suggest that two factors are contributing to the trend: developers' inexperience with security issues, and the ease with which attackers can find and exploit a weakness.[2]

Internet Security Systems emphasizes that the single most important systems-security issue faced by companies is crime for financial gain. However, people who are motivated by ideology or adventure are also a concern. In 2007, Estonia was the victim of three weeks of *denial-of-service attacks*, which are efforts to make a Web site or other resource unavailable; in this case, by flooding Web sites with requests. A group of young Russian activists claimed responsibility for the incident, which brought chaos to Estonian banks and prompted NATO to create a research center to explore ways to defend against cyber attacks.[3]

Companies are also responding, to an extent. In March 2009, the Open Web Application Security Project (OWASP) reported that despite the economic situation, "Web application security spending is expected to either stay flat or increase in nearly two thirds of [the 51] companies" that responded to a survey. The authors also highlighted the following detail: "Organizations that have suffered a public data breach spend more on security in the development process than those that have not."[4]

Threats by Type

Authors Michael Howard and David LeBlanc suggest use of the acronym STRIDE to categorize security threats:[5]

- **S**poofing identity. In the relationship of user and Web site, two kinds of masquerades are possible: an attacker accesses a Web site with another person's user ID and password; or the attacker somehow causes the user to access a Web site—for example, a banking site—that seems legitimate but is under the attacker's control.

- **T**ampering with data. Attackers seek to update data that is stored in a database or file or is in transit between machines.

- **R**epudiation. Attackers seek to hide proof of an online intrusion or other illegal act; or they seek to argue (repudiate) the validity of a contract or transaction. The term *non-repudiation* often refers to online commerce. Each party to an agreement seeks assurance that the other party cannot honestly claim (a) that contractually binding data was not sent; (b) that the data came from a different originator; (c) that the data was changed in transit; or (d) that the data was not delivered. A further aspect of non-repudiation is the use of timestamps to document when communication occurred.

- **I**nformation disclosure. Confidential information may become known to those who have no right to pry. This type of security opening can lead to tampering.

- **D**enial of service. Attackers seek to make a Web site or other resource unavailable, as noted earlier.

- Elevation of privilege. Attackers seek to access a resource at a higher level of trust than was intended. For example, a non-manager might use a Rich Internet Application to retrieve salary details but—as a result of an elevation in privilege—might gain access to a Web service that gives details on salary data for all employees. In general, elevation of privilege refers to undeserved access to the administrative levels of a machine or system.

The STRIDE categories represent effects that can build on one another. For example, a spoofing identity or an elevation of privilege might let an attacker tamper with a Web site article that provides data about a company's financial condition. The purpose of the action might be to create a short-term rise in the company's stock price, benefiting the attacker but damaging the company's reputation and legal standing.

Security by Location

In relation to Web 2.0, your company is vulnerable in many ways: data is in transit at run time, and both data and logic are stored on server machines, where some of the logic runs. In relation to client-side scripts—including Rich Internet Applications and potentially malicious code—the logic runs in a browser and interacts periodically with the server that transmitted the code.

We'll consider data in transit, server-side security, and client-side security.

Data in Transit

Attackers can access messages passing between server and browser or between a server-side proxy (as described later) and one or another service. The messages are passed in constituent parts known as *data packets*, with each packet crossing a network that may not be trustworthy, even if trusted.

The packets follow a route, from one machine or router to the next; and the route may be different for different packets (Figure 3.1).

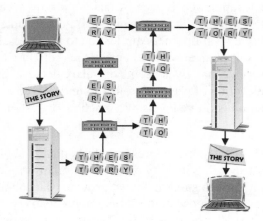

Figure 3.1: Data in Transit

The structure of the packets is defined by a *protocol*, which is a set of rules for transmitting and receiving data. Two related protocols are of interest to us. First, Transmission Control Protocol / Internet Protocol (TCP/IP) handles the kind of low-level packet-organizing tasks illustrated in Figure 3.1. Second, HyperText Transfer Protocol (HTTP) provides a standard way for Web sites, browsers, and Web services to communicate details that are meaningful in a business sense. For example, a Web site uses HTTP to transmit a Web page.

An attacker who gains even remote access to a hardware device on the route may be able to use a *protocol analyzer*, which is software (or hardware and software) that gives access to details about the packets in transit. Access to one or more packets may provide the detail needed to mount a *man-in-the-middle (MITM) attack*, which involves a two-way spoof: the attacker masquerades as the Web site provider during contact with a requester and masquerades as the requester during contact with the Web site provider. In most cases, the purpose of an MITM attack is to collect confidential information such as credit-card numbers.

What *is* a packet? To remove some of the mystery, we'll say a few words about the technical detail.

Packets

A packet is a unit of meaning, with business content at the center and protocal-specific detail at the front and back. For example, the packet format for the protocol TCP/IP is used for a variety of reasons, including email, file transfer, and Web-page request or response. We represent the business data in a packet by a single letter (Figure 3.2).

Figure 3.2: Packet Format for TCP/IP

If the TCP/IP packet is part of a message whose purpose is to request or present a non-secure Web page, the packet is supplemented, front and back, with detail that is specific to the protocol that handles Web pages: HTTP (Figure 3.3).

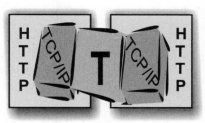

Figure 3.3: Packet Format for HTTP

An attacker able to access the packet can review the business content without difficulty.

Transport Layer Security

The TCP/IP packet may be part of a message whose purpose is to request or present secure data—that is, data encrypted so that it is decipherable only to the receiver. An encrypted packet is supplemented, front and back, with detail that is specific to Transport Layer Security (TLS).

The TLS detail is itself embedded in HTTP.

Figure 3.4: Packet Format for HTTPS

The secure version of HTTP is identified as *HTTPS* (the *S* is for *Secure*). Most of the HTTP detail is treated as part of the TLS front matter, and almost the whole packet is encrypted (Figure 3.4).

Incidentally, an older variant of TLS is named *Secure Sockets Layer (SSL)*.

Encryption

The purpose of Transport Layer Security is to help "prevent eavesdropping, tampering, or message forgery."[6] Central to this purpose is the use of *cryptosystems*, which are processes for encrypting and decrypting data.

Encryption includes the following components: the data to be encrypted; a *cipher*, which is an algorithm used to encrypt the data; and a *key*, which is a numeric string that is mathematically related to a similar string used later, during decryption. The output of encryption is *ciphertext*, which is the value to be decrypted (Figure 3.5).

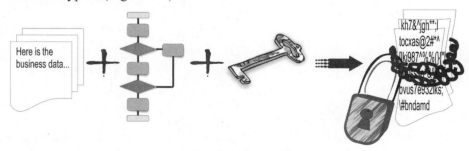

Figure 3.5: Encryption

Decryption includes the following components: the ciphertext to be decrypted; a *reverse cipher*, which is an algorithm used to decrypt the data; and a key. The output is the business data (Figure 3.6).

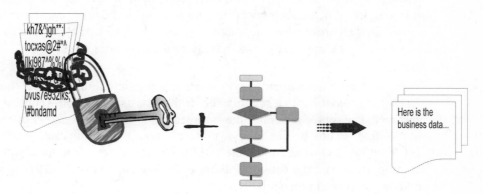

Figure 3.6: Decryption

Two cases are possible in relation to the encryption and decryption of messages between a specific sender and a specific receiver. In a *symmetric cryptosystem*, the keys that are used for encryption and decryption are identical for all uses.

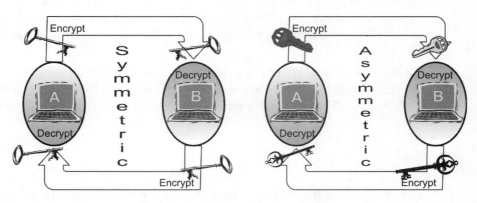

Figure 3.7: Symmetric and Asymmetric Crytosystems

In an *asymmetric cryptosystem*, one pair of keys is used to handle one direction of the conversation, and a second pair of keys is used to handle the other direction, and even the keys in a given pair are different from one another, although mathematically related (Figure 3.7).

When the keys are identical for all uses, decryption is faster than when they are different. However, the symmetric alternative has two problems. First, sender and receiver need to exchange keys in a confidential way before a business communication can occur. Each party needs the one, shared key. Second, to ensure confidentiality, each participant in a social network needs a different key when communicating with any *one* of the other participants. In a network of *n* participants, the number of shared, confidential keys is as many as *(n²-n)/2*. That number grows quickly as the network grows.

Business use of a symmetric cryptosystem is possible. For example, the *Kerberos protocol* uses a security server that is trusted by both sender and receiver. The server generates the symmetric key for a particular conversation at run time, so companies have no concern about the administration of many confidential keys or about the theft of the generated keys from persistent storage. However, the network cannot exchange data securely if the server and its backups are unavailable.

For the initial stage of a communication between sender and receiver, the more common pattern is the asymmetric one, which is often called *public key cryptography*. In this case, each participant has the following keys: a *public key*, which is available to others; a *private key*, which is meant to be held in the tightest confidence; and the public key of any other participant with whom an online communication is intended. In a network of *n* participants, the number of shared, confidential keys is 0; the number of confidential keys is *n*; and the total number of keys is *2n*, which is far less than in the alternative.

In public key cryptography, a sender encrypts a message by using the *public* key of the receiver. The receiver decrypts the message by using the receiver's *private* key. The keys used in one direction are always from the same person.

Digital Signatures

What is the purpose of a signature? In American law, a signature provides evidence that a document is attributable to a specific person and that the document reflects the signer's intent. Also, the act of signing helps focus the signer's attention on the promise being made. And a signature is future oriented, providing a point of finality so that subsequent transactions can occur efficiently, without people's raising questions about the status of a prior agreement.[7]

A *digital signature* is an outcome that results from a process of data transformations, including encryption. Other kinds of electronic signatures—for example, written signatures stored in graphic files—may have legal value, but are not in our current scope.

Here's how a digital signature is formed. When a sender submits data for transport by HTTPS, the protocol adds a timestamp, along with details that identify the sender. Transport Level Security then uses one or another technique to create a *digest*, which is a value derived from the submitted data (Figure 3.8).

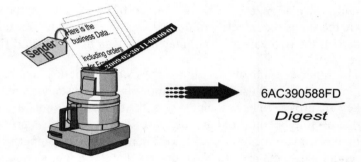

Figure 3.8: Digest

The digest is *not* an encrypted version of the message but is merely a value that represents the message. The message cannot be re-created from the value. However, the algorithm used to create the digest is so complex that the value would have been different had the message been even slightly different. The digest is a kind of digital fingerprint, but not yet a signature.

The last step is to encrypt the digest with the sender's private key, which is usually used for decryption. The digest encrypted in this way is the sender's digital signature (Figure 3.9).

Figure 3.9: Digital Signature

The signature is sent with the message and identifies the signed *portion* of the message (Figure 3.10).

Figure 3.10: Signed Message

The digest is not necessarily protected from view. Anyone who accesses the digest can use the sender's public key to read the digest. But that's the point. The ability to use the sender's public key to access the digest proves that the digest was from the sender.

The receiver decrypts the message and creates a second digest by using the same calculation as used by the sender. If the expected and calculated values are the same, the integrity of the message is assured: no one tampered with the data. If the two values do not match, the data has been modified in transit.

The American Bar Association suggests that digital signatures conform to the requirements and uses of a signature. First, if the sender's public and private key are proven to be associated with the sender, the signature is attributable to that person. Second, an equivalence of digest values is a proof of message integrity and indicates that the document reflects the signer's intent. Third, the sender's use of a private key indicates that the signer's attention was focused on the signing at the time of signing. Last, the digital signature offers a guarantee that is in some ways superior to that of a written signature, providing the social benefits expected of a signature.[8]

Public Key Infrastructure

The presence of a pair of public and private keys does not verify that the pair is from any particular individual or company. What is needed is a *Public Key Infrastructure*, which is an Internet or intranet function that uses public key cryptography and a set of organizations to verify the authenticity of network participants.

When a Web site receives a request for secure data transfer from a client, the site responds with a *digital certificate*—a file that holds the detail necessary to prove the Web site's authenticity. The detail includes the Web site's name and public key, as well as the certificate's expiration date.

A certificate is provided by a *Certificate Authority (CA)*, which is an organization trusted by both the Web site provider and the requesting browser.

A browser comes installed with details on major CAs and provides a way for the user to register others. Any company can become a Certificate Authority. Also, a company or department sometimes fulfills the CA role to support network communication that is internal to the company; and sometimes acts as a *Registration Authority*, which verifies information for a CA.

Digital certificates vary by purpose. Some allow a server to make a secure connection with a browser. Others prove that downloadable software is from a given manufacturer or that an email is from a given person. Certificates also vary by how thoroughly the CA checked the details being certified. In any case, the certificate has nothing to do with the content of a Web site or the integrity of the Web site provider.

Before requesting certification, a requester uses cryptographic software in the requester's machine. The software generates a number at random and uses it to generate a private and public key. The request for certification includes the public key, as well as details that identify the requester.

When issuing the certificate, the CA uses its own private key to sign the details. That signature is the essence of a certificate. Later, when the certificate owner is about to provide the certificate to another party on the Web, the owner signs the certificate as well.

The receiver of the certificate uses public keys to verify a chain: the certificate owner in fact provided the certificate, which in fact was issued by the CA. However, the chain may be longer. The owner may have included a certificate—as issued by a second CA—to prove the authenticity of the first CA. The end of the chain is a certificate that is self-signed by a *root CA*, which is a company that a browser accepts as being of unquestioned authority.

Server-Side Security

Server-side security is challenging, especially for providers of social Web sites. In our necessarily brief treatment of the subject, we emphasize two principles that apply to security in general:

- Do not trust input data

- Defend the system in multiple and even redundant ways

We focus on a phenomenon called *code injection*, which is the placement of logic into a runtime process from an external source. The effect may be beneficial—some products *feature* code injection—but is harmful in most cases.[9]

Here's an example. A Web application transmits a userID and password to a Web service whose purpose is to authenticate a user. The service uses Structured Query Language (SQL) code to *select* (retrieve) a row from a relational-database table. If the row is found, the service informs the invoking Web application that the user can access additional logic in the application.

Here is the SQL code, as constructed in a single string.

```
myString STRING =
              "SELECT 'OK' " +
              "FROM USERLIST " +
              "WHERE USERID = '" + userID + "' " +
              "AND PASSWORD = '" + password + "'"
```

The expectation is that the statement passed from the service to the database management system (DBMS) is somewhat as follows.

```
SELECT 'OK' FROM USERLIST
WHERE USERID = 'SMITH'
AND PASSWORD = '928TR41'
```

The problem here is that the passed value might be from a malicious user or might represent a successful man-in-the-middle attack. Consider what happens if the assignment to **userID** is as shown in the following entry.

```
SMITH' OR 1=1 --
```

The service provides the following statement to the DBMS, partly because the double hyphen identifies the beginning of an SQL comment.

```
SELECT 'OK' FROM USERLIST
WHERE USERID = 'SMITH' OR 1=1
```

The clause 1=1 is always true and causes the DBMS to return a row in all cases. The user gains access to the Web application (beyond the login screen), independent of the user's credentials.

Other damaging effects are possible. For example, if the DBMS can accept a request to run multiple database-access statements, one after the next, the malicious input could direct the DBMS to delete tables. The effect could be merely disruptive, with the company required to do as follows: stop normal activities, rewrite the software, and restore data from backup copies of the database. But the effect could be disastrous, with the company losing data about recent transactions or about details that are central to the firm's success.

The solution is to format the SQL statement in a way that prevents user input from overriding the developer's intent. For example, an EGL developer can structure the following **get** statement, which includes an SQL SELECT statement.

```
get userRecord with sql#{
    SELECT 'OK' FROM USERLIST
    WHERE USERID = :userRecord.userid
    AND PASSWORD = :userRecord.password };
```

This SQL SELECT statement includes *host variables*—variables that are embedded in the SQL syntax but are from the host language; in this case, from EGL. This use of host variables avoids the kind of free-form possibilities that we've just described, because the application does not provide the DBMS with a single, valid string. Instead, the following two DBMS processes are separated: the *parsing*—that is, the analysis of the SQL statement as a whole—and the runtime identification of data values. The details of DBMS processing add safety in this case.

Our SQL example is a specific instance of code injection, which can occur with many runtime technologies. A developer protects the company by handling user input with an eye on what malicious input could do.

We suggest that you never assume that data transmitted from one trusted platform is safe on another platform, even if the data was already validated. You may find this a curious suggestion, as we earlier described technology that helps protect against a man-in-the-middle attack.

Our point is twofold. First, the safest practice is to layer your security, with multiple lines of defense. A successful MITM attack is possible even with the protections described earlier. Second, modern software relies on more-or-less independent components. Although a given unit of logic—a Web application or service—might receive safe data today, that unit of logic might receive data from a different and less carefully coded source in the future.

Client-Side Security

As described next, client-side vulnerabilies include cross-site scripting, drive-by downloads, and running malicious JavaScript returned from a Web service.

Cross-Site Scripting

A Web page is composed of presentation structure (headers, paragraphs, and so forth); displayable data; and, optionally, client-side logic, or *script*. Malicious users can sometimes trap others into running a script that resides in a part of the Web page that appropriately contains data. The phrase *cross-site scripting (XSS)* refers to the presence of the undesired logic, which in turn makes possible the exploitation of other weaknesses.

Here's an example. A Web site allow users to enter search queries. The site retains those queries in a database for review by an administrator, for the purpose of identifying user interests. However, if a malicious user submits a script rather than a search term, the unwanted logic might run in the administrator's browser when the report runs. As a result, the browser might read confidential data from different Web sites on the company's intranet and might email the data.

The problem arises because the Web site did not properly screen the data accepted from one browser and did not properly screen the data provided to another.

A variant of cross-site scripting involves the use of *cookies*, which are strings that are sent from a Web site to a browser when the user accesses the Web site. The browser holds the strings in memory or stores them in files on the user's machine. The cookies do not include logic but can include the detail needed to maintain a conversation with the Web site. A cookie is often used to customize the user's interaction so that (for example) only a desired set of Web site features are presented when the user logs in.

One result of cross-site scripting might be to send cookies to someone who can then hijack the user's conversation with the Web site. In this way, XSS can lead to a man-in-the-middle attack.

One aspect of the solution—better input and output screening—is important for code security in general. When writing code that runs differently depending on a data value, developers should test for *valid* data, excluding all data that does not conform, rather than testing for invalid data. The reason is that a test for valid data will handle the case in which values that were initially considered neutral, offering no security issues, ultimately become an issue.

Drive-By Download

Here's a client-side scenario that does not necessarily involve logic where data should be. The user of a social site reads a message from someone else who accesses the same site. The message includes an appealing offer, along with a link that seems to refer to a second, well-known site. But the displayed address is simple text that hides a link to a different address. The user clicks the link, causing the silent download of code that thereafter monitors user activity.

The immediate cause of this kind of attack is the user's action; for example, clicking a link, moving the mouse over an area on a Web page, or even opening a Web page. And the *success* of the attack is often made possible by insufficient maintenance: the user's browser might not be current or have the latest security patch; or the machine might lack a *firewall*, which is software that would otherwise give protection against intruders. Firewalls also let the user prevent outgoing communications that violate privacy. (Note that the word *firewall* can refer to network devices that provide similar function.)

In our scenario, the problem is twofold. First, the user's out-of-date software failed to issue a warning before accepting a download. Second, the user clicked the link without first reviewing the address that was displayed on the bottom of the browser. Maintenance and education are ways to minimize this threat, which is known as a *drive-by download*.

JavaScript Code from a Web Service

If a Rich Internet Application invokes a Web service and receives a return string that conforms to JavaScript Object Notation (JSON) format, the content is expected to hold data alone but can include malicious JavaScript code. The effect (for example) might be to display a graphic that, if clicked, sends cookies to an external Web site.

A protection exists if you've written the RIA with EGL Rich UI. Specifically, if a Web service returns a JSON string that includes potentially malicious

JavaScript code, the EGL Runtime issues an error message rather than evaluating the string.

Use of an LDAP-Compliant Server

Authentication—proving an identity—and *authorization*—proving the right to access a particular resource—require that user credentials such as userIDs and related passwords be stored in an area of persistent storage such as a file or relational database.

A popular kind of repository for storing user credentials is an *LDAP-compliant server*, which is a specialized database that returns data quickly. LDAP stands for Lightweight Directory Access Protocol (LDAP).

EGL-generated code can access an LDAP-compliant server.

Security for a Rich Internet Application

Figure 3.11 illustrates the runtime relationship of a *Rich UI application*—that is, a Rich Internet Application written with EGL—and multiple servers.

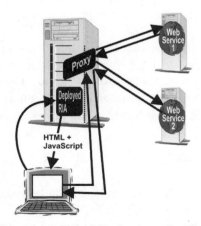

Figure 3.11: Rich UI Application at Run Time

The Rich UI application is deployed on a server machine, and the server responds to a browser request by transmitting a file—specifically, a Hypertext Markup Language (HTML) file—that includes the Rich Internet Application, which is in JavaScript format. The browser runs the application, which in turn can access one or more Web services. To access a Web service, the application contacts the *EGL Rich UI proxy*, which is logic deployed on the server machine that transmitted the file. In most cases, the Web service is on yet another machine.

Please note that the HTML and JavaScript delivered to the browser are visible to any user who wants to view the source code there. We suggest that your company avoid putting confidential logic in the application. Instead, hide that logic in the Web services that are called from the application. Similarly, avoid transmitting confidential data to the RIA; process such data in a Web service.

Web Servers and Application Servers

Before we describe security issues that are specific to the Rich UI application, we need to clarify an aspect of the server.

As noted earlier, a *Web server* is software that receives browser requests and that transmits Web pages and other content in response. In most enterprise computing, the Web server is merely a front end for the more complex processing that is available from an *application server*. The Web server is an intermediary, receiving the user's request and passing it to software such as the EGL Rich UI proxy, which runs directly in the application server.

In the context of EGL technology, an application server supports *Java Enterprise Edition (JEE)*, a Java Runtime that provides special handling for security, database access, and other areas of enterprise processing. Some server-side products—such as WebSphere Application Server—are fully compliant with JEE; and some—such as Apache Tomcat—are partially compliant. For purposes of this discussion, both kinds of products are JEE-compliant application servers. In contrast, some server-side products—such as Apache HTTP Server—have no JEE support and may not even be written in Java. That kind of product is a *standalone Web server*.

The point is this: At this writing, if a Rich UI application accesses services, the application must be installed on a JEE-compliant application server. If a Rich UI application does not access services, the application can be installed on either a JEE-complaint application server or on a standalone Web server.

A server is said to be the *container* of the applications deployed to it.

Container-Managed Authentication

Container-managed authentication is a user-validation process that relies on a container's access of stored credentials. The deployer of a given application identifies the repository that the container will access at run time.

We outline two kinds of container-managed authentication: basic, which is available on all containers that support Rich UI, and form based, which is available only on JEE-compliant application servers.

Each type of authentication is secure only when accompanied by Transport Layer Security.

Basic Authentication

When *basic authentication* is in effect, the runtime behavior is as follows: If the browser requests a secure resource such as a Web page and fails to specify a valid userID and password, the container directs the browser to display a login dialog that the browser itself provides. In response to any login error, the container directs the browser to re-display the same dialog.

In general, the appearance of the browser-provided login page is not consistent with the appearance of pages in the application.

Basic authentication is called *HTTP basic access authentication* on standalone Web servers and is called *JEE basic authentication* on JEE-compliant application servers.

JEE Form-Based Authentication

When *JEE form-based authentication* is in effect, the runtime behavior is as follows: If the browser requests a secure resource but fails to specify a valid userID and password, the container responds by transmitting a login page that the developer provides. The page is transmitted from the server and is in *JavaServer Page* (JSP) format. The developer can create that page with any product that supports Rich UI.

In this case, the appearance of the login page and related error page can be made consistent with the appearance of pages in the application.

Security Options

We now consider what aspects of a Rich UI application your company might choose to secure. In each case, we assume that security includes use of TLS.

We suggest that a company always secure the proxy, if one is present. If the proxy is available but not secure, an attacker may be able to use it to access Web services anonymously, including services that the application itself does not access. For this reason, we see the alternatives as follows: secure only the proxy or secure the proxy and other resources.

Secure Only the Proxy

When only the proxy is being secured, the alternatives are as follows:

- If the application calls no Web services, the developer removes references to the proxy from a configuration file.

- If the application calls a Web service, the developer sets up basic authentication for the proxy.

  Two options are in effect for JEE basic authentication. First, the developer can accept the default behavior, in which case the user's first invocation of a Web service causes the browser to display a browser-specific login page.

  Second, the application can stay in control by a three-step process: first, provide a custom login page to request user credentials; second, invoke an EGL system function to provide those credentials to JEE to log in to the proxy; and third, handle any errors returned from JEE. A security benefit of staying in control in this way is that the application can gather details about every login attempt.

We discount the possible use of JEE form-based authentication when only the proxy is being secured, because the login page transmitted from the server would interfere with the client-based Rich UI application.

Secure the Proxy and Other Resources

In relation to securing the proxy and other resources, note that the options for runtime access work only if the same set of user credentials is available in every repository that is inspected during the security checks.

Here is how a company secures both the proxy and other resources:

- The company can use JEE form-based authentication to protect the Rich UI application and the proxy. The user logs in once and is authenticated to the requested application and to the proxy.

  The company cannot use form-based authentication to secure a Web service, which is always directly invoked by the proxy. The user would not see the login page. However, the company can use JEE basic authentication to secure a service. In this case, the application invokes an EGL system function to pass credentials.

- Instead of using JEE form-based authentication, the company can rely on a combination of basic and custom authentication. We highlight one scenario.

  An example Rich UI application has a variety of capabilities and includes a login page. In this case, you can use *EGL single sign-on*, which is a way to receive credentials from the user and to use them for providing access to multiple resources.

  After the user provides a userID and password, the application acts as follows:

  a. Invokes an EGL system function that uses basic authentication and passes credentials to the proxy.

  b. Accesses an authentication service. The service in turn accesses a respository such as an LDAP-compliant server, as noted earlier.

  c. Directs the now-authenticated user to the secured areas of the application, as appropriate.

    d.   Invokes an EGL system function that uses basic
        authentication and passes credentials to one or another
        Web service.

The security model for a given application may be complex, but the task
required of the user can be simple.

Risk

The threats are real, as is the technology for mitigating them. A company that
sees opportunity in the Web needs to analyze and manage the risk.

In general, a measurement of risk is based on several factors, including the
potential losses and the probabilities that each kind of loss will occur. A fuller
analysis includes the cost of reducing risk, as well as the cost of the
opportunities that are left for others. The company's level of risk aversion is
another measure that helps inform decisions.

Assessing Risk

In 2003, Howard and LeBlanc—who suggested the acronym STRIDE as a
way to categorize threats—described a formula for rating the security risks
that come from vulnerabilities in application software.[10] Many in the
computer industry are now rating those risks in simpler ways; for example, as
critical, important, moderate, or low.[11] We'll present some of the earlier idea,
without arithmetic, to highlight the issues involved.

Five parameters are of interest, and the happy acronym in this case is...
DREAD:

- **D**amage potential. How much damage might be done if the
  vulnerability were exploited? Give added weight to vulnerabilities
  that might cause elevation of privilege or that might otherwise
  compromise sensitive data.

  The value of this first parameter is likely to be given greater weight
  than the others.

- **R**eproducibility. What is the likelihood that the attack, if it comes, can
  be replicated? The value is lower if the vulnerability is in effect only

on February 29. The value is higher if the vulnerability was found in a software component that is installed by default.

- **Exploitability.** What is the level of resource necessary for the vulnerability to become an attack? The value is lower if exploitation of the vulnerability requires a high level of privilege. The value is higher if exploitation requires only a personal computer and a grudge.

- **Affected Users.** How many users might be affected? The value is likely to be particularly high in the case of server vulnerabilities that can affect many client machines.

- **Discoverability.** What is the likelihood that a vulnerability will be discovered? The value is lower if discovery takes time, patience, and intelligence. The value is also lower if discovery requires the use of automated tools, although those who use such tools are more likely to mount an attack.

You can safely assume that most vulnerabilities will be discovered.

The Affected Users parameter reminds us that popular software attracts a large number of attacks. For example, Internet Explorer is probably not the most *vulnerable* browser. Rather, the return on investment for criminals is greater if Internet Explorer is targeted because the number of users who would be affected by a successful attack is greater.

An implication is this: software development in-house has a security benefit. In most cases, the criminals' interest in the delivery of custom software is less than their interest in the delivery of commercial software.

Responding to Risk

You can respond to risk in any of the following ways:

- You can *accept* risk, after deciding that the likely return outweighs the danger.

- You can *transfer* risk, either by establishing an insurance policy in some sense (and perhaps literally) or in the sense of assigning the problem—however tactfully—to someone else. In the context of Web security, the other party might be the head of a department that has a greater stake in the decision; for example, the manager of a different line of business or of another software-development group.

- You can *avoid* risk, after deciding that the danger outweights the likely return. For example, you might decide against deploying vulnerable software.

- You can *mitigate* risk. In the context of Web security, one principle is to analyze security issues repeatedly as you design, develop, and deploy software, with each vulnerability given a relative priority and, as appropriate, assigned to an expert for remediation.

CHAPTER 4

Service-Oriented Architecture

We continue the SOA overview started in the Introduction, including details on service-oriented applications and on some of the underlying technology.

Structure of a Service-Oriented Application

A *service-oriented application* is an application composed largely of services, which are often in a hierarchy (Figure 4.1).

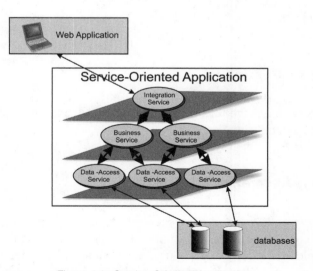

Figure 4.1: Service-Oriented Application

The topmost level contains one or more *integration services*, each of which controls a flow of activities such as processing an applicant's request for insurance coverage. Each integration service invokes one or more business services.

The second level is composed of services that each fulfill a relatively low-level business task. For example, an integration service might invoke a series of *business services* to verify the details provided by an insurance-policy applicant. If the business services return a set of values that are judged to mean "issue a policy," the integration service invokes yet another business service, which calculates a quote and returns the quote to the software that invoked the service-oriented application.

The third level consists of *data-access services*, each of which handles the relatively technical task of reading from and writing to data-storage areas such as databases and message queues. A data-access service is most often invoked from the business layer, but the easy access of services allows for different uses; for example, a requester such as a Web application can access a data-access service to assign initial values in a form.

The central point is flexibility. Some integration services provide different operations to different requesters, and some invoke other integration services. In addition, a requester might access different kinds of services from *within* a service-oriented application. The requester might access an integration service at one point and a business service at another.

Aspects of a Service

A service has the following aspects: a service implementation, elementary access details, and a contract.

Service Implementation

A *service implementation* is the core business logic, which might be written in EGL or any other programming language. The terms "service" and "service implementation" are often used interchangeably, and the second term is most appropriate when the focus is on the details of the business logic.

Elementary Access Details

Elementary access details include the *location*, which is an address where the service implementation resides, and the *binding*, which identifies the protocol that formats a message at the start of transmission and unformats the message at the end of transmission. For Web services, the protocol is Hypertext Transfer Protocol (HTTP). Formatting occurs when the invocation message originates at the requester; in that case, unformatting occurs when the message arrives at the service location. Formatting also occurs if the service issues a response; in that case, unformatting occurs when the response arrives at the requester.

Note that the location of a service is set when the service is deployed. The question is, "When is the location known to the requester?"

- The details on service location can be embedded in the business logic of the requester, but that usage is inflexible. If the service location changes, the requester must be recompiled and redeployed.

- In most cases, the details on service location are provided by configuration files at the site where the requester is deployed. That usage is more flexible because the configuration files can change during the years when the requester is in use, and the requester can access the service even if the service is deployed to a new location.

- In some cases, location details are passed to the requester at run time or the message is redirected by the SOA runtime software. These usages are flexible but add complexity that is not required for most purposes.

Contract

A *contract* describes the service's intended behavior and is independent of the implementation details. The contract has two elements: a service interface and a Quality of Service.

Service Interface

The *service interface* provides a description of the data that can pass between a requester and a service, along with details on each operation the service provides. The interface includes information on the messages and answers the questions such as "What is the format of a message (for example, two strings and an integer)?" and "What are the restrictions on content?" The interface also includes details on the message exchange pattern, which indicates how the requester and service interact. The primary question here is, "Does the service always respond to the requester?"

Some aspects of the service interface are implicit in the service interface. For example, a service might provide a stock quote but return an error message if the submitted stock symbol is invalid.

An interface is an aspect not only of a service but also of a high-level design for the service. The interface precedes the implementation in most cases, and the service is said to *implement* the interface.

Quality of Service

The second part of the contract is the *Quality of Service (QoS)*, which is a set of interaction rules that go beyond those implied by either the elementary access details or the service interface. QoS includes the following issues:

- Reliability. For example, what percentage of time is a service promised to be available?

- Security. For example, what ensures that a specified requester is authorized to access a specified service?

- Coordination. For example, is the service allowed to revise database changes that were made but not *committed* (made permanent) by the requester?

- Runtime update of message content or destination. For example, can a message be reformatted at run time to allow transmission to a computer that uses a different protocol?

Loose Coupling

An important aspect of an SOA is loose coupling, which means that one unit of software is largely independent of another. This independence implies that changes to one unit of software cause less turmoil and cost to an organization than when the software is more interdependent. It also means you can substitute one unit of software for an already deployed unit relatively easily. The value of loose coupling is greatest when technical changes are expected over time.

The following questions identify a few of the ways that someone might measure how loosely coupled are a service and its requester:

- How easily can the service be revised without changing how the service is invoked?

  The logic and programming language of a service implementation should be independent of the service contract. You can change the service internals for greater efficiency without changing the requester in any way.

- How protected is the requester from disruption in the face of increased service capabilities?

  In general terms, two kinds of service interfaces are possible. In the case of a *Remote Procedure Call (RPC)*, the requester submits a set of arguments to a particular service operation as if invoking a local function. The alternative kind of interface is *document oriented*, in which case the requester submits a string of arbitrary length. The service reviews that string to determine what operations to perform.

  The RPC and document-oriented categories overlap, as when an RPC invocation submits a single string. However, the point is that if the contract between requester and service features a long string rather than a set of arguments and if a later version of the same service adds new functionality, the service interface is unaffected. Updates to the requester, as necessary to use the new functionality, may be needed over time rather than in urgent response to a change in the service.

- Can the requester continue running in the absence of a response?

  If the requester can invoke a service and continue running, the requester is less dependent on the service.

Service Registry

A requester must be able to reference a service's access and proposed contract details, which are often available in an online registry. Such a registry often conforms to the rules of Universal Description, Discovery, and Integration (UDDI).

A company can create its own registry for internal use and can create public registries, often in concert with other companies in the same industry.

In theory, the requester can retrieve the registered information after a runtime search; however, this kind of programmatic retrieval is rare in practice. In most cases, the registered information is available to the requester at development time.

Service Level Agreement

A Service Level Agreement (SLA) is a document that gives human readers the information necessary to decide how and whether to invoke a particular service from other software. The presence and use of an SLA varies by SOA vendor and corporate user. If present, the SLA

- Includes elementary-access and contract details in most cases

- May be written by software designers to help negotiate what functionality is to be included in a given service

- May communicate plans to potential service users and other interested parties

- May be the basis of a legal document that indicates what level of reliability the service offers; for example, how many hours per week the service is available

- May be used as an input to an automated process that creates invocation details for use when developing a requester

Web and Binary-Exchange Services

What is the defining characteristic of a Web service? For some, the answer has been that the service exchanges data in a text-based format called SOAP, which once stood for Simple Object Access Protocol but no longer has that name. Leonard Richardson and Sam Ruby sensibly insist that the defining characteristic of a Web service is that the service exchanges data over HTTP.[2]

To understand the different styles of Web service, consider a bit of technical detail as we outline the structure of an HTTP request message, which is the data transmitted from browser to Web server, and the structure of the HTTP response message, if any, that returns.

The HTTP request message has three components:

1. The message begins with an *HTTP action* to identify what the receiver is to do with the message.

2. Several subsequent entries are headers that provide information that is not specific to your company's business data; for example, details on the *user agent* (that is, the requesting browser). Each header is a name-and-value pair such as a partial one shown here.

    ```
    User-Agent: Mozilla/4.0 ...
    ```

3. The entity-body is the request data, if any. If the HTTP action is GET (a request for data), the entity-body is empty in most cases.

The HTTP response message has three components:

1. The message begins with an *HTTP response code* to indicate whether the request data was processed successfully.

2. Several subsequent entries are headers, including one (**Content-Type**) that identifies the format of the data provided in the entity body of the response. The format is quite specific; for example, one is for a picture of type JPEG. If the format is Hypertext Markup Language (HTML), the response is a Web page. At least three other text-based types are of interest to us because they provide business data for use in a Web application or other requester. Those types are Extensible Markup Language (XML); SOAP, which is an XML dialect; and

JavaScript Object Notation (JSON), which is data easily processed by JavaScript.

3.   The *entity-body* is the response data, if any.

The phrase *Web service* implies the transmission of data in a text-based format. In contrast, a *binary-exchange service* exchanges data in a format associated with a particular computer language or a specific vendor. For example, a service written in EGL can be deployed as a Web service or as an *EGL service*. The latter exchanges binary data in a proprietary format.

The use of binary-exchange services provides several benefits:

* Allows a faster runtime response than is possible with Web services

* Avoids the need to maintain configuration files

* Avoids the need to learn the technologies related to traditional Web services

However, the cost is reduced accessibility. A binary-exchange service is directly accessible only to software that transmits data in the binary format expected by the service.

Our focus hereafter is on Web services.

Architectural Styles in Web Services

A Web service can represent any of three styles: Remote Procedure Call (RPC); a document-oriented style that is associated with Representational State Transfer (REST), as described later; or a hybrid style called REST-RPC.[2]

Web services traditionally fulfill the *RPC style*. In this case, you use a business-specific operation name—for example, **UpdatetEmployeeData**—and a set of arguments, as if invoking a function. In many cases, you expect a return value.

In contrast, the *RESTful* style is based on the transfer of a single unit of business data, at most. The service implementation can do whatever is necessary, but the operation name is generic: for example, GET or UPDATE.

The idea here is to hide detail. For instance, an employee record is said to be handled in only one of a few ways, regardless of what is done with the data. A business-specific operation name such as **UpdateEmployeeData** is not meaningful in determining what operation to perform.[4]

REST-RPC services use business-specific operation names. In most cases, these services use an RPC style of data exchange, but don't use the complex administrative files that are needed to handle traditional Web services.

Traditional RPC-Style SOAP Services

A traditional Web service receives and returns data in SOAP format. The so-called *SOAP envelope* is the primary content of the HTTP entity-body and is structured as shown here.

```
<Envelope>
   <Header>
      <!-- SOAP Headers here, for QoS -->
   </Header>
   <Body>
      <!-- Business data -->
   </Body>
</Envelope>
```

The SOAP message is not complex. The headers provide the main benefit of SOAP, allowing for support of security and of service coordination. The body holds the data used by the service implementation during a service request or by the requester during a service response.

In the traditional Web service, the content of the SOAP envelope is related to the content of Web Services Description Language (WSDL) files, which *are* complex. Here is how those files are used, primarily:

- At service design time, to communicate the service interface to developers and other designers.

- At the time of developing the requester, to aid the process by which the developer defines the data that will be exchanged with the service.

- At run time, to fulfill two purposes; first, to specify the service location, and second, to allow for runtime validation of the SOAP message.

One benefit of the traditional technology is that a company can cause the requester to access the same-named service at a different location simply by updating the WSDL file that is used by the requester at run time. In this way, the company responds quickly to technical change, as might accompany a merger.

In general in the software industry, automated tools help developers and deployers work with the WSDL file.

REST Services

For purposes of this book, a REST service is one that uses Web facilities to fulfill the RESTful style. Two aspects of that style were already mentioned: the transfer of a single unit of business data, at most, and the use of a narrow set of operation names. A third aspect is that the service address includes information on the data being operated on. For example, consider the following address, which is composed of three qualifiers.

```
www.example.com/employee/123
```

The address doesn't refer to a Web page, but to information about an employee, as indicated by the second qualifier; and, in particular, about a *specific* employee (number 123), as indicated by the third qualifier.

Like a Web site, a REST service is associated with many addresses. In the case of a Web site, an address provides access to a Web page. In the case of a REST service, an address provides access to a unit of business data.

As described in this book, a REST service provides at least one of the following four operations: GET, for reading data; POST, for creating data; PUT, for updating data; and DELETE, for deleting data. These operations correspond to the major HTTP actions that can be specified in the HTTP request message.

REST services generally do not involve WSDL definitions. To allow for flexibility over time, EGL provides a way to quickly update the service locations accessed by a requester. The update requires the requester's redeployment. However, the details of operation name and service interface are simpler, and complex administrative files are not required.

When an HTTP message is used for a REST service, the entity-body often holds business data in the form of Extensible Markup Language (XML) or JavaScript Object Notation (JSON). In most cases, a SOAP envelope is not present.

Richardson and Ruby anticipate a greater use of the SOAP envelope for data exchange with REST services; or at least a greater use of SOAP (or HTTP) headers so that the SOA runtime software can better handle QoS issues.[5]

We distinguish between REST and SOAP services in this book. However, a change in terminology may be necessary in the future. The real distinction is between the RPC and RESTful *styles*.

REST-RPC Services

The industry provides many kinds of REST-RPC services. We use the phrase *EGL REST service* to refer to the type of REST-RPC service provided by EGL. At this writing, the EGL REST service is accessible only to a Rich UI application.

Access of an EGL REST service involves an RPC style. In this case, parameters and a return value identify the data to exchange, and the developer can think in terms of a business-specific operation name such as **GetEmployeeData**. The request message always uses an HTTP POST action, but that detail is not visible to the person developing the Rich UI application or the EGL REST service.

Incidentally, a Rich UI application can also access SOAP services and third-party REST services, as noted in the next chapter, which details the scope of EGL.

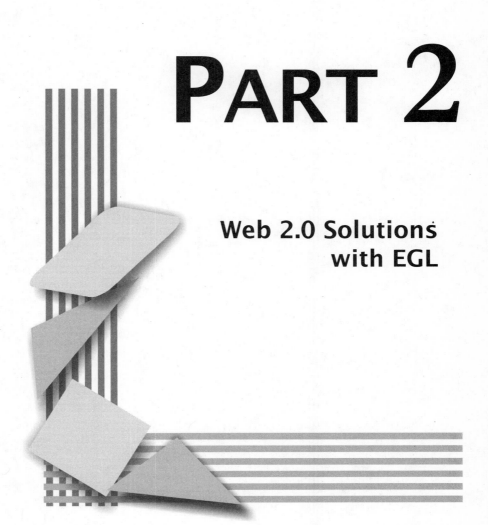

PART 2

Web 2.0 Solutions with EGL

CHAPTER 5

EGL Scope

Before we explore additional details about EGL, we describe its scope.

Uses of EGL

EGL lets developers create business software without requiring them to have a detailed knowledge of runtime technologies or to be familiar with object-oriented programming. Developers can focus on business issues, and your company can retain those people and their business savvy as technology changes.

The Rational products that support EGL are based on *Eclipse*, which is the integrated development environment (IDE) described at *http://www.eclipse.org*. Developers familiar with Eclipse will be familiar with the most basic product features, including the *Workbench*, which is the interactive component.

The Workbench includes several *wizards*, each of which is a sequence of dialog boxes that elicit developer input. The input is then used to automate an aspect of the development process. Some wizards are similar to those in Eclipse and set up folders to contain the developer's source code. Other wizards go beyond the ones available in Eclipse, creating skeletal source code or Web pages.

The EGL developer writes and changes EGL source code in a text editor that provides interactive assistance. Also, the developer can use a source-code debugger to verify the code's runtime behavior and to test the effect of different data values. The debugging session switches seamlessly from technology to technology as the runtime situation changes. You might debug a program, for example, along with a service that is invoked by the program and is intended for use on a remote machine.

After the developer codes and debugs the EGL source, the next step is specific to EGL: with a keystroke, the developer submits the source as input to a process called *generation*. The primary output is Java or COBOL source code, which is the basis of an executable, or JavaScript. The JavaScript is subsequently included in a Web page, which is written in Hypertext Markup Language (HTML).

The use of EGL is illustrated in Figure 5.1.

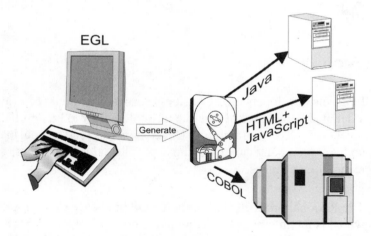

Figure 5.1: Generation and Deployment

The abstractions of EGL allow for simple coding and update. The output of the generation process is only an intermediate form. If you wish to make changes to the logic, you change the EGL source code and regenerate the output.

The products that support EGL can place Java or COBOL output on a deployment platform separate from the machine where development occurs. In the case of COBOL output, the creation of an executable occurs on the deployment platform. EGL also produces supplementary files to help the deployment staff install the executable.

Another aspect of the overall development process is that each product that supports EGL provides two ways to generate output. A developer working in the Workbench interacts with the capabilities described earlier, including editors, debuggers, and wizards. In contrast, a developer or administrator working with the EGL software development kit (SDK) uses a command-line interface that includes none of the interactive features characteristic of the Workbench.

An organization might use the SDK in an automated build process. Developers prepare an application for testing, for example, and then store the EGL source files in a software-library system. A batch job periodically runs: first, to extract the files from the library system; second, to trigger generation; and third, to prepare and deploy the generated output. In response to errors found by the testers, the developers update and store the source code for another round of testing, which can occur only after the batch job runs again.

Each product runs on any of several Microsoft Windows platforms (Windows 2000®, Windows 2003®, Windows XP®, and Windows Vista®) or on Linux. Each product includes WebSphere® Unit Test Environment, which is a component for serving Web pages to browsers and for running applications under Java Enterprise Edition (JEE). You can use the WebSphere environment to test Web and JEE applications as you develop them. Moreover, you can test Rich UI applications directly in the Rich UI editor.

Supported Technologies

We describe the commercial technologies supported by EGL. The breadth of support has a long-term implication: the language and skills taught in this book are likely to remain useful even as your organization changes technologies.

Runtime Environment

EGL-generated code runs under any of the following environments.

- *Java Platform, Standard Edition (JSE)*. JSE is the simplest Java runtime. EGL-generated Java JSE code runs on the platforms AIX®,

HP UX, IBM i, Linux®, UNIX System Services (on System z™), and the supported Windows platforms.

HTTP servers such as the Apache HTTP server are JSE environments.

- *Java Platform, Enterprise Edition (JEE)*. JEE is a Java runtime that provides special handling for database access, Web applications, and other technologies. Developers can generate code that will run in one of the following three ways: first, as an *application client* (a Java program, but one that does not compete for all the resources needed to present data to a browser); second, in a *Web application* (logic that interacts with a browser); or third, as an *Enterprise JavaBean stateful session bean* (a modular unit of business logic). EGL-generated Java JEE code runs on the platforms AIX, HP UX, IBM i, Linux, Solaris®, UNIX System Services, and the supported Windows platforms.

  You can run JEE Web applications in Apache Tomcat, which you can download from *http://tomcat.apache.org*, and you can run any kind of Web or JEE application on WebSphere Application Server. EGL helps you to work with JEE security on either server.

- *IBM i*. On the midrange IBM Power Systems, in the context of the operating system IBM i, EGL-generated COBOL code includes interactive programs, batch programs, and services. Moreover, EGL lets you quickly create Web services that expose the logic available in any of the following kinds of programs: rpgle, cbl, cblle, sqlrpgle, sqlcbl, and sqlcblle.

- *z/OS®*. On the mainframe computer System z, in the context of the operating system z/OS, EGL-generated COBOL code runs in any of the following environments:

  - *z/OS batch* is the z/OS batch-processing environment.

  - *Customer Information Control System (CICS)* is a *transaction manager*, which is a runtime for handling large numbers of business transactions such as customer orders. Developers can generate interactive programs, batch programs, and SOAP services, all in COBOL.

  - *Information Management System (IMS™)* is another transaction manager. Developers can generate COBOL programs that use any of the major IMS facilities on System z. Generated interactive programs can be IMS Message Processing programs (MPPs). Generated batch programs can be IMS Batch Message Processing programs (BMPs), DL/I Batch programs, or MPPs. EGL also supports the IMS FastPath facility.

- *z/VSE*™. Also on System z, in the context of the operating system z/VSE, EGL-generated COBOL code runs in either of the following environments:

  - *z/VSE batch* is the z/VSE batch-processing environment.

  - CICS is available; in this case, developers can generate interactive or batch programs.

EGL offers a special benefit when you are writing interactive code for CICS or IMS. In this case, you structure your code as if the user were having a conversation with a program that is always in memory, even though the runtime code (in the usual case) is repeatedly brought into memory and taken out of memory during the program's interaction with the user. The complexity of the conversation is handled in the logic generated by EGL and not in your EGL source code, which is relatively simple to write and understand.

Persistent Data Storage

The EGL developer uses intuitive I/O statements (such as **add** and **get**) to access data from a relational database, a hierarchical database, a message queue, or a file:

- *Relational databases*. The standard language for accessing relational databases is Structured Query Language (SQL). For simple applications, the developer can rely on the SQL statements used by default in EGL I/O statements. For complex applications, an EGL developer familiar with SQL can go beyond the defaults. Moreover, EGL is structured so that an SQL developer can write sophisticated database-access code for other developers to use.

  EGL supports access of DB2® Universal Database (DB2 UDB) from COBOL code and supports access of the following databases by way of Java Database Connectivity (JDBC): DB2 UDB, Informix®, Microsoft SQL Server®, Oracle®, Cloudscape®, and Derby.

- *Hierarchical databases*. The standard language for accessing hierarchical databases is Data Language/I (DL/I). The developer can rely on default EGL I/O statements, can go beyond the defaults, and can write database-access code for other developers.

  EGL supports access of hierarchical databases on IMS, CICS, and z/OS batch.

- *WebSphere MQ message queues*. WebSphere MQ calls allow program-to-program communication that involves a set of queues managed by WebSphere MQ rather than by either program. The application that sends data is not dependent on the immediate availability of the application that receives the data, yet message delivery is assured.

  When accessing a message queue, the EGL developer usually relies on default EGL I/O statements. Specialized expertise is not as necessary as in the case of database access.

  EGL supports access of WebSphere MQ message queues on all platforms.

- *Files*. EGL supports access of *sequential files,* whose constituent records are accessed in record order. Access of those files is available for any target platform. EGL also supports access of two other types of files, for target platforms that allow the choice. Those other types are *indexed files*, whose records are each accessed by the value of a key in the record, and *relative files*, whose records are each accessed by an integer that represents the record's position in the file.

  For some platforms, you can associate a sequential, indexed, or relative file with any of several file technologies. You write your EGL code, then choose a file technology at generation time. The generated source code includes the I/O statements that are specific to the technology chosen.

Here are the technologies:

- *Virtual Storage Access Method (VSAM)*. EGL supports VSAM files, each of which is organized as a sequential, indexed, or relative file. EGL-generated code that runs on any of several platforms can access either local VSAM files or (in the case of IBM i) an equivalent type of file.

  The platforms for local access are AIX; IBM i; CICS; z/OS batch; and IMS (but only for EGL-generated BMPs on IMS). In addition, EGL-generated code that runs on a supported Windows platform can access VSAM files that reside on a remote System z.

- *CICS-specific technologies*. EGL supports access of the following kinds of data stores on CICS: spool files, which primarily hold program output for subsequent printing; temporary storage queues, which hold data for subsequent processing in the same or another program; and transient data queues, which submit data to another program.

- *IMS-specific technologies*. EGL supports using I/O statements to access *IMS message queues*, whether to submit data to another program or, in some cases, to retrieve data into a program.

  EGL also supports *Generalized Sequential Access Method (GSAM)* files, which are sequential files accessed by way of DL/I calls. Those calls allow processing to resume, after a failure, from the middle of a file rather than from the start.

  GSAM files are available to BMPs and on z/OS batch.

EGL supports access of two file types that are specific to IBM i: *physical files*, each of which contains data, and *logical files*, each of which provides a subset of the data in a physical file.

User Interface

With EGL, developers can create applications that interact with users in one of several ways, depending on the target system where the code runs. EGL supports a Web-based interface; a traditional character-based interface (for CICS COBOL, IMS COBOL, IBM i COBOL, and Java applications); and a more interactive, largely character-based interface (for Java applications migrated from Informix 4GL).

Web-Based Interface

EGL supports Web-based interactions in three ways: first, by providing Rich UI, which is a new technology for writing Rich Internet Applications that will be deployed on JEE-compliant application servers or on JSE Web servers; second, by providing support for JavaServer Faces (JSF), which is a technology that runs on JEE; and third, by offering a migration path for the VisualAge Generator Web transaction, which also runs on JEE but is older and less flexible than the alternatives.

Each of the three mechanisms allows for elementary processing. The user can receive a Web page, type input into a form, and click a button to provide data for subsequent processing by application logic. Also, each mechanism allows a division of labor. A graphics designer who has minimal knowledge of software can create a Web page by dragging controls from a palette, dropping them on a drawing surface, and customizing them in a variety of ways.

Rich UI. In Rich UI, the application logic is EGL-generated JavaScript that runs in a browser. The developer writes the code in EGL.

For advanced purposes, the developer can write custom JavaScript or use JavaScript libraries instead of relying on the default behavior provided by EGL. For example, the developer can use Rich UI to access the following software:

- The Dojo Toolkit (http://dojotoolkit.org/)

- Microsoft® Silverlight (http://silverlight.net/)

We describe Rich UI in Chapter 6.

JavaServer Faces (JSF). Many Web applications are not based primarily on client-side processing; instead, they are server-centric. Logic on a server guides the construction of a stream of HTML and transmits that stream to the browser. The user periodically submits data back to the server, which processes the input as appropriate and responds with another HTML stream.

An important technology for developing server-centric Web applications is *JavaServer Faces (JSF)*. We describe JSF in Chapter 14.

Web transactions. As mentioned earlier, EGL also provides a third, less flexible way of serving business data to Web browsers. The developer in this case writes a program called a *Web transaction*, which is a pre-set flow of logic that transmits Web pages and receives data back. A JEE-compliant application server is required. The primary purpose of Web transactions is to migrate code from IBM VisualAge Generator.

Text UI

EGL-generated programs can process business logic and periodically display a *text form*—a set of character-based fields that are presented at a standalone terminal or in a workstation window. After displaying the form, the program waits for user input. A particular keystroke (ENTER or a specified function key) causes the program to receive the user's input and continue processing.

This interface technology is called *Text UI*. It provides support for interactive COBOL applications running on CICS, IBM i, or IMS. Text UI is also available for interactive Java applications; specifically, for JSE applications and JEE application clients. Use of this technology in Java is primarily to migrate code from IBM VisualAge Generator.

Console UI

EGL offers a user-interface mechanism called *Console UI*, primarily for code migrated from Informix 4GL. In this case, the users interact with buttons, drop-down lists, and the like, in a workstation window. Console UI is available for JSE applications and JEE application clients.

Support for Service-Oriented Architecture

EGL strongly supports the business use of service-oriented architecture (SOA) and includes a construct that helps the developer to create a service, which may be deployed in one of three ways:

- As a *Web (SOAP) service*, which exchanges data in a text-based format called SOAP. We refer to this kind of service as a SOAP service. The Workbench also provides ways to create and use a Web

Services Description Language (WSDL) file, which tells how to access a SOAP service.

An EGL-generated SOAP service can be deployed on any of three platforms: WebSphere Application Server, Apache Tomcat, or CICS. This kind of service can be accessed by many kinds of logic, including EGL-generated Java code, Rich UI applications, and EGL-generated COBOL code running on CICS or IBM i.

- As a *Web (REST) service*, which provides a simple way of exchanging data in a variety of text-based formats. We refer to this kind of service as an EGL REST service.

  An EGL REST service can be deployed on any JEE-compliant application server and, at this writing, is accessible only to a Rich UI application.

- As an *EGL service*, which uses a proprietary format for data exchange. The main benefits of using an EGL service are first, it gives faster response than is possible with either kind of Web service, and second, it reduces your company's need to maintain WSDL and related files.

  An EGL service can be deployed on and made available to almost any EGL target platform. One exception is IMS. A second exception relates to an EGL Rich UI application. The Rich UI application can access SOAP or REST services from any source, but cannot access the EGL services that exchange data in a proprietary format.

Last, you can expose the logic in an IBM i called program or service program as if that logic were provided from a SOAP service or EGL REST service.

Network Communication

EGL lets your company avoid some of the effort needed to integrate logic that runs on different platforms. Specifically, your organization has less need to write *interface code*, which is software whose purpose at run time is illustrated in Figure 5.2.

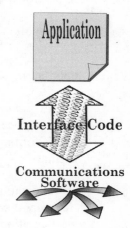

Interface code transfers application data to and from communications software, which in turn transmits the data from one platform to another. Your organization avoids the burden of writing interface code when EGL-generated Java logic calls a remote program deployed on IBM i, CICS, or IMS. Supported communications software for IBM i is IBM Toolbox for Java; for CICS, CICS Transaction Gateway; and for IMS, IMS Connector for Java.

Figure 5.2: Interface Code

Report Production

The EGL developer code can create output reports using either of several tools: Business Integration and Reporting Tools (BIRT), EGL text reporting, and print forms.

Business Intelligence and Reporting Tools (BIRT))

Business Intelligence and Reporting Tools (BIRT) is a reporting technology that delivers formatted business data to printers and screens. The technology produces sophisticated output in PDF or HTML format, including graphics, tables, charts, and graphs. The developer can sort and otherwise manipulate data from databases, variables, or Web services. For additional background details, see *http://www.eclipse.org/birt*.

An EGL program invokes the BIRT report engine to create the report. The engine can then invoke EGL functions used as *event handlers*, which are logical units that respond to a particular kind of runtime event. For example, the engine might invoke one event handler at the start of the report, one event handler at the start of a predefined report group (such as the sales data for a single type of product), and another event handler at the end of the report. For another example, an event handler might change the color of report text in response to a value received into the report from the EGL program or from a database or file.

BIRT reports are available for logic that runs under JSE or JEE.

EGL Text Reporting

EGL text reporting creates reports that deliver the output of sophisticated business processes when you need neither graphical content nor an HTML- or PDF-formatted deliverable. The benefit is speed at both development and run time.

Several details described for BIRT reporting also hold true for text reporting. A text report can include values submitted by the EGL program that drives the report-creation process; EGL functions can act as event handlers; and EGL text reporting is available for logic that runs under JSE or JEE.

Print forms

An EGL *print form* is a set of character-based fields that a program writes periodically to a printer, either directly or by way of a file. Print forms are available for COBOL programs, JSE applications, and JEE application clients.

Integration with Existing Code

Your company can integrate EGL-generated code with existing software. EGL-generated COBOL code can interact with *native* (non-generated) programs on the same platform, whether the platform is CICS, IBM i, IMS, or z/OS batch. Similarly, EGL-generated Java code can call local, native programs written in C, C++, or Java; and can call remote CICS, IBM i, or IMS programs.

EGL provides two additional ways to integrate EGL-generated and native Java code. First, EGL lets you access a native Java interface or class from within your EGL code. You're able to use EGL syntax to work with the Java-based logic.

Second, you can cause a native Java class to call an EGL-generated program. This kind of integration involves a *Java wrapper*, a set of Java classes that will be deployed with the native class. The Java wrapper acts as an intermediary between the externally created code and the EGL-generated program.

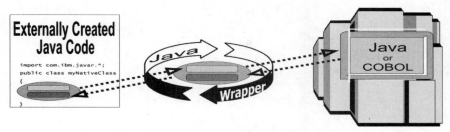

Figure 5.3: Use of a Java Wrapper at Run Time

As suggested in Figure 5.3, the EGL technology hides the details of data conversion. The native code invokes the Java wrapper, submitting data for transfer to the program. The wrapper then calls the program, which may be on a remote platform. The wrapper accepts the data returned from the program and relays the data back to the native code.

The Java wrapper is specific to the EGL-generated program being called, and the wrapper and program can be generated at the same time (Figure 5.4).

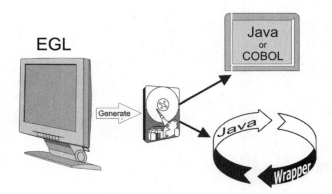

Figure 5.4: Generation of a Program and a Related Java Wrapper

Integrating Multiple Products that Support EGL

You can install an IBM Rational product that supports EGL and also install compatible products on the same machine. You have the option of working in a single, integrated development environment for all products.

CHAPTER 6

EGL Rich UI in Context

O ur intent is to introduce the EGL facility for writing Rich Internet Applications and to show example code. Later chapters detail the structure of EGL as a whole, in a more formal way.

Multiple Tiers

An EGL Rich UI application is likely to be the front end of a complex runtime environment (Figure 6.1).

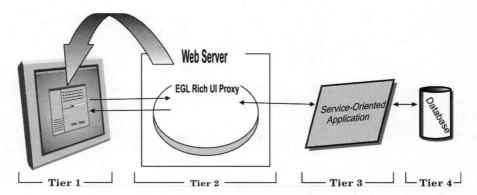

Figure 6.1: The Rich UI Application at Run Time

Our example includes four logical *tiers*:

• Tier 1 is a Web browser where the Rich UI application runs

- Tier 2 is a Web server that transmits the Rich UI application and handles the code's subsequent access of services

- Tier 3 is the software that runs the service-oriented applications

- Tier 4 is the software that supports database access

A tier is logical in the sense that some or all of the tiers can be on the same machine. For example, as you write a Rich UI application, at least tiers 1 and 2 are on the machine used for development, and a simulated proxy allows for access of tier 3.

Support for Old and New Programming Models

A traditional interactive application is based on interactive forms. The typical steps may be familiar to you:

1. Transmit a form from a server, to request user input

2. On the client, validate the input for a given field; for example, to ensure that a numeric field contains only digits

3. Receive the user's data submission, which occurs when the user takes an action such as clicking a SUBMIT button or pressing ENTER

4. On the server, validate the submitted data to ensure (for example) that one field value—such as U.S. state—is compatible with a second— such as zip code:

   ♦ If the cross-field validation fails, redisplay the same form, including an error message and the user's input

   ♦ If the cross-field validation succeeds, store the data in a database and, if necessary, transmit a different form to the user

Whatever the variations in these steps, the form-based processing model has widespread and continued value. When you use EGL Rich UI, you can organize data fields into a set of forms, can enforce a pre-specified ordering of user tasks, and can perform cross-field validation on a form or multiform basis. The new EGL technology lets you simulate use of the old.

However, even if you simulate use of the old technology, Rich UI applications offer specific benefits. First, the cross-field validations can occur in logic that runs in the browser, so you can move from form to form quickly, without contacting the server. Second, any contact with the server is *asynchronous*, which means that the user does not wait for a response, but keeps interacting with the application. Later, we show how a new variation in the EGL **call** statement makes this behavior possible.

Beyond leading the user through a sequence of forms, you can devise an application flow that updates different areas of the screen from within the application in response to the user's choice or to some combination of application data. Again, changes to the displayed Web page reflect statements that run in the client-side code.

The DOM Tree

We now describe how browsers handle a Rich Internet Application at run time. The purpose is twofold:

- To help you learn the Rich UI technology faster, as is possible by clarifying the runtime effect of what you code at development time

- To make it easy for you to respond to advanced technical requirements

When a user enters a Web address into a browser, the browser transmits a request to a Web server, which is usually on a second machine. The address identifies a specific server and indicates what content is to be returned to the browser. For example, if you enter the address *http://www.ibm.com*, a server replies with a message that the browser uses to display the IBM home page. The question that is of interest now is, how does the browser use the message?

The browser brings portions of the message into an internal set of data areas. The browser then uses the values in those data areas to display on-screen controls, which are commonly called *widgets*. Example widgets are buttons and text fields.

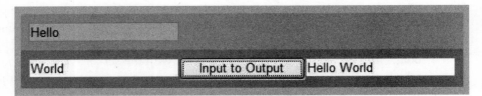

Figure 6.2: Example Web Page

The Web page in Figure 6.2 displays seven widgets:

- The enclosing box is **myBox**

- The upper box within myBox is **myBox02** and includes the text field **myHelloField**

- The lower box within **myBox** is **myBox03** and includes the text field **myInTextField**, the button **myButton**, and the textField **myOutTextField**

The internal data areas used by the browser are represented by an inverted tree (Figure 6.3).

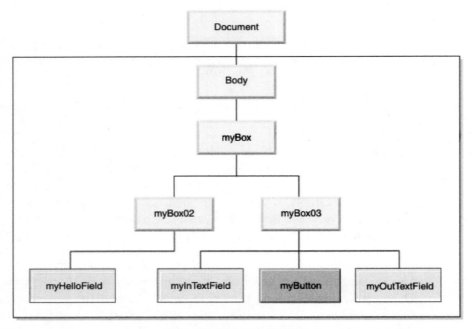

Figure 6.3: Example DOM Tree

The tree is composed of a root—named *document*—and a set of *elements*, which are units of information. The topmost element that is available to you is named *body*. The elements subordinate to body are specific to your application.

A set of rules describe both the tree and how to access the data that the tree represents. That set of rules is called the *Document Object Model* (*DOM*). We refer to the tree as the *DOM tree*; and we refer to the relationships among the DOM elements by using terms of family relationships:

- **myBox03** and **myInTextField** are *parent* and *child*

- **myBox** and **myButton** are *ancestor* and *descendant*

- **myInTextField**, **myButton**, and **myOutTextField** are *siblings*

In the simplest case (as in our example), a widget reflects the information in a single DOM element. In other cases, a widget reflects the information in a subtree of several elements. But in all cases, the spacial relationship among the displayed widgets reflects the DOM-tree organization, at least to some extent. Here are the rules:

- A widget that reflects a child element is displayed within the widget that reflects a parent element.

- A widget that reflects a sibling element is displayed below or to the right of a widget that reflects the immediately previous sibling element

We often use a technical shorthand that communicates the main idea without distinguishing between the displayed widgets and the DOM elements. Instead of the previous list, we might say, "A widget is contained within its parent, and a sibling is displayed below or to the right of an earlier sibling."

The DOM tree organization does not completely describe how the widgets are arranged. A parent element may include detail that causes the child widgets to be arranged in one of two ways: one sibling below the next or one sibling to the right of the next. The display also may be affected by the specifics of a given browser; for example, by the browser-window size, which the user can update at run time in most cases. Last, the display may be affected by settings in one or more *cascading style sheets*, which are files that set display characteristics for an individual widget or for all widgets of a given type.

When you develop a Web page with EGL Rich UI, you declare each widget by specifying a widget name such as **myButton**, a widget type such as **Button**, a set-value block (as described in a later chapter), and a semicolon.

```
myButton Button{};
```

The widgets are displayable only if your code also adds those widgets to the DOM tree. Your code can also update the tree—adding, changing, and removing widgets—in response to runtime events such as a user's clicking a button. The central point is this: *Your main task in Web-page development is to create and update a DOM tree.*

Some of the tasks needed for initial DOM-tree creation are handled for you automatically when you work with the EGL Rich UI editor; in particular, when you select a widget from a palette and drag the widget to your Web page. Alternatively, you can create a DOM tree by writing EGL definitions in source code and can even reference DOM elements explicitly.

In general terms, you create and update a DOM tree in three steps:

1. Declare widgets of specific types—Button for buttons, TextField for text fields, and so forth—and customize the widget properties. For example, you might set the text of a button to "Input to Output," as in our example. Here is EGL code to set the text.

```
myButton Button {text = "Input to Output"};
```

2. Add widgets to the initial DOM tree. A field named **initialUI** identifies the children of the DOM-tree body element; and a widget-specific field named **children** relates one widget to the next.

Although we have not described the EGL syntax, you can look at a fuller example to get a sense of how to build a DOM tree.

```
handler MyHandlerPart
    type RUIhandler { initialUI =[myBox] }

    myBox Box{ children = [myBox02, myBox03] };

    myBox02 Box{ children = [myHelloField] };

    myBox03 Box{ children = [myInTextField,
                myButton, myOutTextField] };

    myHelloField TextField { text = "Hello" };

    myInTextField TextField{};

    myButton Button { text = "Input to Output" };

    myOutTextField TextField{};
end
```

3. Alter the DOM tree by adding, changing, and removing widgets at those points in your code when you want the changes to be displayable. Here is EGL code that resets **myBox03** so that the only child of that box is **myOutTextField**.

```
myBox03.children = [myOutTextField];
```

Given the Web page in Figure 6.2 as a starting point, the revised Web page is as follows (Figure 6.4).

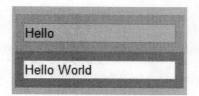

Figure 6.4: Revised Web Page Example

We say that a widget or its changes are "displayable" rather than "displayed" because a widget in a DOM tree can be hidden from view.

Appendix B is a reference guide to the supported widgets.

Rich UI Handler

To create an EGL Rich UI application, you code a Rich UI handler. The handler holds the EGL logic to add widgets to an initial DOM tree and to respond to events such as a user's click of a button.

Let's consider our example Web page again (Figure 6.5).

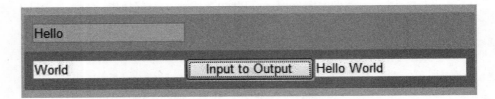

Figure 6.5: Example Web Page

The content shown there is displayed after the user types *World* in the field **myInputTextField** and clicks the button.

Here is the EGL Rich UI handler that provides the logic for displaying that Web page.

```
handler MyHandlerPart
    type RUIhandler {initialUI =[myBox],
                     onConstructionFunction = start}

    myBox Box{padding = 8,
            children =[myBox02, myBox03],
            columns = 1,
            backgroundColor = "Aqua"};

    myBox02 Box{padding = 8, columns = 2,
              children =[myHelloField],
              backgroundColor = "DarkGray"};

    myBox03 Box{padding = 8, columns = 3,
          children =[myInTextField, myButton,
                  myOutTextField],
          backgroundColor = "CadetBlue"};
```

Listing 6.1: Code for the Example Web Page (part 1)

```
myHelloField TextField
    {readOnly = true, text = "Hello"};

myInTextField TextField{};

myButton Button
    {text = "Input to Output", onClick ::= click};

myOutTextField TextField{};

function start() end

function click(e EVENT in)
    myOutTextField.text =
        myHelloField.text + " " + myInTextField.text;
    end
end
```

Listing 6.1: Code for the Example Web Page (part 2)

Consider the following components of the part **MyHandlerPart**:

- The definition statement at the beginning of the part has the identifier **RUIHandler**, which indicates that the handler logic will be transformed into client-side JavaScript.

- The part includes a set of widget declarations from **myBox** through **myOutTextField**.

- The part includes an *on-construction function*, which is a function that runs when the handler is first invoked by the browser. In this example, the on-construction function is named **start** and does nothing. Later, we give example logic for the function.

- The part includes an event handler. In this example, the function **click** runs as soon as the user clicks the button **myButton**.

  You can also configure your code so that an event handler responds to an event that is internal to the code. Such an event might be receipt of a message that was returned from a service.

You can see how to create an initial DOM tree by reviewing **MyHandlerPart**:

- The **initialUI** field indicates that the only child of the body element is **myBox**, which is a widget of type **Box**. This widget is a rectangular control that can contain other widgets.

- The **children** fields indicate which other widgets are descendants of the body element. In our example, **myBox** is the parent of **myBox02** and **myBox03**. The code also shows that **myBox02** is the parent of **myHelloField** and that **myBox03** is the parent of **myInTextField**, **myButton**, and **myOutTextField**. We illustrated these relationships earlier, in Figure 6.3.

Here's a revised example of the on-construction function, followed by a revised display (Figure 6.6).

```
function start()
    myButton.text = "Click here!";
    initialUI = [myBox03];
end
```

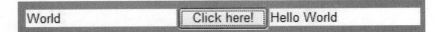

Figure 6.6: Revised Web Page

The display includes only **myBox03**. However, what happens if the on-construction function is as follows?

```
function start()
    myButton.text = "Click here!";
    initialUI = [myBox03, myButton];
end
```

At a given point in runtime processing, a widget can be the child of only one parent. In this example, the on-construction function removes **myButton** from **myBox03** and places the button below the box (Figure 6.7).

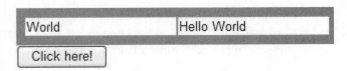

Figure 6.7: A Widget Has Only One Parent

Rich UI Editor

You can use the Rich UI editor to modify a Rich UI handler and to preview the handler's runtime behavior.

The Rich UI editor includes three views:

- The *Design surface* is a rectangular area that shows the displayable content of the Rich UI handler. You can drag-and-drop widgets from the palette onto the Design surface and then customize those widgets by setting values in the Properties view.

- The *Source view* provides an embedded version of the EGL editor, where you update logic and add or update widgets. The Design view and Source view are integrated: changes to the Design view are reflected in the Source view; and, if possible, changes to the Source view are reflected in the Design view.

- The *Preview view* is a browser, internal to the Workbench, where you can run your logic. You can easily switch to an external browser if you prefer.

  The ability to make small changes and immediately see the effect increases productivity and a sense of control. The quickness of the feature demonstrates that EGL Rich UI is well suited for prototyping and agile development.

We now show the Design surface, along with the palette at the right and, at the bottom left, a Properties view (Figure 6.8).

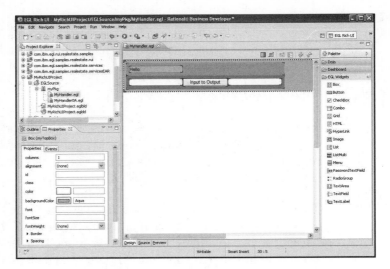

Figure 6.8: EGL Rich UI Editor

When you drag a widget from the palette to the Design surface, the areas that can receive the widget are called *potential drop locations*, and the color of those areas is yellow by default. When you hover over a potential drop location, the area is called a *selected drop location*, and the color of that area is green by default. You can customize those colors.

When you first drag a widget to the Design surface, the entire surface is a selected drop location, and the effect of the drop is to declare the widget and to identify it as the first element in the **initialUI** field of the Rich UI handler. (Again, that field identifies the children of the DOM-tree body element.)

When you drag another widget to the Design surface, you have the following choices:

- You can place the widget adjacent to the initially placed widget. The effect on your source code is to declare the second widget and to identify it as another element in the **initialUI** array. Your placement of the new widget is either before or after the first widget and indicates where the widget is placed in the array at development time. The ultimate effect is to specify another child of the DOM tree body element at run time.

- If the initially placed widget was a container—for example, a box— you can place the second widget inside the first. The effect on your source code is to add an element to the **children** property of the container. The ultimate effect is to specify a child of the container element at run time.

Your subsequent work continues to build the DOM tree. You can repeatedly fulfill drag-and-drop operations, with the placement of a widget determining what array is affected and where the widget is placed in the array. The drag-and-drop operation is an alternative to writing a widget declaration and array assignment in the code itself.

Embedded Handlers

You can use multiple Rich UI handlers to compose a single application. However, by saying "embedded handlers" we do not mean to say that you physically embed one handler in another. Instead, one handler—an EGL part that presents the user interface—declares a variable used to access the functions and widgets in a second handler. For example, the following statement declares a variable that provides access to the handler **secondHandlerPart**.

```
myVariable secondHandlerPart{};
```

A reasonable practice is to use embedded handlers for service invocation and for other business processing that lacks a user interface.

If the embedded handler (**secondHandlerPart**) has an on-construction function, the function runs when the declaration for the related variable (**myVariable**) runs.

You use a dot syntax to access the widgets and functions in an embedded handler. In the following outline, the handler **secondHandlerPart** is assumed to have declared a button named **itsButton**.

```
handler SimpleHandler type RUIHandler
    { initialUI = [ myVariable.itsButton ] }
    myVariable secondHandlerPart{};
end
```

The previous example attaches the button **itsButton** to the DOM tree. (The assignment to **initialUI** happens after all declarations in SimpleHandler run.)

You can access a function or property in an embedded widget by extending the dot syntax. For example, the following statement retrieves the displayed text of the embedded Button **itsButton**.

```
myString STRING = myVariable.itsButton.text;
```

The **initialUI** array of an embedded handler has no effect at run time.

Service access

We turn now to service access, returning later to a review of the application structure.

A Rich UI application invokes services *asynchronously*, which means that the user can still interact with the user interface while the Rich UI application is waiting for the service to respond. However, if the user needs the information to continue a task, you can (for example) disable widgets and present a simple animation until the service responds.

To invoke a service, you fulfill a four-step process. The main step is writing a **call** statement, as shown here.

```
call myService.getEmployee(123)
    returning to myCallback
    onException serviceLib.serviceExceptionHandler;
```

The example references two functions. The first is a *callback function*; here, **myCallback**. The callback function receives the business data returned from the service. The second function is an *onException function*, which receives error details if business data cannot be returned.

The example uses a built-in capability (**serviceLib.serviceExceptionHandler**) to handle errors. However, you can code your own onException function.

You never write an EGL statement to invoke the callback or onException function. Instead, the runtime technology ensures that the invocation occurs as soon as a message arrives from the service.

The process for invoking a service often requires an EGL *Interface part*, which describes the data that can pass between the application and service.

The Interface part tells the names of the service operations and, for a given operation, the kinds of data that the application exchanges with the service.

The Interface part includes no logic. Here's an example that identifies two operations: **getEmployee** (as used in our example) and **getMinimumBonus**.

```
Interface EmployeeInterfacePart
    Function getEmployee(employeeCode STRING IN)
        returns (STRING);
    end
    Function getMinimumBonus()
        returns (BIN (5,2))
    end
end
```

In many cases, you'll click a Workbench menu option to create an Interface part automatically from a service written in EGL or from a Web Services Description Language (WSDL) file.

You declare a variable based on the Interface part. Here is a declaration of **myService**, which is used in our example.

```
myService EmployeeInterfacePart {@WebBinding{}};
```

In short, here is the four-step process for invoking a service:

1. Create an EGL Interface part

2. Declare a variable based on that part

3. Code a **call** statement to invoke the service, using the variable to identify the operation

4. Code the functions referenced in the **call** statement

If you have not written the functions referenced in the **call** statement by the time you write that statement, you can click a Workbench menu option to create empty functions for later customization.

Use of Libraries

An EGL library contains functions, variables, and constants that can be accessed from other EGL code running on the same platform. Libraries allow for reuse of local code.

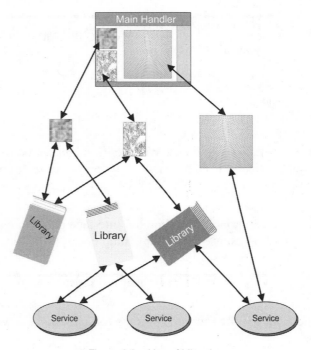

Figure 6.9: Use of Libraries

A Rich UI application can access libraries from handlers, whether to fulfill general tasks or to access services (Figure 6.9).

Model, View, Controller

An organizing idea in modern application development is that the following kinds of issues are handled separately: choices related to a user interface, and choices related to the data in persistent storage. We'll review the separation in a general way, without reference to a particular kind of technology. Our language is general because the technologies are so varied, but we'll follow up by noting how the separation applies to EGL Rich UI.

The back-end aspect of processing is the *model*, which is defined in various ways: the business data found in persistent storage, the business data brought from persisent storage into a specific application, or the logic that accesses the data in persistent storage.

The front-end aspect of processing is the *view*, which is also defined in various ways: the business data received from and presented to the user, the overall mechanism by which data is exchanged with the user, or the visual characteristics of the user interface.

The separation of model and view allows for a division of labor. A developer might handle database access and business-data manipulation while a Web-page designer focuses on the user interface. This division lets people fulfill a task appropriate to their training and lets different tasks proceed in parallel.

The *controller* is the logic that oversees the interaction between the model and view.

In many cases, the acronym MVC refers to processing that involves multiple platforms. For example, a Rich Internet Application on a Windows platform might be considered to be the view and controller; the two are mixed together because of the nature of client-side Web processing. A service-oriented application that accesses a database might be considered to be the model.

The notion of Model, View, and Controller (MVC) can affect the design of logic provided on a single tier, as shown next.

MVC in EGL Rich UI

In an EGL Rich UI application, the following terms have a constant meaning:

- The model is a data field that is internal to the application

- The view is a widget in the user interface

- The controller is an EGL **controller** definition, which ties a specific view to a specific model

Rich UI also provides a second definition, **validating form**, which lets you reference a set of controllers and in this way simulate traditional form processing.

Figure 6.10 shows a set of widgets, including a validating form that allows input of a user name, password, and email address.

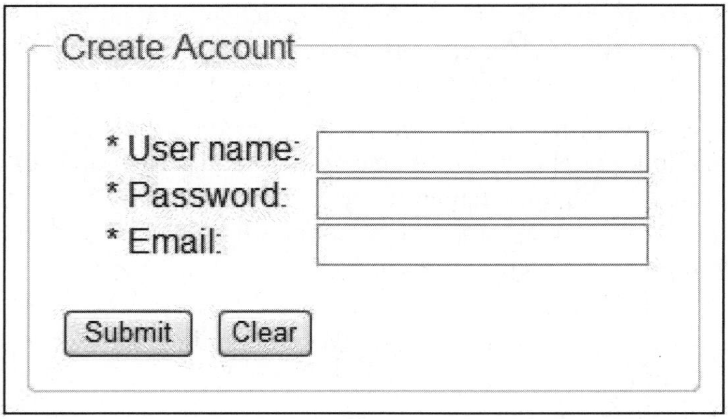

Figure 6.10: Traditional Form in EGL Rich UI

Listing 6.2 outlines how you can accomplish the display.

```
handler MyHandlerPart02
    type RUIhandler {initialUI =[myDiv]}

    myDiv Div {
        width = 310,
        borderStyle="solid",
        borderWidth=1,
        padding=10,
        children=[ myGrouping ]};

    myGrouping Grouping {
        text="Create Account",
        legend.font="Arial",
        children=[
            myForm,
            new Box {
                marginTop=3,
                children=[ submitButton, clearButton ]
            }
        ]};
```

Listing 6.2: Outline of Code for the Traditional Form (part 1)

```
    myForm ValidatingForm{};

    submitButton Button{ text = "Submit",
        onClick ::= submitForm };

    clearButton Button{ text = "Clear",
        onClick ::= clearForm };

    myService MyInterfacePart{@BindService{}};

    myRecord MyRecordPart{};

    // other declarations are not displayed
end
```

Listing 6.2: Outline of Code for the Traditional Form (part 2)

The topmost widget is a *div*, which is a container that offers flexibility in Web-page design. Here, the div includes a single child—a *grouping*, which is a widget collection preceded by customized text. The text in this case is *Create Account*. The grouping in turn includes a validating form—our main concern—and a box that contains two buttons.

Also present in the preceding code are two declarations:

- **myService**. This variable is based on an Interface part **MyInterfacePart**. You might use the variable to access a SOAP service with the validated input; for example, to store the data in an LDAP-compliant server.

- **myRecord** is a record that points to an area described by the Record part **MyRecordPart**. We'll use the record to work with **myForm**, the validating form.

Validating Form

Consider the full declaration of **myForm**.

```
myForm ValidatingForm {
    marginTop=20, marginLeft=20, marginBottom = 20,
    entries = [
        new FormField
            { displayName="* User name:",
              controller = usernameController },
        new FormField
            { displayName="* Password:",
              controller = passwordController },
        new FormField
            { displayName="* Email:",
              controller = emailController }
    ]
};
```

The first assignments in that declaration separate the form from other content. However, at the heart of the declaration is the **entries** field, which specifies an array of validating-form fields. Each field includes a label (for example, ** User name:*) and a controller. Here are the controllers.

```
usernameController Controller
    { @MVC { view = userNameField,
             model = myRecord.userName } };

passwordController Controller
    { @MVC { view = passwordField,
             model = myRecord.password } };

emailController Controller
    { @MVC { view = emailField,
             model = myRecord.email },
      validators ::= validateEmail };
```

Each of the three controllers includes **@MVC**, which ties a view to a model:

• Here are the view declarations.

```
userNameField TextField{};
passwordField PasswordTextField{};
emailField TextField{};
```

Each view in this case is basically a text field. Any widget of type **PasswordTextField** additionally ensures that the user's input is displayed as a series of unreadable characters, for user security.

- The model declarations are fields in the record (**myRecord**) that is based on the following Record part.

```
Record MyRecordPart
    userName string {
        MinimumInput=6,
        ValidationPropertiesLibrary = ValidationMessages,
        MinimumInputMsgKey = "usrMinInput" };
    password string {
        MinimumInput = 8,
        ValidationPropertiesLibrary = ValidationMessages,
        MinimumInputMsgKey = "pwMinInput" };
end
```

The declaration for a model such as **myRecord.userName** can include simple properties that cause the EGL runtime to validate user input. In our example, the property **MinimumInput** indicates that the minimum number of characters for the user name is 6 and for the password is 8. Two of the models also identify a Rich UI properties library and a message key. Those last details are part of a mechanism by which you assign displayable text in an external file; in this case, to control what error message is displayed if the user's input is invalid.

Validators

In addition to specifying validations as shown in the previous code, you can write *validators*, which are customized functions that also

validate field input. In our example, the controller **emailController** references
the validator **validateEmail**.

```
emailController Controller
    { @MVC { view = emailField,
             model = myRecord.email },
       validators ::= validateEmail };

function validateEmail(input String in) returns(String?)
    i int = StrLib.indexOf(input, "@");
    if (i > 0)
        i = StrLib.characterLen(input) - 3;
        if (i == StrLib.indexOf(input, ".", i));
            return("");
        end
    end
    return(ValidationMessages.emailError);
end
```

The example function ensures that the "at sign" (@) is in the input email
address and that a period is three characters from the end of the address.

In general, you can code a validator of any complexity. A returned blank or
null from the validator indicates success, and a returned string is displayed as
an error message at the right of the validation-form field. We'll explain
ValidationMessages.emailError after we outline how to validate the form
as a whole.

Form Validation, Commit, and Publish

You validate the form as a whole by coding an event handler that
responds to the user's click of a button. In our example, the function
is named **submitForm**.

```
function submitForm(event Event in)
    if (myForm.isValid())
        myForm.commit();

        call myService.register
            (myRecord.userName,
             myRecord.password,
             myRecord.email)
             returning to myCallback;
    end
end
```

When the function **myForm.isValid** runs, the validations for each controller are handled in turn, in form-field order. The function **myForm.commit** is invoked only if all validations succeed. Each controller-specific validation includes several steps; and then the function **myForm.commit** causes a second series of steps, invoking controller-specific **commit** functions to transfer data from views to models.

You can use a validation form to display the business data retrieved from a service; that is, to transfer data from models to views. The function you use in this case is **publish**; for example, **myForm.publish**. Such a function invokes the controller-specific **publish** functions to transfer the data.

Rich UI gives you much control over the runtime behavior described here. For convenience, system defaults are available.

Defining Displayable Text in an External File

Rich UI lets you define displayable text in an external file used at run time. The mechanism is useful for the following reasons:

- To override the runtime messages that are available, by default, for failed input validations or for incorrect formatting on output

- To assign text to widgets without hard-coding that text in the Rich UI application

- To display text in one or another language

The basic idea is that you set up variables in a library and then provide the runtime content of those variables in a properties file that is referenced in the library. Here is an example library.

```
Library ValidationMessages type RUIPropertiesLibrary
    { propertiesFile="myFile" }
    emailError STRING;
    otherContent STRING;
end
```

The content in a properties file can include *inserts*—substitution variables—whose values are specified in your code. This feature lets you embed business data—for example, a specific employee number—in a message.

You can have several properties file for a given library, one file for each language you are supporting. The naming convention is crucial:

- You specify the root of the name as the value of **propertiesFile** (in this case, the root is **myFile**).

- When you create the properties files, you specify names that include locale information. For example, the file **myFile-en.properties** has content in English, while the file **myFile-es.properties** has content in Spanish

The invocation of the Rich UI application determines which locale to use. For example, to ensure use of Spanish files, the user might invoke an application as *www.example.com/MyApplication-es.html*. A set of rules determines which properties file to access if the invocation does not match an available locale.

Simulating Page Flow

We'll now explore a couple of ways to simulate a transfer from one Web page to the next.

Here is the first page (Figure 6.11).

Figure 6.11: Web Page 1

Here is the second (Figure 6.12).

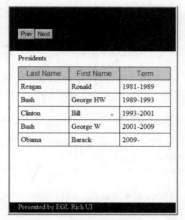

Figure 6.12: Web Page 2

Here is the third (Figure 6.13).

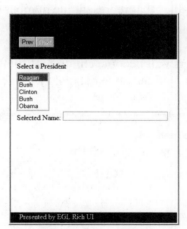

Figure 6.13: Web Page 3

For simplicity, we show only the code that demonstrates the flow. In every case, a single handler named **ControlHandler** controls the navigation. Here's a first look.

```
handler ControlHandler type RUIhandler

    {  initialUI = [thePage],
       onConstructionFunction = start }

    thePage Box{ columns=1, width=250 };

    possibleContent Widget[]{};
    numberOfPages INT = 3;
    currentPageNumber INT = 1;

    // here are other declarations and functions
end
```

The value of **initialUI** is a box (**thePage**) that contains all the displayed widgets. The handler also declares an array of widgets (**possibleContent**) and initializes variables that represent the number of distinct pages and the number of the current page.

Three containers will become children of **thePage**. Here are the declarations of two of them, without style details: the boxes **topBox** and **bottomBox**.

```
topBox Box{
    columns=3,
    children = [prevBtn, nextBtn]};

prevBtn Button{text = "Prev", onClick ::= PrevPage,
                disabled=1 };
nextBtn Button{text = "Next", onClick ::= nextPage};

bottomBox Box{
    columns = 1,
    children=[myTextLabel]};

myTextLabel TextLabel{ text = "Presented by EGL Rich UI"};
```

The content in the two boxes is largely constant. The box **topBox** includes two buttons for user navigation, and the first of those—the button that displays **Prev**—is initially disabled. The box **bottomBox** displays a phrase. The top and bottom boxes define a template that makes the overall display consistent. Not yet shown is the middle box, which varies in response to a user click.

The on-construction function (in this case, **start**) is as follow.

```
function start
    page1Var Page1Handler{};
    page2Var Page2Handler{};
    page3Var Page3Handler{};

    possibleContent.appendElement(page1Var.loginBox);
    possibleContent.appendElement(page2Var.presGridBox);
    possibleContent.appendElement(page3Var.presListBox);

    numberOfPages = possibleContent.getSize();

    thePage.children=[
                        topBox,
                        possibleContent[currentPageNumber],
                        bottomBox ];
end
```

After declaring a variable for each embedded handler, the function appends content from those handlers into the **possibleContent** array and calculates the number of elements in the array.

The main idea of paging is that each element in the array is a widget that is assigned (at one time or another) as the middle box; that is, as the middle child of **thePage**. The assignments in the on-construction function initialize the DOM tree so that page 1 is rendered when the function ends.

Switching Pages in the Simplest Case

What causes the **Next** and **Prev** buttons to work? By clicking a button, the user causes invocation of a button-specific event handler. Here are the event handlers that respond to the user's click of **Next** or **Prev** in the simplest case we'll cover.

```
function nextPage(e Event in)
    currentPageNumber = currentPageNumber + 1;
    switchPage();
end

function prevPage(e Event in)
    currentPageNumber = currentPageNumber - 1;
    switchPage();
end
```

Each event handler changes the value of **currentPageNumber** and invokes the function **switchPage**.

```
function switchPage()
    nextBtn.disabled=0;
    prevBtn.disabled=0;

    if (currentPageNumber==numberOfPages)
        nextBtn.disabled = 1;
    end

    if (currentPageNumber==1)
        prevBtn.disabled = 1;
    end

    thePage.children=[
                    topBox,
                    possibleContent[currentPageNumber],
                    bottomBox ];
end
```

The function enables the two buttons and disables them as necessary. The change to the field **thePage.children** updates the DOM tree so that the requested page is rendered when the function ends.

Switching Pages and Updating the Address Bar

If you view the pages of this example in an external browser rather than in the Workbench, you'll find that the address bar does not change as you move from page to page. The browser interprets all the different displays as being in the same Web page. The interpretation is correct, but unhelpful.

We'll now show how to cause the address bar to change; in particular, how to add a string to the initial Web page name so as to distinguish one apparent page from the next. For example, if the Web page name for the deployed application is **myPages.html**, the first page might be **myPages.html#page_1**.

To set the scene, we return to **ControlHandler**.

```
handler ControlHandler type RUIhandler
    {  initialUI = [thePage],
       onConstructionFunction = start }

    myHistory History{};

    // here are other declarations and functions
end
```

The variable **myHistory** is based on **History**, which is a handler that is always available to you. We use the variable in the on-construction function to establish the first page name.

```
function start
    // here are other statements

    myHistory.addToHistory("page_1");
end
```

The effect of invoking **myHistory.addToHistory** is to add an entry to an internal history list. We also need to consider what happens when the user clicks the **Next** and **Prev** buttons.

```
function nextPage(e Event in)
    currentPageNumber = currentPageNumber + 1;
    switchPage();
    myHistory.addToHistory("page_" + currentPageNumber);
end

function prevPage(e Event in)
    currentPageNumber = currentPageNumber - 1;
    switchPage();
    myHistory.goBack();
end
```

The user's click of the **Next** button adds another entry to the history list. The user's click of the **Prev** button returns to a previously listed string.

In four statements, we've further simulated page flow. Additional function is available; for example, you can cause some task to occur when the user moves from one page to another.

Please note that the mechanism we've described only updates the address bar and keeps an internal list of the page names. You'll need to code any related behavior that makes sense for your application.

You can combine the browser-history technique with a sophisticated mechanism for exchanging data within an application. We turn to this issue in the next section.

The **History** handler also provides a feature that comes into play when the user tries to exit the application. If you want to require that the user confirm the exit, declare a variable for **History**, as before, and invoke the function **keepUserOnPage**.

```
function start
    // here are other statements

    myHistory.keepUserOnPage(warning);
end
```

The event handler you reference (in this case, **warning**) can add a custom message to the message displayed by the browser. Here is the example event handler.

```
function warning() returns (STRING)

    return("If you continue out, " +
          "you will need to complete the work later."
end
```

Figure 6.14 shows the message that will be displayed by Internet Explorer 7 if the user tries to close the browser.

Figure 6.14: Confirmation Message

Handler Communication with Infobus

EGL Rich UI includes the *Infobus*, which is a mechanism that works as follows:

• A Rich UI handler subscribes to an event of a specified name. Here's an example subscription.

```
InfoBus.subscribe("userSelection", showInGrid);
```

The statement references an event handler; in this case, **showInGrid**. The Infobus registers the event handler and ensures that after the named event occurs, the event handler runs.

• In a different Rich UI handler (or, less often, in the same one), a function publishes the event and can include data that is specific to the event. Here is an example **publish** invocation.

```
InfoBus.publish("userSelection", entryNumber);
```

In short, the subscription sets the stage for responding to a later event, and the publish reports the event.

In our example, the string "userSelection" refers to an event published by **Page3Handler**. The event is the user's choosing a list-box entry on Web page 3 (Figure 6.15).

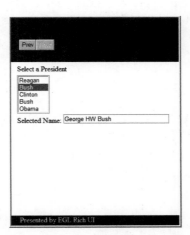

Figure 6.15: Choice on Web Page 3

The **publish** invocation identifies **entryNumber**, which is an integer that will identify, at run time, the user's selection (1 for Ronald Reagan, 2 for the elder George Bush, and so forth).

Here is partial code from **Page3Handler**.

```
handler Page3Handler type RUIhandler
    {onConstructionFunction = start }

    entryNumber INT;

    myTextLable TextLabel {text="Select a President"};
    myList List{onChange ::= mySelect};
    displayBox Box{ columns = 1,
                    children = [ myTextLable, myList]};

    function start()
        // place values in list box
    end

    function mySelect(e Event in)
        entryNumber = myList.getSelection();
        InfoBus.publish("userSelection", entryNumber);
    end
end
```

The declaration for the list box **myList** identifies the function (**mySelect**) that will respond to the user's choice of a list-box entry. The function **mySelect** in turn publishes the event "userSelection". After the user's selection, the EGL Runtime runs **showInGrid** (not shown), which highlights the appropriate row in the grid on Web page 2. When the user clicks the **Prev** button from Web page 3, the grid is displayed (Figure 6.16).

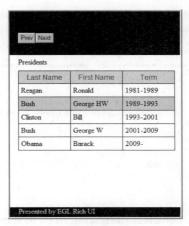

Figure 6.16: Web Page 2

Note that a **publish** invocation does not include the name of the event handler (here, **showInGrid**) that ultimately responds to the event. Instead, the Infobus acts as a mediator and ensures that the appropriate event handler is invoked. The function that publishes an event is independent of the function that subscribes. Many functions can publish the same named event, and many functions can subscribe to that event.

A subscription is most likely in an on-construction function because the purpose of that function is to do set-up tasks. For example, the subscription mentioned here is in the on-construction function of **Page2Handler**.

```
handler Page2Handler type RUIhandler
    {  onConstructionFunction = start }

    function start()
        InfoBus.subscribe("userSelection", showInGrid);
    end
end
```

An important use of the Infobus is to update sections of a display. For example, a subscription might also be in **ControlHandler**.

```
handler ControlHandler type RUIhandler

    {  initialUI = [thePage],
       onConstructionFunction = start }
    page2Var Page2Handler{};

    function start()
        InfoBus.subscribe("userSelection", goToPrev);
    end
end
```

The handler **ControlHandler** subscribes to the same event as does handler **Page2Handler**. However, the subscription in **ControlHandler** does not refer to **showInGrid** but to an event handler that we display now: **gotoPrev**.

```
function goToPrev(eventName String IN, data ANY IN)
    genericGoBack();
end

function genericGoBack()
    currentPageNumber = currentPageNumber - 1;
    switchPage();
    myHistory.goBack();
end
```

An event handler always receives an event name (in this case, "userSelection") and receives the runtime data, if any, that was specified during publish. In this case, the event handler ignores the runtime data.

Let's trace some of the steps that occur when the user runs **ControlHandler**:

1. The runtime declaration of a variable based on **Page2Handler** causes invocation of the on-construction function of the embedded handler. The effect is that **Page2Handler** subscribes to "userSelection".

2. The on-construction function in **ControlHandler** runs next, causing a second subscription to "userSelection." When the user selects a list-box entry on Web page 3, the publishing of "userSelection" causes invocation of **showInGrid** (in **Page2Handler**) and then **goToPrev** (in **ControlHandler**). The user sees the Web page 2, where the appropriate grid row is highlighted.

CHAPTER 7

Services and EGL Rich UI

Many companies need to bring business information *up* from older platforms and *out* to the Web. Services are essential.

Services can include new logic and can expose the data returned from other services and from called programs. EGL can even make the logic in decades old mainframe programs widely available. EGL offers *end-to-end processing*: your company can write the user interface, the service logic, and, if necessary, new back-end programs, all in EGL.

In response to a simple requirement, one person can code all aspects of end-to-end processing. Alternatively, programmers can share expertise with colleagues who are handling different aspects of a complex requirement and who share both the development environment and the coding language.

We'll start our overview with a description of Web service support on CICS and IBM i.

CICS Web Services

Customer Information Control System (CICS) is a *transaction manager*, which is a runtime that handles large numbers of business transactions such as customer orders. CICS became available in 1969 and is now central to the IT operations of many companies.

As introduced in 2004 and now supported by EGL, CICS Web Services is a facility to let mainframe programmers create logic that receives or sends messages over HTTP. A CICS program on z/OS can act as a Web service, as a Web service requester, or both. The implication is that logic running on the mainframe can participate easily in a service-oriented application. Moreover, CICS programs can access z/OS batch programs. The tie of one kind of logic to another means that a huge amount of mainframe-based data is now available to Web browsers.

EGL developers can create SOAP services for use on CICS. In this case, generation of the EGL service part creates a COBOL program; and generation of the deployment descriptor creates a data file of type wsbind and a second COBOL program that we'll call the wrapper program (Figure 7.1).

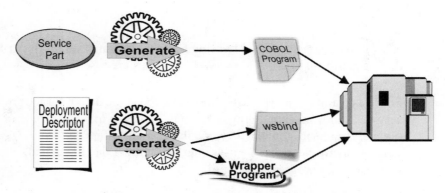

Figure 7.1:   Generation and Deployment of a CICS Web Service

When the CICS runtime needs to handle a request to a particular SOAP service or a response from that service, the CICS runtime reads the wsbind file and guides the conversion of binary data to or from a SOAP envelope (Figure 7.2).

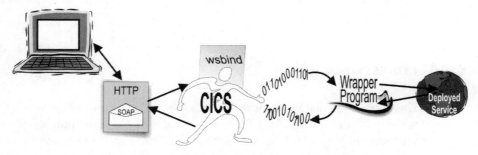

Figure 7.2:   Runtime Processing of a CICS Web Service

The COBOL wrapper stands between the data conversion just described and the EGL-generated service. The wrapper identifies the service operation—in CICS terms, the *entry point*—that was requested; and communicates with the entry point.

Access of IBM i Programs as Web Services

The IBM Power Systems support midrange computing, which is a technology in between that of a mainframe and a personal computer. Mainframes are characterized by an ability to process huge quantities of data, but the distinctions between mainframes and midrange computers are blurring as the latter become faster.

One of the operating systems supported by the IBM Power Systems is IBM i, which has attracted many third-party applications and provides backward compatibility such that 30-year-old business logic can run without modification.

EGL lets you expose the logic in an IBM i called program or service program in an unusual way. With a few clicks, the developer generates a SOAP service or EGL REST service so that a service requester on another platform can access any of several kinds of non-EGL-generated IBM i programs.

The technology even lets Web users access IBM i programs that are *stateful*. A stateful program is one that retains information between invocations so that the user and program can participate in a multistep conversation.

The effect of this support is to allow an exchange of IBM i-stored data with customers or suppliers and with people in the company, when the exchange previously required access to a "green screen" or terminal emulator, if an interactive exchange was possible at all.

End-to-End Processing

The sophisticated use of database-query techniques, exception handling, and the like are available in EGL, and we give you a sense of the language's power in later chapters. For now, we offer some background on the Workbench and then a small example of end-to-end processing there.

EGL Projects and Deployment

A development effort uses Workbench facilities such as an *EGL project*, which is a collection of files that represent a subset of a development effort. The following kinds of EGL projects are of particular interest in this book:

- A *Rich UI project* is used to develop Rich UI applications, custom widgets, or both.

- A *Web project* is used for several purposes, including to develop most Web services. The project is designed to let a developer easily transmit deployable content to a Web server or application server.

- A *General project* is used for several purposes, including to develop COBOL services for CICS.

After a software requirement is at least tentatively defined, a team proceeds as follows:

- Creates one or more Web projects to write and generate Web services; and to specify whether to deploy a given service as a SOAP service (for wide distribution), an EGL REST service (for less administrative complexity), or both. Similarly, creates General projects to write and generate SOAP services for CICS.

- Creates one or more Rich UI projects to write and debug the Rich UI handlers that access those services.

- Prepares to deploy the Rich UI project by working through the Rich UI deployment wizard, which creates an HTML file that embeds the previously generated JavaScript. The wizard copies the HTML file and others (for example, graphics files) from the Rich UI project to a Web project.

- Deploys the Web projects to application servers and CICS.

Example of End-to-End Processing

Assume that you've created an EGL Web project for service development, as well as a Rich UI project for handler development. We'll assume that your first task is to develop a service in the Web project. Here's the source code.

```
service MyService

    value string = "Hello ";

    function myEcho(myString STRING IN) returns (STRING)
        return (value + myString);
end
```

The function **myEcho** accepts an input string such as "World" and returns the concatenation of "Hello " and the input. When you create the service, you specify how you intend to deploy it, and the information is stored in the EGL deployment descriptor, as described later.

You generate the service, start the WebSphere Test Environment, and click a menu option to deploy the service. You then start a wizard that helps you fulfill the following tasks: create an Interface part from the preceding code and place that part in the Rich UI project. Here is the Interface part.

```
Interface IMyRESTService

    value string = "Hello ";

    function myEcho(myString string in) returns (string);
end
```

You'll use the Interface part as the basis of a variable in the Rich UI handler. The variable provides access to the operations in the service.

You work in the Rich UI project to create the handler that invokes the service. The handler displays three widgets, which are, from left to right, a textbox for the user input. a button, and a textbox for the service response (Figure 7.3),

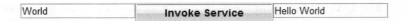

Figure 7.3: Display of Service Request and Response

The handler invokes the service when you click the button. Here is the handler.

```
handler MyHandler type RUIhandler {initialUI = [myBox]}

   myBox Box{columns = 3,
             children=[myInputText, myButton, myOutputText]};

   myInputText TextField{};
   myButton Button{ text="Invoke Service",
                    onClick ::= respondToClick };
   myOutputText TextField{};

   myInterface IMyRestService {@BindService{}}

   function respondToClick(e Event IN)
      call myInterface.myEcho(myInputText.text)
           returning to myCallback
           onException serviceLib.serviceExceptionHandler;
   end

   function myCallback(returnValue string in)
      myOutputText.text = returnValue;
   end
end
```

The Interface declaration indicates (by the use of **@BindService{}**) that information on service location is available, not in the code, but in an entry in the EGL deployment descriptor, which is a file you customize.

EGL Deployment Descriptor

The *EGL deployment descriptor* is central to the EGL support for SOA. This development-time file is available in every project and can store information on two different issues: the services that are requested by the logic being developed and, if you are developing a service, the characteristics of the service deployment.

The EGL deployment descriptor is an input to the EGL generator. The output varies by target platform and always facilitates data transport. EGL is shielding the developer from details that are specific to a target platform.

Service Client Bindings

If your EGL source code requests a service, you specify access details for the service in the EGL deployment descriptor, in a section reserved for *service client bindings*. You specify a binding that describes how to access the service:

- A *SOAP Web binding* for a SOAP service.

- A *REST Web binding* for a REST or EGL REST service.

- An *EGL binding* for a proprietary EGL service. This option is available in various cases, but a Rich UI application requires the previous alternatives.

- A *Native binding* for an IBM i service program that is made directly available to EGL-generated requesters.

Incidentally, system functions in the EGL ServiceLib library let an EGL-generated requester retrieve and set the service client bindings. That is, a requester can direct processing to a different version of a service in response to a runtime condition. One version of a service might be appropriate for a user who needs access to confidential data or is paying a premium.

Web Service Deployment

If you create a Service part, the New Part wizard in the Workbench adds details to the deployment descriptor, to a section reserved for *Web service deployment*. You can update that section so that, for example, a subsequent generation of a service previously deployed as a REST service will generate both a REST and a SOAP service.

How Do You Set the Location Data for Service Access?

A technical detail has a business implications. In regard to accessing a service from a Rich UI application, we'll consider where the service-location details reside at run time and how the details are specified at development time.

The general rule is as follows: you can put location details in your source code, but the best practice is to put those details in the EGL deployment descriptor. If you follow the best practice and then a runtime detail changes, your company gains the following benefits:

- Only a small amount of work is needed to retest the requester and to preprocess the generated output for deployment, as compared to the amount of work needed to handle a code change

- The requester is not offline as long as would otherwise be necessary

- You won't add errors to the source code, as might occur from even the most trivial change to the logic

Here is the general procedure if you follow the best practice: change the deployment descriptor for the requester, regenerate only the deployment descriptor, and redeploy only the output of that generation.

The following sections outline how the general rules apply when a requester is accessing a service of one or another style. The illustrations in these sections also suggest some programming details, for your future reference.

Access of SOAP Services

The runtime access of SOAP services always involves access of a WSDL file (Figure 7.4).

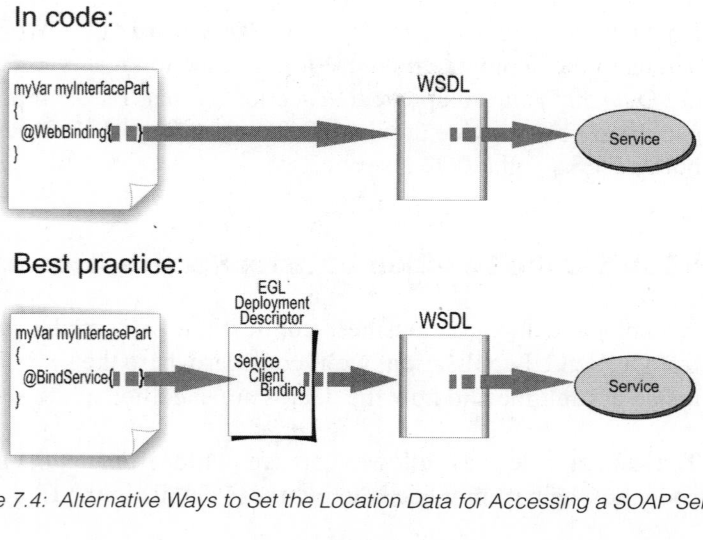

In code:

```
myVar myInterfacePart
{
    @WebBinding{   }
}
```

WSDL

Service

Best practice:

```
myVar myInterfacePart
{
    @BindService{   }
}
```

EGL Deployment Descriptor

Service Client Binding

WSDL

Service

Figure 7.4: Alternative Ways to Set the Location Data for Accessing a SOAP Service

If a service location changes, no change to the code or deployment descriptor is necessary. Your company only needs to change the WSDL file that is accessed by the requester. However, if the location of the WSDL file changes, your company benefits from having followed the best practice.

Access of EGL REST Services

The runtime access of an EGL REST service involves no WSDL file, but the relationships are otherwise similar to those of the previous section (Figure 7.5).

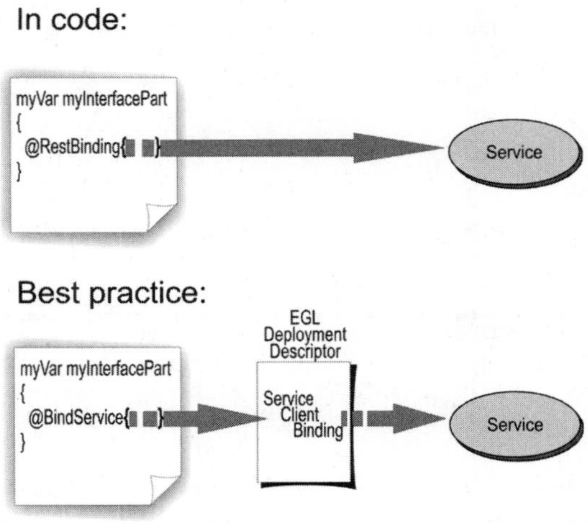

Figure 7.5: *Alternative Ways to Set the Location Data for Accessing an EGL REST Service*

Access of Third-Party REST Services

The runtime access of a third-party REST service involves a distinction between the following kinds of information:

- *Base URI*, which is a set of high-level qualifiers for the service location; for example, *www.example.com/myproject/restservices/employee*.

- *URI template*, which is a set of lower-level details that are concatenated to the base URI. These details are specific to an operation such as GET.

  If you change the URI template, you must change it in the Interface part and regenerate the code. You can't include the template in a configuration file because the template generally includes variables that are set at run time.

Here's an example. The Interface part identifies a single function, which is specific to the GET operation (as indicated by the use of **@GetREST**).

```
Interface EmployeeInterfacePart
    Function employeeData(employeeNumber string in)
        returns(myEmployeeDetail)
    {@GetREST{uriTemplate="/{employeeNumber}",
                requestFormat = JSON,
                responseFormat = JSON }};
    end
```

Here is the variable declaration and the **call** statement in the requester.

```
myEmployeeService EmployeeInterfacePart;
call myEmployeeService.employeeData("123")
    returning to myCallback
    onException serviceLib.serviceExceptionHandler;
```

The requester passes "123", which the Interface part indicates is the value of **employeeNumber**. The presence of **employeeNumber** in the template URI means that, by passing "123", the requester directs the service request to an address whose low-level qualifier is 123. If the base URI is *www.example.com/myproj/restservices/employee*, the runtime access detail is *http://www.example.com/myproject/restservices/employee/123*.

Figure 7.6 shows the alternative ways to specify the base URI.

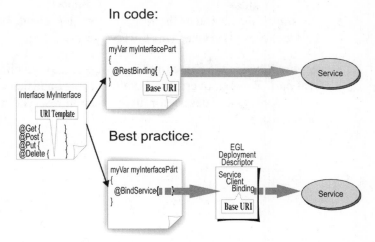

Figure 7.6: Alternative Ways to Set the Location Data for Accessing a Third-Pary REST Service

You can omit the base URI and rely solely on the template URI to access any of the REST operations that are referenced in the Interface part. Also, if the Interface part lacks a template URI for a given operation, you can rely solely on the base URI.

What is the Location for an EGL-Generated Service?

When you deploy an EGL-generated service, the service-location detail has the following pattern,

```
http://domain&Port/projectName/constantName/serviceName
```

Here is the meaning:

- *domain&Port* is an Internet identifier such as localhost:9080, www.example.com, or a machine-specific Internet Protocol (IP) address; however, depending on the machine to which the service is deployed, *domain&Port* also may include a colon (:) and an *HTTP port*. The port is an address that is internal to the deployment machine. HTTP "listens" for an incoming request at the port.

- *projectName* is the name of the project to which output was generated.

- *constantName* is one of the following values: **services** (for a SOAP service) or **restservices** (for a REST service).

- *serviceName* is the name of the Service part, or an alias specified in that part. You can override the value of this qualifier when you work in the deployment descriptor, in the section reserved for *Web service deployment*.

PART 3

Programming
with EGL

CHAPTER 8

Overview of Generation

"Any sufficiently advanced technology is indistinguishable from magic."[1]

Arthur C. Clarke

We've indicated that EGL is used in a development process that has defined steps, from coding a source to generating an output (Java, COBOL, or JavaScript) to preparing and deploying that output. Now that you've seen some EGL code, we'd like to give you a more detailed overview of generation. You'll want to have this background if you work with the language or supervise people who do.

The steps leading to generated output are twofold: EGL build and EGL generation (Figure 8.1).

Figure 8.1: From Source Code to Generated Output

EGL build itself includes an EGL-specific compilation of source code.

EGL Compilation

As you develop EGL source code in the product Workbench, the interface responds to your changes. For example, if you write invalid syntax, the EGL editor signals an error with a red X in the **Outline** view. After you fix the error, the red X goes away (Figure 8.2).

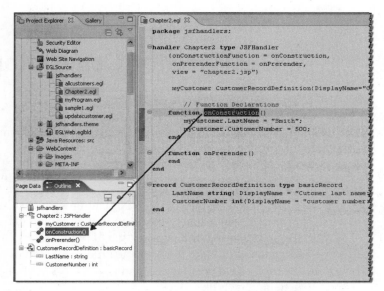

Figure 8.2: Outline View

How does the Workbench respond to your code, signaling errors in the EGL editor and suddenly displaying data in a different view? Those behaviors are made possible by hidden EGL compilations, which convert your source code to an internal format of a kind later used as input to the EGL generator.

Each compilation validates whether the syntax of the source code is correct. The validation lets the Workbench respond interactively to syntax errors but does not catch errors that are specific to a target platform.

The *EGL compiler* is the system code that compiles your source code.

EGL Build

An *EGL build* is a process that compiles your EGL source-code files and stores the output in a set of *intermediate representation (IR)* files that are used for debugging and generation (Figure 8.3).

Figure 8.3: EGL Build

By default, the product performs an EGL build automatically each time you save your EGL source code. We suggest you accept the default behavior. If you don't re-create the IR files each time you save the EGL files, you may accidentally use old EGL source code when debugging the code or when generating output.

Most builds are incremental, adding content to existing IR files. The Workbench also provides the **Clean** option, which removes and rebuilds the IR files.

EGL Generation

An *EGL generation* is a process that requires not only IR files, but a set of rules that are specific to the target platform. Before generation, you provide those rules by specifying a set of definitions that are called *build parts*. The build parts affect how output is generated, as well as how output is built at deployment time.

The most important build part is the *build descriptor*, which identifies the target platform and that references other build parts as appropriate (Figure 8.4).

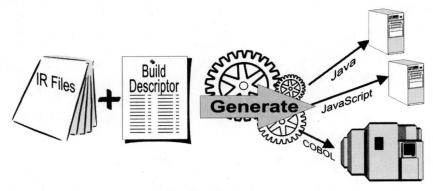

Figure 8.4: EGL Generation

EGL generation includes a second validation step to ensure that the input to generation is appropriate to the target platform. This validation step is the source of most messages from the EGL generator.

In regard to EGL generation, we suggest that you accept the default behavior. In most cases, your development task is to repeatedly write, build, and debug, leaving generation for later in the process. However, generation occurs automatically in some cases; for example, when deployment descriptors and JSF handlers are saved and when your keystrokes stop for a few seconds during development of a Rich UI handler.

CHAPTER 9

Language Organization

EGL has characteristics of Java and COBOL and includes innovations all its own. This chapter outlines how the language organizes data, logic, and presentation.

Data Types

In the broadest sense, a *data type*—for example, integer or string—defines a set of values and a set of operations that can act on those values. You can add two integers, each of which has a numeric range, or concatenate two strings, each of which has characters that are found in a particular set. The number 65 is said to be "of the type" integer.

As a developer, you associate digital values with data types (Figure 9.1).

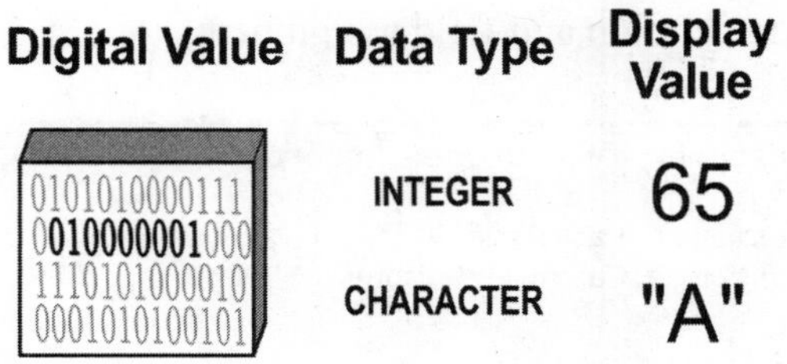

Digital Value	Data Type	Display Value
0101010000111 0010000001000 1110101000010 0001010100101	INTEGER	65
	CHARACTER	"A"

Figure 9.1: Digital Value and Display Value

A variable or constant is a name that refers to an area of memory. In EGL, the variable or constant is said to be *based on* a type, meaning that the value in the area is of the specified type.

EGL provides you with a set of primitive types—for example, STRING and INT (for integer)—and lets you create complex types. Each complex type is subdivided into fields, and any value based on a complex type is subdivided into fields as well.

An *instance* is a value to which you've applied a type. The type is a model of format, much as a blueprint is a model of a house (Figure 9.2).

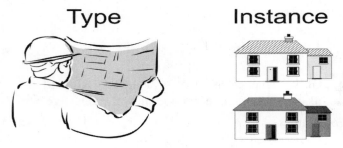

Type   Instance

Figure 9.2: Type and Instance

Let's assume that you define the type **My_Customer_Record_Definition** to include the field **LastName**, which is of type STRING, and the field **CustomerNumber**, which is of type INT. Here's the EGL syntax.

```
Record My_Customer_Record_Definition
    LastName STRING;
    CustomerNumber INT;
end
```

A variable of type **My_Customer_Record_Definition** itself has a name (for example, myCustomer) and includes a customer name and number. Here's a variable declaration and field assignments.

```
myCustomer My_Customer_Record_Definition;

myCustomer.LastName = "Smith";
myCustomer.CustomerNumber = 500;
```

In EGL, the values of most types—for example, the field values "Smith" and 500—are available at business-application run time. You can also provide *annotations*, which are values that give directions to the EGL compiler or generator prior to run time.

Categories of EGL Data Types

The simplest EGL data types are called *primitive types*. Categories include numeric types; character types; date/time types, including timestamps (instances in time) and intervals (durations); large-object types (for memos, graphics, multimedia, and so on); and a single logic type, BOOLEAN.

The other data types are called *data parts*. The most elemental of these is the *DataItem part*, or more simply, a *data item*, which assigns a business-specific name in place of a primitive-type name. For example, a data item might assign the name **NumberOfCars** in place of INT.

A *Record part* lets you create a customized type that includes primitive types and data parts. Our example type **My_Customer_Record_Definition** was a Record part.

A *Dictionary part* offers storage and retrieval of runtime data in property-value pairs. The part allows you to write code that handles some advanced tasks in a more straightforward way than would be possible without the runtime flexibility.

EGL also offers a *DataTable part*, or more simply, a *data table*. This is a data collection in which you store, for example, a list of U.S. states, their postal abbreviations, and their populations. Often, the purpose of a data table is to help validate user input. The data table is a *static part*, which means that the distinction between data type and variable is not meaningful because you use the part as needed, without declaring a variable.

Whenever the distinction between data type and variable *is* meaningful, you can create an array of elements of the type. A variable that is of type STRING array, for example, names a data area that addresses a series of elements, each of type STRING. We describe arrays in Chapter 10.

Many organizations maintain a collection of data-type names and related details. That collection is traditionally called a *data dictionary*, and it helps ensure that a data definition is the same for many programs or services. The two kinds of EGL data types that are most appropriate for a data dictionary are data items and Record parts.

Data Item

Here's the definition for the data item **NumberOfCars**.

```
DataItem NumberOfCars INT end
```

The definition assigns a name that you can use instead of a primitive-type name such as INT. If you assign a name that is meaningful in a business sense, the data item provides clarity.

For example, the following code first declares a variable for the number of cars in an insurance policy and then assigns a value.

```
myCarCount NumberOfCars;
myCarCount = 2;
```

The effect at run time is the same as if you had declared a variable of type INT.

```
myCarCount INT;
myCarCount = 2;
```

Figure 9.3 illustrates the runtime equivalence.

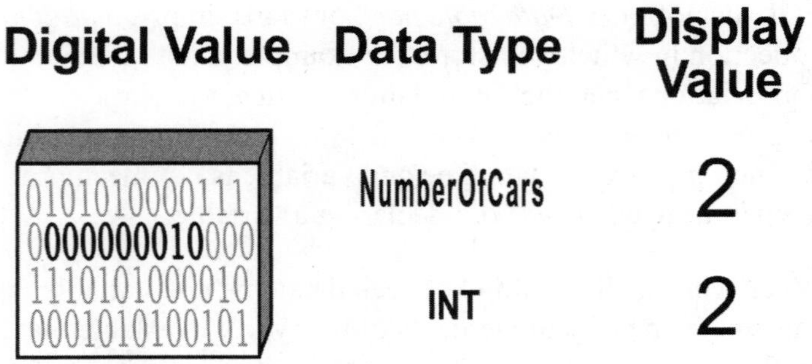

Digital Value	Data Type	Display Value
0101010000111 0000000010000 1110101000010 0001010100101	NumberOfCars	2
	INT	2

Figure 9.3: Equivalence of NumberOfCars and INT at Run Time

Your use of a data item helps you to focus on a business issue, and those who maintain your code gain the same benefit. And if the name reflects your organization's usual vocabulary, you gain the efficiency that comes from better communication among developers, Web designers, and business analysts.

Record Part

Business processing often requires you to create a sequence of fields that are processed as a unit. A *Record part* defines such a sequence. Here's an example.

```
Record CarPolicy type BasicRecord
    policyID STRING;
    carCount NumberOfCars;
    driverCount NumberOfDrivers;
end
```

The part has a name—in this case, **CarPolicy**—as well a list of fields. Each field is a declaration that includes a name, data type, and semicolon. The part is a model of format and is used for declaring a *record*, which is a variable that's based on the Record part. For example, here's a record declaration and subsequent record-field assignments.

```
myCarPolicy CarPolicy;

myCarPolicy.policyID = "ABC123";
myCarPolicy.carCount = 2;
```

Record Stereotypes

The use of the word *type* in the Record part can be misleading. Here, the word means *kind* and not a model of format.

We'll work with the following kinds of Record parts in this book:

- **BasicRecord**. Records of this kind are for general processing, but not for input/output (I/O) against an external file or database.

- **SQLRecord**. Records of this kind are for exchanging data with a relational database.

- **Exception**. Records of this kind are for error handling.

Several other kinds of Record parts are available. A record based on a particular kind of part can exchange data with a particular kind of data storage such as sequential files, indexed files, and message queues.

The different kinds of Record parts provide our first example of a pattern we'll see again. A "type" category includes different "kinds." For example, the Record part category includes SQLRecord and Exception kinds of Record parts. Each kind has a distinct syntax and a distinct business or technical purpose.

The technical term for "kind," in the sense described here, is *stereotype*. The distinction between EGL stereotypes such as SQLRecord and Exception is not that records of the two kinds have a different format at run time. The distinction is that records of the two kinds are processed differently by the EGL system code.

The notion of stereotypes comes from the Unified Modeling Language (UML), which is a graphical language used for business-process modeling and other purposes. Potentially, UML diagrams that reference EGL stereotypes can be an input to an automated process that creates EGL source code. The creation of source code from business models is generally described as Model Driven Development (MDD), and our use of the term *stereotype* points to the potential use of EGL in MDD.

Structured and Non-Structured Records

In addition to distinguishing Record parts as BasicRecord, SQLRecord, and so on, EGL distinguishes Record parts as *structured* or *non-structured*. Our previous examples represented the non-structured variation, which is useful for general processing and for accessing relational databases.

When you create a record based on a non-structured Record part, some fields in the record can reference areas that grow or shrink in size at run time. A field of type STRING, for example, might reference an area that contains the word *sedan* at one moment or the phrase *sports car* at another.

In contrast, a structured Record part is required when you need a specific runtime order of fixed-length fields. A record that's based on a structured Record part can act in several ways: accessing a file whose every field has a known, fixed length; transfering fixed-length data to or from another program; or accessing a DL/I database.

A field in a structured Record part can be based only on a type that provides a fixed length. For example, a field of type STRING is not valid; but a field of type CHAR(*size*) is, where *size* is the actual number of characters in the field.

If you create a field of type CHAR(6) and assign *sedan*, the field size remains the same, with a blank added after the last letter. If you later assign *sports car*, the field size remains the same, and the extra characters are truncated, leaving *sports*.

When you define a structured Record part, you must assign level numbers, which can indicate a complex structure. Here's an example.

```
Record PersonPart type BasicRecord
    05 name CHAR(30);
        10 lastName CHAR(15);
        10 firstName CHAR(15);
    05 Address CHAR(51);
        10 line01 CHAR(15);
        10 line02 CHAR(15);
        10 city CHAR(10);
        10 stateCode CHAR(2);
        10 zip CHAR(9);
            15 zip5 CHAR(5);
            15 zipExtension CHAR(4);
end
```

The use of level numbers lets you reference a sub-field by name. To set the sub-field **city** to the value *Boston*, for example, write the following variable declaration and assignment statement:

```
personVar PersonPart;
personVar.address.city = "Boston";
```

Although the maximum length of a structured record is fixed, your code can decide, at run time, to exclude the last fields in some situations. Those situations don't apply to any of the Record parts described elsewhere in this book; but we'll give you an idea of the capability without specifying every detail. Here's an example of a structured Record part.

```
Record PersonPart02 type SerialRecord
    { filename = "myLogicalFileName",
      numElementsItem = numberOfDegrees }
    05 name CHAR(30);
        10 lastName CHAR(15);
        10 firstName CHAR(15);
    05 numberOfDegrees SMALLINT;
    05 degrees[5]
        10 year SMALLINT;
        10 degree CHAR(10);
        10 school CHAR(20);
end
```

A record of type **PersonPart02** might include from zero to five educational degrees. The exclusion of unused degree-related entries is possible when your code writes data from the record into a file and in other cases.

Dictionary Part

Unlike the data parts we've described so far, the Dictionary part is predefined and in that sense is like a primitive type. The purpose of the part is to declare a variable—a *dictionary*—to store and retrieve data whose identifier may be known only at run time.

As you work with a dictionary, you include *dictionary entries* such as those shown in the following variable declaration.

```
stockPrices Dictionary
{
    IBM = 165.25,
    GE  =  52.75
};
```

Each entry is composed of two components: a key (such as **IBM**) that lets you access a business value, and the business value itself. The entry can accommodate any type of value, and the values across entries can represent different types of data.

Once you've declared a dictionary, you can add, change, and delete entries; retrieve the keys and values; determine the number of entries in the dictionary; and test whether a given key is present.

Our example includes entry details that were set at development time. At run time, you can use data retrieved from whatever source as a key. For instance, you can create an application that retrieves stock symbols from the user and can organize the input in a dictionary, where each key is a different stock symbol.

After you retrieve an entry, you are likely to assign it to a variable of an appropriate type. The following example is possible if you know the type of data that was retrieved.

```
price DECIMAL(5,2);
price = stockPrices.IBM;
```

However, you may have stored several kinds of entries in a single dictionary at run time. For example, some value might be of a numeric type, for holding the price of a common stock; and some values might be based on a Record part, for holding the details of a stock option. After retrieving a value, you can use the operator **isa** to test the type of the value so as to ensure that subsequent processing is appropriate to the type. The operator **isa** returns a Boolean; in the following case, *true*.

```
if (stockPrices.IBM isa DECIMAL(5,2))
    ;
end
```

A real-world stock-quote application would use a bracket syntax, as described in Chapter 10. For now, we'll show you an example that's equivalent to the previous one.

```
mySymbol STRING = "IBM";
if (stockPrices[mySymbol] isa DECIMAL(5,2))
    ;
end
```

Data table

A *data table* is a data collection that other EGL code can access. Here's an example.

```
DataTable myErrorMessages type MsgTable
  msgNum INT;
  msgText char(30);

  { contents = [ [ 101, "File not found" ] ,
                 [ 102, "Read error" ] ,
                 [ 103, "Write error" ] ]
  }
end
```

As shown, the data table has a name, *myErrorMessages*. and a stereotype such as **MsgTable**. Next, variables indicate the type of data in every row; in this case, two columns are in use, one of type INT and one with as many as 30 characters. Last, a set-value block (as described later) includes the value of the **contents** field, which is an array of arrays of type STRING.

Each inner array such as *101, "File not found"* holds the initial data for a row of the data table.

The following data-table stereotypes are available:

- **BasicTable**. A data table of this kind is for general processing; for example, a list of U.S. states, their postal abbreviations, and their populations.

- **MsgTable**. A data table of this kind contains runtime messages.

- **MatchValidTable**, **MatchInvalidTable**, or **RangeChkTable**. A data table of any of these kinds helps validate user input to a Web-page field or other onscreen field. In the first case (MatchValidTable), the input must match a value in the first data-table column. In the second case (MatchInvalidTable), the input must be different from any value in the first data-table column. In the third case (RangeChkTable), the input must match a value between the first and second column of at least one data-table row. If a validation fails, EGL displays an error message.

The data table is *generatable*, which means that you can request code to be generated by acting on the file that contains the part; for example, by right-clicking the file in the Workbench and selecting **Generate**. The output created for a generated part is a standalone unit such as a program or binary file.

A data table is different from a dictionary in several ways, as outlined in Table 3-1.

Table 9-1: Comparison of Data Table and Dictionary		
	Data Table	**Dictionary**
Kinds of Data	Fixed length	Any kind of data
Number of Columns	Any number	Two
Number of Rows	Set before run time	May vary at run time
Validations	Special support	No special support

A data table can handle only fixed-length data, as was described in relation to structured records. A dictionary can handle any kind of data. A data table can have multiple columns. A dictionary can be used as a table, but only as a two-column table. You set the number of rows in a data table at development time. You can vary the number of entries in a dictionary at run time. Last, several kinds of data tables are helpful for validation, and EGL provides special support so that you can easily use data tables for that purpose. The language does not provide special support for dictionary-based validation.

Logic Parts

EGL includes a variety of *logic parts*, which process data. All have the following characteristics:

- Each logic part includes a set of functions. Each function is composed of EGL statements such as assignments, as well as identifiers— variables and constants—that are *local*: available only to the statements inside the function.

- Each logic part includes a set of identifiers that are at least *program global*: available to statements in every function in the part.

- Each logic part is generatable.

Consider the following logic part, a program that resides in the file MyProgram.egl.

```
program MyProgram

    const GREETING string = "Hello, ";
    suffix string;

    Function main()
       myName string = "Dave";
       suffix = "!!";
       SayHello(myName);
    end

    function SayHello(name string IN)
       sysLib.writeStdOut(GREETING + name + suffix);
    end
end
```

The function **main** runs first in any program. In this example, main assigns content to two variables and invokes the function **SayHello**. There, the plus sign (+) concatenates three strings. A system function, **sysLib.writeStdOut**, writes the text to the standard output, which is a file or display area that is specific to the runtime operating system. If you run a program in the Workbench, the standard output is the Console view.

The output string is "Hello, Dave!!"

As used in any of the logic parts, a function can return a value of a specified type; and can include parameters, each corresponding to an argument in the function invocation. Each parameter includes a modifier, whether explicitly or by default:

- When the modifier is **IN** (the default), the parameter receives a value from the invoker, and the invoker does not receive any changes made to the parameter.

- When the modifier is **OUT**, the parameter is set to an initial value according to initialization rules. For example, a parameter of type STRING has an initial value of spaces. When the function updates the parameter, the corresponding argument is updated in the invoker.

- When the modifier is **INOUT**, the parameter receives a value from the invoker and updates the argument when updating the parameter. If the argument is a constant such as the string "Smith," the behavior is the same as when the modifier is **IN**.

Categories of EGL Logic Parts

The EGL logic parts include *programs*, which define logic that starts at the same statement in every situation; *libraries*, which give local EGL code access to functions and data areas that are treated as part of the running code; *services*, which contain functions that can be accessed—possibly remotely— from other code; and *handlers*, which define a series of interactions that are specific to a runtime technology such as Rich UI, JSF, or BIRT reports.

In some cases, EGL logic parts—and other parts we'll describe later—can be models of format. For example, to access a function in a service that you created, you might write code similar to the incomplete code shown here.

```
myService myServicePart;
myEmployee STRING = myService.getEmployee("910");
```

In this example, you declare a variable that's based on a Service part and use the variable to access a function coded in the part. The general rule is as follows: when a part is a model of format, the related variable provides access to data, logic, or both. The specific capability depends on the kind of part.

Program Within a Run Unit

A *program* always starts running at the same logical statement; in other words, has a single entry point. A *main program* is invoked by an operating-system command; by a transfer from another main program, in which case the transferring program ends; or by the function **vgLib.startTransaction**, in which case the invoking program continues running. A *called program* is invoked from a main or called program, and the caller waits for the called program to return control.

A called program can include parameters, which are program global. If the caller passes a variable, any change made to the corresponding parameter is available to the caller when the caller receives control again; and that rule applies even if one of the programs is written in a language other than EGL.

A *run unit* is not a logic part, but a collection of runtime software that works together such that a severe error in any of the code causes the operating system to remove all the code from memory. A main program and any program it calls, for example, are always in the same run unit and therefore share runtime properties, which assign resources such as files and database connections.

The details of what constitutes a run unit vary by platform.

Library

A *library* contains functions, variables, and constants that can be accessed from other EGL code running on the same platform. Each variable or constant that's external to any function is *run-unit global*, which means that the identifier is specific to a run unit and is available throughout the run unit. Each function is a separate entry point and, in a sense, so is each of the global identifiers, with an exception mentioned later.

Here's an example of a library, including two constants and a function.

```
library myLibrary type BasicLibrary {}

    const PREFIX STRING = "A1";
    const MINIMUM_BONUS BIN(9,2) = 100.00;

    // Function Declarations
    function getEmployee(employeeCode STRING) returns (STRING)
        if (employeeCode == "011")
            return (PREFIX + employeeCode);
        else
            return (employeeCode);
        end
    end
end
```

You can explicitly declare a library function, variable, or constant to be *private*, which means that the identifier can be accessed only from within the library. In the previous example, the constant named PREFIX could have been declared to be private.

```
private const PREFIX STRING = "A1";
```

Here's an example of a program that accesses the previous library and writes the string "A1011".

```
Program myProgram

    use myLibrary;

    Function main()
        myEmployee STRING = getEmployee("011");
        sysLib.writeStdOut(myEmployee);
    end
end
```

The program includes a **use** statement, which lets you reference names from the library as if they were local to the program. We'll revisit the **use** statement later.

Service

A *service* contains public functions that can be accessed from other code, potentially from anywhere in the world. The service can include private functions and global variables, but those functions and variables are solely for use by functions that are within the service.

At run time, a service written in EGL is *stateless*, which means that the internal logic never relies on data from a previous invocation. For example, a stock-quote service receives a trading symbol and returns a quote, and the data used in one invocation is independent of the data used in the next. In contrast, the variables in a library retain their values in a given run unit.

Here's an example of a service.

```
service myServicePart

    const PREFIX STRING = "001";
    const MINIMUM_BONUS BIN(9,2) = 100.00;

    // Function Declarations
    Function getEmployee(employeeCode STRING) returns (STRING)
        if (employeeCode == "910")
            return (PREFIX + employeeCode);
        else
            return (PREFIX);
        end
    end

    Function getMinimumBonus() returns (BIN (9,2))
        return(MINIMUM_BONUS);
    end
end
```

Additional details are needed to access the service at run time; first, to identify the *protocol*, which is software that oversees the runtime transmission of data to and from the service, and second, to identify the service location. The details are stored in a file named the *EGL deployment descriptor*. In many cases, you accept the values that are provided for you. A deployer can update the location details at deployment time.

Here's an example of a program that accesses a service.

```
Program myProgram

    Function main()
        myService myServicePart
            {
                @BindService
                    {bindingKey = "myServicePart"}
            };
        myEmployee STRING = myService.getEmployee("910");
        sysLib.writeStdOut(myEmployee);
    end
end
```

The example declares a variable based on the previously described service part, invokes the function **getEmployee**, and writes the string "001910".

The declaration of **myService** includes the annotation **BindService**, which identifies a *service client binding*. The service client binding details how the program accesses the service. In the example, the binding is named **myServicePart**. You must specify the **BindService** annotation, but if you don't specify the **bindingKey** field, the name of the binding is assumed to be the name of the Service part. The following declaration is also valid.

```
myService myServicePart { @BindService{} };
```

The service client binding is stored in the *program's* EGL deployment descriptor.

Any technique for working with a service is a variation on what we've shown here: create a variable, bind it to a service client binding, and access a function by way of the variable. Advanced techniques involve variables that are based on Interface parts, which we describe later.

Handler

A *handler* is code that defines a series of potentially complex interactions with the user. Handlers guide the behaviors of Rich UI applications (see Chapter 6); of business reports written either with BIRT or with EGL text reporting (see Chapter 13); or of Web pages that run under the JSF runtime (see Chapter 14).

Prototype Parts

The word *prototype* reflects its use in C++, where a *function prototype*—the function name, parameters, and return type—includes the details needed to access a function but does not contain the function. Similarly, each EGL prototype part includes the details needed to access a particular kind of logic but does not contain the logic itself, which is defined elsewhere.

Categories of EGL Prototype Parts

The EGL prototype parts include *Interface parts*, which identify operations in a service; *external types*, which provide access to non-EGL code from within your code; and *Delegate parts*, which provide an advanced capability like that of function pointers in other languages. Each is of these parts is similar to a data part and is intended to be used as the basis of a variable.

Interface Part

An *Interface part* includes function prototypes that describe the operations in a service. Here's an example.

```
Interface MyInterfacePart
    Function getEmployee(employeeCode STRING IN)
        returns (STRING);
    end
    Function getMinimumBonus()
        returns (BIN (9,2))
    end
end
```

The Interface part has two purposes. First, your organization can use the part as a tool for design. In this usage, a designer specifies a part that describes the service. You then code the service, which is said to *implement the interface*. The service contains every function described in the Interface part, which provides a kind of contract that the service must fulfill.

Second, the Interface part lets you access a service whose logic is not available. The lack of availability may result from the service being outside your company. For example, a business partner can deploy a remote Web service and make the interface details available. Those details are usually in the form of a Web Services Description Language (WSDL) file, which the Workbench can convert into an Interface part.

The lack of availability also might result from a decision. The service provider (your company or another) may want you to access the service by way of a variable that's based on the Interface part. Use of the part lets the provider avoid disclosing details of the service logic, either for competitive reasons or to reduce complexity. In either case, your focus is on the functionality that the service provides rather than on details that are internal to the service.

Here's an example of code that includes a variable based on an EGL Interface part.

```
Program myProgram

    Function main()
        myInterface myInterfacePart
            {
                @BindService
                    {bindingKey = "myInterfacePart"}
            };
        myEmployee STRING = myInterface.getEmployee("910");
        sysLib.writeStdOut(myEmployee);
    end
end
```

The variable provides access to the service. As shown, the declaration and access syntax are the same as in an earlier example, when we used a variable based on a Service part.

ExternalType Part

An *ExternalType* part, or *external type*, gives you a way to interact with non-EGL code from within your EGL logic. Three stereotypes are available. You can use a **JavaObject** stereotype to access or create Java code. You can use a **JavaScriptObject** stereotype to access native JavaScript from a Rich UI application; in this way, you can use existing widget libraries such as Dojo and Silverlight when creating a user interface. Last, you can use a **HostProgram** stereotype to access an IBM i called or service program as if that program were a Web service.

Delegate Part

A *Delegate part* provides an advanced capability. The part is the basis of a variable that lets you write code to invoke a *kind* of function—a function that has a given prototype. The variable lets you defer, until run time, the decision as to which function to invoke. The capability is used in applications that handle events. For example, when you develop a Rich UI application, you might specify an EGL function to respond to a user's opening a menu. The function matches a Delegate part that has particular types of arguments and return value, as noted in the Appendix B section on Menus.

We illustrate the general capability in an example that has no practical use. First, we'll define **Responder**, a Delegate part.

```
Delegate Responder
   (howOld INT) returns (STRING)
end
```

Responder describes a function that accepts an integer (the age of a car, in years) and returns a string (the message to be displayed after a user's request for an insurance quote is processed).

Here's **Responder**, along with a program that uses it.

```
Delegate Responder
   (howOld INT) returns (STRING)
end

Program ProcessQuote(VIN STRING)

  Function AntiqueCarQuote(howManyYears INT) returns (STRING)
     return ("We can insure your antique!");
  end

  Function RecentCarQuote(thisOld INT) returns (STRING)
    return ("We can insure your car!");
  end

  Function main()
    response Responder;
    message STRING;
    age INT = 30;

    if (age >= 25)
       response = AntiqueCarQuote;
    else
       response = RecentCarQuote;
    end

    message = response(age);
    sysLib.WriteStdOut(message);
  end
end
```

Listing 9.1: Delegate part

The program **ProcessQuote** itself accepts a string (**VIN**, the Vehicle Identification Number) and includes two functions other than **main**. Both of those functions have the same prototype as the function described in the Delegate part.

Three declarations are in the function **main**: one for **response**, a variable based on the Delegate part; one for **message**, a string to display; and one for **age**, an integer that contains the car's age, which is set to 30 in this case. An **if** statement specifies which function to assign to **response**:

```
if (age >= 25)
   response = AntiqueCarQuote;
else
   response = RecentCarQuote;
end
```

Next, the variable **response** is used as if its name were the name of a function:

```
message = response(age);
```

Last, the EGL function **sysLib.writeStdOut** writes the value returned from the selected function.

```
sysLib.WriteStdOut(message);
```

The output from this example is "We can insure your antique!".

User Interface Parts

Some EGL parts fall into multiple categories. Handlers include logic and affect user interface; and the Console UI parts are external types that also affect user interface. For our purposes, EGL provides two user interface parts: *Form* and *Form Group*.

Form Part

A *Form part*—usually called a *form*—is a set of character-based fields that are organized for presentation. Like a data table, the form is a static part; it is not the basis of a variable, but is a data collection that other EGL code can access directly. You create the form with an editor in the Workbench.

Two kinds of forms are possible. A *text form* is a form displayed at a standalone terminal or in a workstation window. This type of form is used by a *textUI program*, which is a program whose only onscreen interaction is by way of these forms. In contrast, a *print form* is displayed by a printer—or in a text file—and is used by a library or by any kind of program. Each form has a fixed, internal structure like that of a structured record, but a form cannot include a substructure.

A form is available to a program or library only if the form is included in or referenced by a form group and only if the program or library identifies the form group in a **use** statement, which we describe later.

FormGroup part

A *FormGroup* part—usually called a *form group*—is a collection of text and print forms and is a generatable UI part. A program can include only one form group for most uses, along with one form group for help-related output. The same form can be included in multiple form groups.

Annotations

An *annotation* is a value that helps the EGL system code to set up an interaction with a runtime technology. Annotations are available only to the EGL compiler and generator, not to the statements in your runtime code.

You specify annotations for various reasons. In one case, you set a database-table name that's embedded in the generated code. In another case, you identify the function to invoke when a user clicks a Web-page button. In a third case, you set the output file name for an EGL-generated program.

Let's look at that last case, which involves the **Alias** annotation. The effect of **Alias** is to help set the name of an output file. The annotation is most useful if you're generating code for an environment that supports only short names. For the Java output emphasized in this book, the following source code ensures that a generated program is named **MyProg.java**.

```
Program AnExtraordinaryProgram { Alias = "MyProg" }

end
```

We'll explain the syntax in a moment, but want to emphasize that an annotation is "of a type"; and the type is always a Record part such as the one shown here.

```
Record Alias type Annotation
    value STRING;
end
```

When you think about an annotation that has only one field, you may find yourself talking about the annotation field as if it were the annotation. For example, you might say that the **Alias** annotation is of type STRING. As EGL moves toward letting developers extend the language, we'd like the underlying detail to be understood. The annotation is never of a primitive type. The annotation is based on a Record part. In this case, the annotation is of type Alias, and an annotation field in that Record part is of type STRING.

Note: The product documentation uses two phrases that are equivalent to annotation field: *property field* and *simple property*.

Annotation Syntax

You can further refine the purpose of a data item by specifying various annotations; for example, **DisplayName** and **InputRequired**.

```
DataItem
    NumberOfCars INT
    { DisplayName = "Number of Cars",
      InputRequired = yes }
end
```

Any annotation in a data item represents a default characteristic that pertains to any variable that is based on the data item. In this case, if a Web-page field is based on **NumberOfCars**, the defaults are as follows: the label "Number of Cars" is on the page, adjacent to the field, and the user is required to enter data.

The annotations that are available for primitive types or data items are called *field-level annotations*. To specify those annotations, you code a *set-value block*, which is an area of code between opening and closing braces. As shown, one annotation is separated from the next by a comma. The *target* of the set-value block is the language element that is affected by the entries in the set-value block. In this case, the target is the data item being defined. The target precedes the set-value block.

The syntax of the previous example is so concise that it may mislead you. The following syntax communicates the relationships more clearly.

```
DataItem
    NumberOfCars INT
    { @DisplayName { value = "Number of Cars"},
      @InputRequired { value = yes } }
end
```

The at sign (@) directs the EGL system code to create a new annotation of the specified type, whether the type is **DisplayName** or **InputRequired**. The embedded set-value block lists all the field-value pairs for the new annotation.

Whenever an annotation type has exactly one field, you can create a new annotation with syntax such as **DisplayName = "Number of Cars"**. You're assigning a value of the appropriate field type—in this case, STRING—and ignoring the name of the field.

Data Items and Variables

The annotations that are valid for any data items are valid for all data items. For instance, in our example, no error occurs if you declare a variable based on **NumberOfCars** and fail to use the variable as a Web-page field. The benefit of this rule is that you can use the same data item to declare several variables, each of which might be used in a different way. One variable of type **NumberOfCars** might be used for data storage, one for general processing, and one for data presentation.

The annotations specified for a data item represent a default that you can override when you declare a variable that's based on the data item. You can accept or override individual annotations from the default set, and you can add annotations from the set of field-level annotations. Here's an example of a variable declaration.

```
myCarCount NumberOfCars
    { DisplayName = "Quantity",
      InputRequiredMsgKey = "Message101" }
end
```

If the variable **myCarCount** is used on a Web-page field, the result is as follows: The label "Quantity" is on the page instead of "Number of Cars"; the user is required to enter data although no mention of that requirement is in the variable declaration; and a failure to enter data will cause the display of a message that is referenced by the string "Message101", which is not mentioned in the data item at all.

You might describe your coding in the following way: you assign a business value like 2 *into* **myCarCount,** and you assign an annotation like DisplayName *onto* **myCarCount.**

Stereotypes

Earlier, we noted that the term *stereotype* in EGL refers to a kind of type—for example, to a kind of Record part that makes your interaction with a relational database easier. Assume now that a systems architect seeks a runtime behavior such as database access. The runtime behavior is affected by the processing of the EGL system code. In short, the architect seeks an annotation.

At the level of EGL source code, a stereotype is an annotation that specifies the extra detail needed to handle an instance of a complex type. For example, here's a Record part whose stereotype is SQLRecord and which defines a relationship with the relational-database table **Policy**.

```
Record CarPolicy type SQLRecord
   { tableNames =
        [["Policy"]],
     keyItems = [policyID] }
   policyID STRING;
   carCount NumberOfCars;
end
```

Here's a declaration of an instance.

```
myCarPolicy CarPolicy;
```

The stereotype SQLRecord identifies what must be done to process the instance.

Let's look more closely at the syntax used to set stereotypes. When we first described a set-value block, we showed a concise syntax that included the annotation name but ignored the annotation-field name. In the current example, **tableNames** and **keyItems** are stereotype-field names—and are therefore annotation-field names. The following definition is equivalent to the previous one.

```
Record CarPolicy
{ @SQLRecord
    { tableNames =
        [["Policy"]],
      keyItems =
        [policyID] }
    policyID STRING;
    carCount NumberOfCars;
end
```

The target of the outer set-value block is the Record part being defined. The at sign (@) directs the EGL system code to create a new annotation of the specified type; here, type SQLRecord. The embedded set-value block lists all the field-value pairs for the new annotation.

Set-Value Blocks

As shown earlier, you can use a set-value block to set annotations. You can also use set-value blocks to set values for run time. The next example assigns a default value to an SQL record field.

```
Record CarPolicy type SQLRecord
    { policyID = "9999",
      tableNames =
          [["Policy"]],
      keyItems = [policyID] }
    policyID STRING;
    carCount NumberOfCars;
end
```

In any record that's based on CarPolicy, the values of field **policyID** is "9999" by default. You can override a field default in the record declaration, as shown next.

```
myCarPolicy CarPolicy
    { policyID = "ABC123",
      carCount = 2 };
```

Here's another example of a set-value block: a dictionary, where you can set annotations such as **CaseSensitive** and entries such as IBM.

```
stockPrices Dictionary
{
    // annotation
    CaseSensitive = No,

    // dictionary entries
    IBM = 165.25,
    GE  =  52.75
}
```

That setting of **CaseSensitive** lets your code refer to the first dictionary entry as *IBM*, *IbM*, or *ibm*.

In some cases, you'll want to use a set-value block to refer to nested fields. Here is a record part that defines a relationship with a relational-database table named **PreferredPolicy**.

```
Record CarPolicyPreferred type SQLRecord
    { tableNames = [["PreferredPolicy"]],
      keyItems = [preferredID] }

    preferredID STRING;
    onePolicy CarPolicy;
    serviceLevel INT;
end
```

When you declare a variable of type **CarPolicyPreferred**, you can nest a set-value block to initialize the field **onePolicy**.

```
Program myProgram

    function main()
        policyVar CarPolicyPreferred
        { preferredID = "ABC123",
            onePolicy{ policyID = "ABC123", carCount = 2 },
            serviceLevel = 1 };
    end
end
```

As shown, the syntax involves preceding the nested set-value block with the name of the field whose own fields are being initialized.

You can nest set-value blocks to reference fields in records that are themselves nested, to any level of complexity.

Packages

The EGL language organizes parts into *packages*. All code—including EGL system code—is in a package and can access all parts in the same package, even if the code is spread across different files.

In general, a package name is a sequence of identifiers separated by periods (.), as in this example: *com.myCompany.myCommonPkg*. Each name corresponds to a subfolder at development time and, for Java output, at deployment time. In this example, the directory structure includes the folder *com*, the subfolder *myCompany*, and the sub-subfolder *myCommonPkg*.

As a result of a collaboration or merger, your work may be combined with the work of another organization. To ensure that your package names are unique, you can make the initial part of a package name an inversion of your company's Internet domain name. If your company's domain name is *ibm.rational.software.com*, for example, your company's package names might start with *com.software.rational.ibm*.

The rules for specifying the lowest-level qualifiers in a package name vary from company to company, with different packages reflecting a difference between development groups, business purposes, runtime platforms, or some other characteristic of the business.

An EGL file in one package can access parts in a second. Consider, for example, a source file that holds the data item parts used in several applications:

```
package com.myCompany.myCommonPkg;

DataItem NumberOfDrivers INT end

DataItem NumberOfCars INT end
```

The package *com.myCompany.myCommonPkg* includes at least the two data item parts. Let's consider a second source file, which holds a Record part in the package *com.myCompany.myApplicationPkg*:

```
package com.myCompany.myApplicationPkg;

import com.myCompany.myCommonPkg.*;

Record CarPolicy type BasicRecord
  policyID CHAR(10);
  driverCount NumberOfDrivers;
  carCount NumberOfCars;
end
```

In general, an **import** statement *imports* (that is, makes available) one or more parts in a package. In such a statement, a period and asterisk (.*) at the end of a package name makes available every part in the package; and in the current example, the **import** statement makes available the data item parts shown earlier.

You can specify a part name instead of an asterisk. The effect is to make a single part available. The following code gives two examples:

```
package com.myCompany.myApplicationPkg;

import com.myCompany.myCommonPkg.NumberOfDrivers;
import com.myCompany.myCommonPkg.NumberOfVehicles;

Record CarPolicy type BasicRecord
  policyID CHAR(10);
  driverCount NumberOfDrivers;
  carCount NumberOfCars;
end
```

The next example shows that you can avoid specifying an import statement altogether:

```
package com.myCompany.myApplicationPkg;

Record CarPolicy type BasicRecord
  policyID CHAR(10);
  driverCount com.myCompany.myCommonPkg.NumberOfDrivers;
  carCount com.myCompany.myCommonPkg.NumberOfCars;
end
```

The parts **NumberOfDrivers** and **NumberOfCars** are available in this case because you've qualified each part name with the name of the package in which the part resides.

Two types or parts cannot have the same name in a given package. However, a given part name can appear in many different packages. When you create an application, you'll need to know the rules for identifying which part is referenced when you use a particular part name:

- If the name of a part is qualified by a package name (as in our example of **com.myCompany.myPkg.NumberOfDrivers**), EGL seeks the part in the specified package.

- If a part name is not qualified, EGL first reviews the single-part **import** statement, if any, that refers to the name; our example is **import com.myCompany.myPkg.NumberOfDrivers**. In a given source file, only one single-part **import** statement is valid for a given part name.

- If the part name is still not resolved, EGL checks the current package.

- If necessary, EGL reviews the parts in multiple-part **import** statements such as **import com.myCompany.myCommonPkg.***. An error occurs if two of those statements provide access to a same-named part.

- If necessary, EGL checks the EGL system scope; primarily to find one of the many EGL system functions or variables.

If you're working in the Workbench, the rules for resolving part names are affected by the *EGL build path*, which is a list of all projects whose parts can be accessed from your project. If you're generating code in the EGL SDK, the rules are affected by the *eglpath*, which is a list of directories whose parts can be accessed when generating code in a batch process. Using projects in the Workbench is similar to using eglpath directories, so for purposes of explanation we'll assume you're working with the EGL build path.

At each of the steps described earlier, EGL searches the current project; then, if necessary, searches the next project in the EGL build path; and then, if necessary, searches the next project. If a part name is resolved in a given project, the search ends.

You can create a source file that identifies no package name at all. In this case, the code resides in a *default package*, which is simply in a high-level folder. However, use of a default package is discouraged because other packages cannot access the parts in such a package.

Use Statement

In most cases, the **use** statement is a convenience that lets you easily reference variables, constants, and functions that are declared in libraries and other generatable parts. For example, assume that a library named **CustomerLib** is in your current package and includes the function **getCustomer**. The following is valid.

```
package com.myCompany.myPkg;

program myProgram type BasicProgram
    function main()
        CustomerLib.getCustomer();
    end
end
```

You can add a **use** statement to save you from having to qualify the
referenced name. The following example is equivalent to the previous one.

```
package com.myCompany.myPkg;

program myProgram type BasicProgram

    use CustomerLib;

    function main()
        getCustomer();
    end
end
```

Depending on your declaration of **import** and **use** statements, a reference—
for example, to **getCustomer**—may be qualified with a package name; with
the package name, a dot, and the name of the generatable part; or with only
the name of the generatable part. The simplest alternative is to have no
qualifier and to reference only the variable, constant, or function in the
generatable part.

CHAPTER 10

Runtime Values

The rules for working with data are an important aspect of EGL, and we cover the issue in detail.

Constants

A *constant* names an unchangeable data area. Here are some declarations.

```
const TOPSCORE, MAXVALUE, UPPER INT = 100;
const COPYSTRING STRING = "Copyright 2010";
const AGES INT[] = [5, 6, 7];
```

As shown, you declare a constant by specifying the reserved word **const**, a name or a list of comma-separated names, a primitive type or array, and an assignment.

You use a constant as if it were the assigned literal. The name helps you to think about a business problem and lets you change every use of the constant by changing the one declaration.

Variables

A *variable* names a changeable data area. Here are some declarations.

```
policyID, counter, salesInQuarter INT;
copyright STRING;
salesByQuarter INT[];
```

As shown, you declare a variable by specifying a name or a list of comma-separated names, followed by a type or array.

Two kinds of variables are available in EGL. A *value variable* names a data area containing a value of direct interest to your application. For example, a variable of type INT might name a data area that holds the number of items sold in a quarter (Figure 10.1).

Figure 10.1: Value Variable

In contrast, a *reference variable* names a data area containing a memory address. The address has no direct interest to your application, but refers to one or more data areas that do.

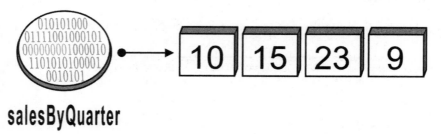

Figure 10.2: Reference Variable

In Figure 10.2, the variable **salesByQuarter** is of type INT array. The named data area in turn references a series of data areas that contain the number of items sold in each of the last four quarters.

Our description of the two kinds of variables doesn't fully express what occurs at run time, but accurately tells what you need to understand as you access data areas in your code.

Given a particular variable, is it a value variable or a reference variable? The determining factor is the data type on which the variable is based (Table 10-1).

Table 10-1: Value and Reference Types		
	Value	**Reference**
Primitive Types and Related Data Items	All numeric, character, and datetime types, as well as BOOLEAN	ANY and the large-object types
Complex Types	Record parts other than Exception	Exception Record; External Type; Dictionary, Service, Interface, and Delegate parts; and Dynamic-array types

Most primitive types are value types, including STRING. Most Record parts are value types, too, with the exception of... Exception.

The simplest reference types are ANY and the large-object types. Among the other reference types are External Types and the following EGL parts: Dictionary, Service, Interface, and Delegate. Also, dynamic array types—for example, INT array—are reference types; and later we'll show how that fact affects what happens when you copy arrays.

If your data structures get complicated, we suggest you draw simple diagrams to reflect the relationships, with circles for the areas named by reference variables and rectangles for the areas named by value variables, as shown in this chapter.

In many cases, a value variable is initialized. For example, a global variable of type BOOLEAN is set to *false* automatically. However, no initialization occurs for a reference variable, and you must initialize the variable before you can use it as a source of data. The phrase "to initialize a reference variable" means to cause the variable to address a data area or, as shown later, to enable use of the variable for function invocation.

When working with reference variables, you can use **null** to indicate explicitly that the variable is not initialized. Here's an example.

```
Program myProgram type BasicProgram

    Function main()
        myDictionary Dictionary = null;
    end
end
```

Using the New Operator

The **new** operator *allocates*—that is, reserves—a data area at run time and places the area's address into a variable. For example, the following code creates an area of type Dictionary, which is a reference type.

```
Program myProgram type BasicProgram

    Function main()
        myDictionary Dictionary = new Dictionary;
    end
end
```

You can use the **new** operator even if you're working with a value type. The following example creates an array of basic records.

```
Record MyCustomerType type BasicRecord
    ID INT;
    name STRING;
end
Program myProgram type BasicProgram

    Function main()
        myCustomers MyCustomerType[] = [
            new MyCustomerType
                { ID = 120, name = "IBM" },
            new MyCustomerType
                { ID = 121, name = "MC Press" }
        ];
        sysLib.writeStdOut (myCustomers[1].name);
    end
end
```

The code writes *IBM* to the standard output.

Using a Set-Value Block with a Reference Variable

You can initialize a reference variable without the **new** operator. In this case, you specify a set-value block in the variable declaration. Each statement in the next example allocates a new data area.

```
Program myProgram type BasicProgram

    Function main()
        myDictionary Dictionary{ };
        myDictionary02 Dictionary { x = 1, y = 2 };
    end
end
```

Specifying the set-value block with a reference variable is not always identical to using the **new** operator. You can use the set-value block to update the fields of an existing data area. Consider the next example.

```
Program myProgram type BasicProgram

    Function main()
        myDictionary Dictionary = null;
        myDictionary{ IBM = 100, GE = 40};
        myDictionary{ IBM = 125, GE = 45};
    end
end
```

The first statement in the function creates a reference variable that doesn't refer to a data area. The second statement allocates a data area, and the third statement reassigns values to the same data area. Consider the following variation.

```
Program myProgram type BasicProgram

    Function main()
        myDictionary Dictionary = null;
        myDictionary{ IBM = 100, GE = 40 };
        myDictionary = new Dictionary{ IBM = 125, GE = 45 };
    end
end
```

That last statement creates a new dictionary, and the area of memory to which **myDictionary** referred in the second statement is made available for other purposes, automatically.

Arrays

EGL supports array literals, dynamic arrays, and structure-field arrays. We'll look at each in turn.

Array Literals

An array literal consists of a pair of brackets enclosing either a comma-separated list of literals—including other array literals—or more complex expressions. Each array literal has a type and can be used anywhere an array of that type is allowed. The following example assigns an array literal of type INT to the reference variable **myArray**.

```
myArray INT[] = [1,2,3];
```

Table 10-2 shows other examples.

Table 10-2: Examples of Literal Arrays	
Array Literal	**Type**
["bye", "ciao"]	STRING[]
[(myPay < 10000), (yourPay > 50000)]	BOOLEAN[]
[[1, 2], [3, 4]]	SMALLINT[][] (a two-dimensional array)
[3, "ciao", 4.5, 6.7]	ANY[]

Dynamic Arrays

A dynamic array is an array whose number of elements is changeable at run time. This kind of array can be based on a primitive type, on a data part, or on a logic or prototype part used as a data part.

You make a size change by invoking an array-specific function such as **removeElement**, **insertElement**, or **appendElement**. Other functions let you increase or decrease the maximum number of elements allowed. However, you cannot invoke any function unless the array is initialized. The following declaration does not specify an initial number of elements but includes a set-value block, which fulfills the initialization requirement.

```
age INT[] {};
```

The following code declares a dynamic array of 3 elements, each of type INT.

```
age INT[3] { maxSize=5 };
```

The example includes the annotation **MaxSize**, which specifies the maximum number of elements. In this case, an attempt to add more than 5 elements to the array causes an exception at run time.

You can assign values to the array at declaration time, whether by assigning an array literal or by including the values in a set-value block.

```
age INT[5]  =  [27, 35, 29, 42, 53];
age INT[5]     {27, 35, 29, 42, 53};
```

Similarly, the following examples assign values to a multi-dimensional array; in this case, an array of 2 rows and 3 columns.

```
myTable INT[2][3] = [ [1, 2, 3], [4, 5, 6] ];
myTable INT[2][3]   { [1, 2, 3], [4, 5, 6] };
```

To reference an element, you use *array indexes*, expressions that resolve to integers and are used to identify the element. Here are examples; first, an array element being assigned to another variable, and second, a value being assigned to an array element.

```
// assign 29 to myAge
myAge INT = age[3];

// replace 2 with 12
myTable[1][2] = 12;
```

Structure-Field Arrays

You declare a structure-field array when you specify that a field in a structured record has multiple occurrences, as in the following example.

```
Record ExampleRecord01
    10 myItem CHAR(1)[3];
end
```

If a structured record variable named **myRecord** is based on that definition, the name **myRecord.myItem** refers to a one-dimensional array of three elements, each a character, and you can reference the second element by typing **myRecord.myItem[2]**.

Also, you can declare a structure-field array of multiple dimensions, as shown next.

```
Record ExampleRecord02
    10 myArray[3];
        20 myEmbeddedArray CHAR(20)[2];
end
```

If a record variable named **myRecord02** is based on that definition, each element of the one-dimensional array **myRecord02.myArray** is itself a one-dimensional array; and you can refer to the second of the three subordinate one-dimensional arrays as **myRecord02.myArray[2]**. The structure field **myEmbeddedArray** declares a two-dimensional array, and the next example demonstrates the preferred syntax for referring to an element of that array.

```
// for row 1, column 2
myRecord02.myArray[1].myEmbeddedArray[2]
```

Assigning One Variable to Another

In this section, we'll illustrate four kinds of assignments and use in-code comments to detail the effect. Table 10-3 gives a summary.

Table 10-3: Assigning One Variable to Another	
Kind of Assignment	**Effect**
Value to Value	Copies the value from the sender to the receiver
Value to Reference	Copies the value from the sender to a new area and causes the receiver to reference that area
Reference to Reference	Causes the receiver to reference the area that the sender was referencing already
Reference to Value	Copies the value from the referenced area to the receiver

This section also shows the practical implications; first, by assigning a customer-contact record that references a list of people at the customer site, and second, and by adding a similar record to an array of records, as might be necessary for contacting people at many customer sites. The array processing is particularly important.

Value Variable to a Value Variable

The assignment of a value variable, literal, or constant to a value variable is a straightforward copying of data from one area to another (Figure 10.3).

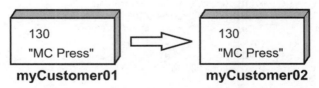

myCustomer01   **myCustomer02**

Figure 10.3: Assigning a Value Variable to a Value Variable

Value Variable to a Reference Variable

You can assign a value variable to a reference variable. In Figure 10.4 and in subsequent sections, the white arrow represents the assignment, the dotted arrow represents a physical copying of data, and the solid black arrow represents a reference.

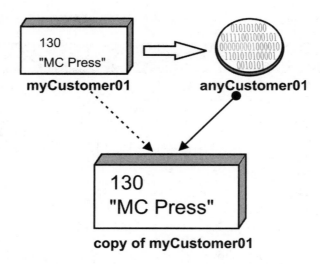

Figure 10.4: Assigning a Value Variable to a Reference Variable

The following code copies a value variable—in this case, a basic record—to a variable of type ANY.

```
Record MyCustomerType type BasicRecord
    ID INT;
    name STRING;
end

Program myProgram type BasicProgram
    Function main()
        myCustomer01 MyCustomerType;
        myCustomer01.ID = 130;
        myCustomer01.name = "MC Press";

        anyCustomer01 ANY = myCustomer01;
        anyCustomer01.name = "IBM";

        sysLib.writeStdOut(myCustomer01.ID);      // 130
        sysLib.writeStdOut(myCustomer01.name);    // MC Press
        sysLib.writeStdOut(anyCustomer01.ID);     // 130
        sysLib.writeStdOut(anyCustomer01.name);   // IBM
    end
end
```

Listing 10.1: Assigning a Value Variable to a Reference Variable

The assignment of **myCustomer01** to **anyCustomer01** does not copy the address of **myCustomer01**. Instead, the assignment copies the content of **myCustomer**01 to a separate data area, and causes **anyCustomer01** to refer to that area. The assigment of *IBM* to **anyCustomer01.name** does not affect **myCustomer01**.

Reference Variable to a Reference Variable

As in the previous example, the next example begins by creating two reference variables, **anyCustomer01** and **anyCustomer02** (Figure 10.5).

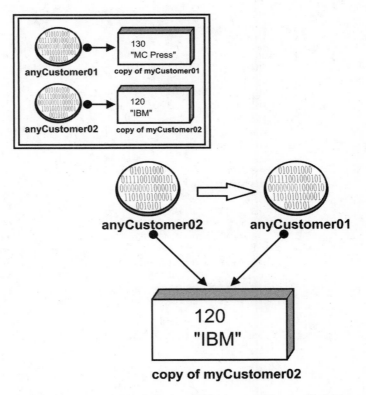

Figure 10.5: *Assigning a Reference Variable to a Reference Variable*

The example then assigns one reference variable, **anyCustomer02**, to the other reference variable, **anyCustomer01**. The inset shows the situation after the two reference variables are created, but before the assignment.

The bottom of the figure shows the result after **anyCustomer02** is copied to **anyCustomer01**. At that point, the two reference variables refer to the same data area.

Now consider the code. To fulfill the inset in Figure 10.5, we create two value variables—again, basic records—and assign them to variables of type ANY. To fulfill the center of Figure 10.5, we then copy one variable of type ANY to the other variable of type ANY.

```
Record MyCustomerType type BasicRecord
    ID INT;
    name STRING;
end

Program myProgram type BasicProgram

    Function main()
        myCustomer01, myCustomer02 MyCustomerType;
        myCustomer01.ID = 130;
        myCustomer01.name = "MC Press";
        myCustomer02.ID = 120;
        myCustomer02.name = "IBM";

        anyCustomer01 ANY = myCustomer01;
        anyCustomer02 ANY = myCustomer02;
        anyCustomer01 = anyCustomer02;
        anyCustomer01.ID = 100;

        sysLib.writeStdOut(myCustomer01.ID);      // 130
        sysLib.writeStdOut(myCustomer01.name);    // MC Press
        sysLib.writeStdOut(myCustomer02.ID);      // 120
        sysLib.writeStdOut(myCustomer02.name);    // IBM
        sysLib.writeStdOut(anyCustomer01.ID);     // 100
        sysLib.writeStdOut(anyCustomer01.name);   // IBM
        sysLib.writeStdOut(anyCustomer02.ID);     // 100
        sysLib.writeStdOut(anyCustomer02.name);   // IBM
    end
end
```

Listing 10.2: Assigning a Reference Variable to a Reference Variable

Again, each time a value variable such as **myCustomer02** is assigned to a reference variable such as **anyCustomer02**, the value variable is unaffected by the assignment. The reference variable addresses a copy of the values that were in the original data area.

The example assignment of **anyCustomer02** to **anyCustomer01** has two effects:

- The data area that previously held a copy of myCustomer01 is made available for other purposes, automatically.

- Both variables of type ANY now address the same data area, which holds a copy of **myCustomer02**. Assigning a value to a field in **anyCustomer01** changes a field that is referenced by both **anyCustomer01** and **anyCustomer02**.

You may want to copy data from one reference variable to another such that, after the operation ends, the two variables point to different data areas. The option is available if you use the EGL **move** statement (Figure 10.6).

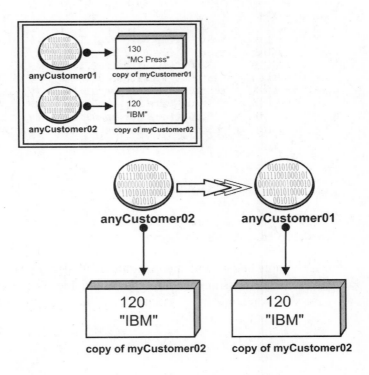

Figure 10.6: Moving a Reference Variable to a Reference Variable

The following example is similar to the previous one, but two boldfaced statements demonstrate the use and effect of a **move** statement in place of an assignment.

```
Record MyCustomerType type BasicRecord
    ID INT;
    name STRING;
end

Program myProgram type BasicProgram

    Function main()
       myCustomer01, myCustomer02 MyCustomerType;
       myCustomer01.ID = 130;
       myCustomer01.name = "MC Press";
       myCustomer02.ID = 120;
       myCustomer02.name = "IBM";

       anyCustomer01 ANY = myCustomer01;
       anyCustomer02 ANY = myCustomer02;
       // we replace this: anyCustomer01 = anyCustomer02;
       move anyCustomer02 to anyCustomer01;
       anyCustomer01.ID = 100;

       sysLib.writeStdOut(myCustomer01.ID);      // 130
       sysLib.writeStdOut(myCustomer01.name);    // MC Press
       sysLib.writeStdOut(myCustomer02.ID);      // 120
       sysLib.writeStdOut(myCustomer02.name);    // IBM
       sysLib.writeStdOut(anyCustomer01.ID);     // 100
       sysLib.writeStdOut(anyCustomer01.name);   // IBM
       sysLib.writeStdOut(anyCustomer02.ID);     // 120
       sysLib.writeStdOut(anyCustomer02.name);   // IBM
    end
end
```

Listing 10.3: One Use of the Move Statement

Reference Variable to a Value Variable

The next example begins with an operation equivalent to an earlier one, when a value variable was assigned to a reference variable. The inset in Figure 10.7 shows the situation that's in effect after the operation is complete.

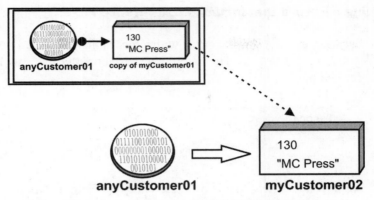

Figure 10.7: Assigning a Reference Variable to a Value Variable

The center of Figure 10.7 shows the effect of assigning a reference variable to a value variable: the value of the referenced data area is copied to the value variable.

Now consider the code. To fulfill the inset in Figure 10.7 we create a value variable—a basic record—and assign it to anyCustomer01, a variable of type ANY. To fulfill the center of Figure 10.7 we then assign anyCustomer01 to the value variable myCustomer02.

```
Record MyCustomerType type BasicRecord
    ID INT;
    name STRING;
end

Program myProgram type BasicProgram

    Function main()
        myCustomer01, myCustomer02 MyCustomerType;
        myCustomer01.ID = 130;
        myCustomer01.name = "MC Press";

        anyCustomer01 ANY = myCustomer01;
        myCustomer02 = anyCustomer01;

        sysLib.writeStdOut(anyCustomer01.ID);      // 130
        sysLib.writeStdOut(anyCustomer01.name);    // MC Press
        sysLib.writeStdOut(myCustomer02.ID);       // 130
        sysLib.writeStdOut(myCustomer02.name);     // MC Press
    end
end
```

Listing 10.4: Assigning a Reference Variable to a Value Variable

Assigning a Record that Includes a Reference Field

In earlier examples, we worked with a record that contained fields of the value types INT and STRING. The record was based on **MyCustomerType**, which is defined here.

```
Record MyCustomerType type BasicRecord
    ID INT;
    name STRING;
end
```

We now add a field that is of a reference type, and the additional field has no effect on the assignment relationships that we described earlier. However, the runtime behavior may seem different because the new field references a data area instead of containing a data area. We'll review the issue with a single example that uses the following updated version of **MyCustomerType**.

```
Record MyCustomerType type BasicRecord
    ID INT;
    name STRING;
    contact STRING[]{};
end
```

Our example copies a basic record to a variable of type ANY, as originally illustrated in Figure 10.4. Figure 10.8 includes the new **contact** field.

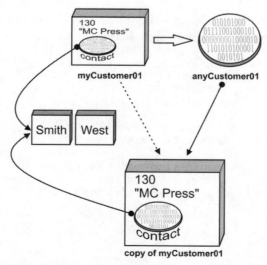

Figure 10.8: Assigning a Value Variable to a Reference Variable, with a Difference

Here's the updated code.

```
Record MyCustomerType type BasicRecord
    ID INT;
    name STRING;
    contact STRING[]{};
end
Program myProgram type BasicProgram
    Function main()
        myCustomer01 MyCustomerType;
        myCustomer01.ID = 130;
        myCustomer01.name = "MC Press";
        myCustomer01.contact.appendElement("Smith");
        myCustomer01.contact.appendElement("West");

        anyCustomer01 ANY = myCustomer01;
        anyCustomer01.name = "IBM";
        anyCustomer01.contact[1] = "Jones";

        sysLib.writeStdOut(myCustomer01.ID);           // 130
        sysLib.writeStdOut(myCustomer01.name);         // MC Press
        sysLib.writeStdOut(myCustomer01.contact[1]);   // Jones
        sysLib.writeStdOut(anyCustomer01.ID);          // 130
        sysLib.writeStdOut(anyCustomer01.name);        // IBM
        sysLib.writeStdOut(anyCustomer01.contact[1]);  // Jones
    end
end
```

Listing 10.5: Assigning a Record that Holds a Reference Variable

In two cases, the function **appendElement** adds an element of type STRING to the array referenced by **contact**. As in our earlier example, the assignment of **myCustomer01** to **anyCustomer01** copies the content of **myCustomer01** to a separate data area and causes **anyCustomer01** to refer to that area. The difference now is that both **myCustomer01** and **anyCustomer01** refer to a data area that itself references a data area.

The assignment of *IBM* to **anyCustomer01.name** still does not affect the value of **myCustomer01.name**. However, the assignment of *Jones* to **anyCustomer01.contact[1]** changes the value of **myCustomer01.contact[1]**.

Adding a Record to an Array of Records

Now that we've assigned a record that references a dynamic array, we'll consider the same issue with a slight twist: adding a record to an array of records. The next example considers the array-specific function

appendElement and is similar to the previous example for the following reason: **appendElement** adds a copy of data to an array, leaving the original data unaffected. Figure 10.9 shows the effect of the next example, illustrating the **appendElement** invocation with a dark arrow.

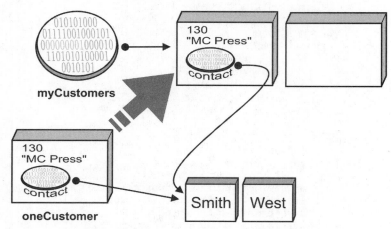

Figure 10.9: Appending a Record to a Dynamic Array

The example program uses the following Record parts.

```
Record MyCustomerType type BasicRecord
    ID INT;
    name STRING;
    contact MyContactType[]{};
end

Record MyContactType type BasicRecord
    lastName STRING;
end
```

The program builds a record named **oneCustomer** and appends it to **myCustomers**, which is an array of records.

```
Program myProgram type BasicProgram
    Function main()
        myCustomers MyCustomerType[]{};
        oneCustomer MyCustomerType;
        oneContact  MyContactType;

        // build oneCustomer
        oneCustomer.ID = 130;
        oneCustomer.name = "MC Press";
        oneContact.lastName = "Smith";
        oneCustomer.contact.appendElement(oneContact);
        oneContact.lastName = "West";
        oneCustomer.contact.appendElement(oneContact);

        // append oneCustomer and then change it
        myCustomers.appendElement(oneCustomer);
        oneCustomer.contact[1].lastName = "Jones";

        // is the update to myCustomers intended?
        sysLib.writeStdOut
            (myCustomers[1].contact[1].lastName);        // Jones
    end
end
```

Listing 10.6: Adding a Record that Contains Reference Variables

The data area to which the **oneCustomer.contact** refers contains the contact list; and that area is identical to the area to which **myCustomers[1].contact** refers. Even after you append **oneCustomer**, some changes that you might have thought would affect only **oneCustomer** also affect **myCustomers**. If you are working with **appendElement** or **insertElement**, you need to be aware of this behavior.

Expressions

An *expression* is a sequence of operands such as constants, variables, literals, and function invocations; operators such as + and -, and special characters such as parentheses. At run time, each expression resolves to a value of a specific type:

- A *numeric expression* resolves to a number of a specific type. The language supports modulus and exponentiation and offers system functions for trigonometry, logarithms, rounding, and numeric comparisons.

- A *text expression* resolves to a value of a character-based type such as STRING or UNICODE. The language supports concatenation and substring processing.

- A *logical expression* resolves to *true* or *false*. Its purpose is to affect the flow of logic in the EGL statements **case** and **if**, which run conditionally, and in statements such as **for** and **while**, which run iteratively.

  To compare two numeric, text, or datetime expressions, you can use the following operators: equality (==), inequality (!=), and the variations of less-than or greater-than (<, >, <=, >=). You can test a variable's content; for example, is it numeric? is it blank? does it conform to a particular string pattern? You can test for the target system in which the code is running; for example, is the code running on AIX? You can determine whether a particular value is in a data table or array by using the **in** operator. You can use the *not* (!) operator to reverse the value of a logical expression; for example, from *true* to *false*. Last, you can combine logical expressions with the *and* (**&&**) or *or* (||) operator.

- A *date/time expression* resolves to a date, interval, time, or time-stamp. You can subtract a timestamp from a timestamp to find the interval between the two values, for example, and can add two intervals to calculate a third. A variety of functions are available, too; for example, to return a date value from a timestamp.

Expressions are evaluated in accordance with a set of precedence rules and, within a given level of precedence, from left to right. However, you can use parentheses to force a different ordering.

Name Resolution in Expressions

Earlier, we described rules for resolving type and part names. Those rules are meaningful primarily in relation to data declarations. A second set of rules is meaningful primarily in the EGL logic statements, for resolving identifiers in expressions.

The main rules of this second kind are similar to those in other languages. Given an expression such as **myVar01 + myVar02**, for example, EGL first considers *local names*, which are identifiers declared within the function where the expression resides. Included in this category are the names of function parameters and of function-specific variables and constants.

If a name in the expression is not matched by a local name, EGL searches in the next category of names, and then (if the name is still unresolved) searches in the next. Eight categories of names are in effect; but in many cases you'll need to be aware only of local names and three other categories, in the following order:

- Program-global names, which identify variables, parameters, and constants that are global to the program or handler in which the function resides

- Run-unit global names, which identify variables and constants that reside in libraries and are available to all logic in the run unit.

- The names of EGL system variables.

You can avoid problems in name resolution if you use container names as qualifiers. If the field **employeeNumber** is in a record named **employee**, for example, you can—and, in some cases, must—use the following syntax.

```
employee.employeeNumber
```

You can use library names as qualifiers and can use package names, as may be necessary when referencing variables and constants that are in libraries, forms, or data tables.

To access an identifier that is program-global even when a local identifier takes precedence, qualify the identifier with the keyword **this**, as in the following example.

```
Program myProgram

    category INT:

    function main()
        category INT;

        // this.category refers to the program-global variable
        this.category = 4;
    end
end
```

Assignment and Reference Compatibility

Compatibility rules tell when an expression of a given type is valid during an exchange of data in memory. The rules apply to an assignment statement, or when a function return value is received into a variable, or when an argument is passed to a function. Two sets of rules apply:

- *Assignment compatibility* is in effect in most cases; for example, when your code assigns an expression of a CHAR type to a STRING type or to some other value variable

- *Reference compatiblity* is in effect in other cases; for example, when you are assigning, passing, or returning a reference variable to a reference variable

Details are in the Workbench help system.

Static and Dynamic Access

In most cases, your code interacts with a variable statically, which means that at generation time, all the details necessary to ensure variable access are in

place. Each reference to the variable is built with a dot syntax such as
employee.employeeAddress.city, as shown in the following example.

```
Record AddressPart
    streeAddress STRING;
    city STRING;
    state STRING;
end

Record EmployeePart
    employeeNumber  SMALLINT;
    employeeAddress AddressPart;
end

Program myProgram

    Function main()
        employee EmployeePart;
        employee.employeeAddress.city = "San Diego";
    end
end
```

The variable name is known to the code at generation time but is not retained
at run time because by then, the name has been replaced by a known (static)
memory address.

Static access is fast because the EGL runtime does not need to locate the
variable or to verify that the access is valid for the data type. The drawback of
static access is a lack of flexibility; but for many business uses, the flexibility
is unimportant.

In contrast to the variable in the previous example, a variable of type ANY is
accessed dynamically, which means that the EGL runtime locates the variable
by name and ensures that the access is valid. Dynamic access occurs, for
example, if your logic assigns any of several types of records to a variable of
type ANY and then accesses a record field. In the following code, a variable

called **person** is accessed dynamically, with each successive field identified by a bracketed string.

```
Record AddressPart
   streetAddress STRING;
   city STRING;
end

Record EmployeePart
   employeeNumber  SMALLINT;
   employeeAddress AddressPart;
end

Record RetireePart
   employeeDetail EmployeePart;
   pensionType CHAR(1);
end

Program myProgram

   Function main()

      isRetiree Boolean = false;
      employee EmployeePart;
      retiree  RetireePart;
      person ANY;

      // assume other processing
      // that assigns values to isRetiree
      // as well as to person, which receives
      // a record of type employee or
      // a record of type retiree
      if (isRetiree)
         person["employeeDetail"]["employeeAddress"]["city"]
            = "San Diego";
      else
         person["employeeAddress"]["city"]
            = "San Diego";
      end
   end
end
```

Listing 10.7: Dynamic Access

The bracket syntax indicates that dynamic access is in effect. The previous example showed literal strings, but a major benefit of dynamic access is that you can use variables of a character type, as in the following variation.

```
Function main()

    isRetiree Boolean = false;
    employee EmployeePart;
    retiree  RetireePart;
    fieldName01 STRING = "employeeAddress";
    fieldName02 STRING = "city";
    person ANY;

    if (!isRetiree) // if isRetiree is false
        person[fieldName01][fieldName02] = "San Diego";
    end
end
```

In most cases, the bracket syntax is optional if you have access to the literal string, so the reference just described can be **person.employeeAddress.city**. However, you must use bracket syntax when accessing an EGL dictionary entry whose key has a space or otherwise does not conform to an EGL naming convention. Consider the following code.

```
Function main()

    miscellaneous Dictionary { };
    category, component, test STRING;

    miscellaneous["Function"] = "EGL reserved word";
    miscellaneous["EGL runtime"] = "Flexible!";
    miscellaneous.dot = "You can use dot syntax here";

    category = miscellaneous["Function"];
    component = miscellaneous["EGL runtime"];
    test = miscellaneous.dot;

end
```

That code assigns "EGL reserved word" to **category**, "Flexible!" to **component**, and "You can use dot syntax here" to **test**.

EGL System Resources

This chapter reviews three EGL resources that are available when you write functions: statements, system libraries, and a mechanism for exception handling.

Our focus remains on core EGL functionality. The Workbench help system provides details on other areas, including the extensive EGL support for the data-access technologies DL/I and WebSphere MQ; for the transaction managers CICS and IMS; and for the user-interface technologies described as Text UI, Console UI, and Web transactions.

EGL Statements

In this section, we describe EGL statements for general use. In the next chapter, we list statements that access files and relational databases.

Table 11-1 list the statements covered here.

Table 11-1: Selected EGL Statements for General Use	
Statement Type	**Purpose**
assignment	To assign the value of an expression to a data area
call	To transfer control to another program; or, in Rich UI, to invoke a service
case	To run one of several alternative sets of statements

Table 11-1: Selected EGL Statements for General Use (Continued)	
Statement Type	**Purpose**
comment	To document code
function invocation	To run a function
continue	To return control to the start of an enclosing loop in the same function
exit	To end the processing of the nearest enclosing statement of a stated kind
for	To define a block of statements that run in a loop until a specified value is reached
forward	To transfer control from a JSF handler to (in most cases) a Web page
if, else	To define a block of statements that run if and only if a specified condition applies; also, to define an alternative block
move	To copy data from a source to a target, with processing not available in assignment statements
return	To return control from a function and optionally to return a value to the invoker
set	To establish characteristics of a record or record field.
transfer	To transfer control from one main program to another
while	To define a block of statements that run in a loop until a test fails

Code Documentation

A comment lets you add documentation to your code and is useful almost anywhere in an EGL source file, not only in functions.

A single-line comment begins with double slashes (//), as shown next, in boldface.

```
i INT = 2;

// a while loop follows
while(i > 0)
    sysLib.writeStdOut(i);
    i = i-1
end
```

A comment that can span multiple lines begins with a slash and asterisk (/*) and ends with an asterisk and slash (*/), as shown next.

```
i INT = 2;

/* a while loop
   does not follow */
sysLib.writeStdOut(i);
```

Data Assignment

You assign data by coding the assignment, **move**, and **set** statements.

Assignment

The primary data-assignment statement copies an expression into a data area. In the following example, **fullString** receives the value *Welcome to EGL*.

```
oneString, fullString STRING;
oneString = "Welcome ";
fullString = oneString + "to EGL";
```

Move

The **move** statement copies data from a source area to a target area, in any of three ways. First, byte by byte; second, by matching the field names in the target and source; and third, by matching the field positions in the target and source. The **move** statement provides additional options for copying values from one array to another.

Here are two Record parts.

```
Record MyCustomerOneType type BasicRecord
    ID INT;
    title STRING;
end

Record MyCustomerTwoType type BasicRecord
    age INT;
    title STRING;
end
```

Here are two declarations.

```
myCustomer01 MyCustomerOneType;
myCustomer02 MyCustomerTwoType;
```

The effect of **move** by name is to copy the values only for fields whose names match. The result of the next example is to copy a value from one field named **title** to another.

```
myCustomer01.ID = 25;
myCustomer01.title = "Doctor";
myCustomer02.age = 40;
myCustomer02.title = "Officer";
move myCustomer01 to myCustomer02 byname;

sysLib.writeStdOut(myCustomer02.age);  // 40
sysLib.writeStdOut(myCustomer02.name); // Doctor
```

In contrast, the effect of **move** by position is to copy the values for each field in a record, without regard to the field names.

```
myCustomer01.ID = 25;
myCustomer01.title = "Doctor";
myCustomer02.age = 40;
myCustomer02.title = "Officer";
move myCustomer01 to myCustomer02 byposition;

sysLib.writeStdOut(myCustomer02.age);  // 25
sysLib.writeStdOut(myCustomer02.name); // Doctor
```

The last example is with arrays. The assumption in each of the following cases is that the target array has the number of elements needed to accept the content being copied.

```
// move "Buy" to elements 2, 3, and 4 in temp
move "Buy" to temp[2] for 3;

// move elements 2, 3, and 4 from temp
//        into elements 5, 6, and 7 in final
move temp[2] to final[5] for 3;
```

Set

The **set** statement establishes characteristics of a record, form, or field. The statement has many variations. For example, in relation to a record, you can reset the field values to those initially specified in the Record part definition. The boldface statement in the following code has that effect.

```
Record DepartmentPart type BasicRecord
    Department STRING = "Sales";
    BudgetCode INT;
end
Function MyFunction()
    MyDept DepartmentPart;
    SysLib.writeStdOut(MyDept.Department);
    MyDept.Department = "Marketing";
    SysLib.writeStdOut(MyDept.Department);
    set MyDept.Department initial;
    SysLib.writeStdOut(MyDept.Department);
end
```

The code writes **Sales** and then **Marketing** and then **Sales**.

Conditional Processing

The **if** and embedded **else** statements provide conditional processing, as does the **case** statement.

If, Else

The **if** statement defines a block of statements that run if and only if a specified condition applies. The **else** statement defines an alternative block of statements.

The following code sets msgText in various cases. If msgStatus equals 1, msgText is set to *Yes!*; if msgStatus equals 0, msgText is set to *No!*; and otherwise, msgText is set to *Service invocation failed!*.

```
if (msgStatus == 1)
    msgText = "Yes!";
else
    if (msgStatus == 0)
        msgText = "No!";
    else
        msgText = "Service invocation failed!";
    end
end
```

Case

The **case** statement runs one of several alternative sets of statements.

You can specify a value for comparison, as shown next.

```
case (msgStatus)
    when(1)
        msgText = "Yes!";
    when(0)
        mgText = "No!";
    otherwise
        msgText = "Service invocation failed!";
end
```

In this example, if **msgStatus** evaluates to 1, **msgText** receives the value *Yes!*; if **msgStatus** evaluates to 0, **msgText** receives *No!*; and if **msgStatus** evaluates to any other value, **msgText** receives *Service invocation failed!*

The **case** statement runs all statements in a given **when** or **otherwise** clause, and control never passes to more than one clause. In the next example, if

myCode evaluates to 1, the functions **myFunction01** and **myFunction02** run and the others do not.

```
case (myCode)
  when (1)
      myFunction01();
      myFunction02();
  when (2, 3, 4)
      myFunction03();
  otherwise
      myDefaultFunction();
end
```

If you don't specify a value for comparison, the **case** statement runs the first clause for which a condition resolves to *true*. In the following example, if **myCode** evaluates to 4, the function **myFunction03** runs.

```
case
  when (myCode == 3)
      myFunction01();
  when (myCode > 3)
      myFunction03();
  otherwise
      myDefaultFunction();
end
```

Loop Control

The **for, while,** and **continue** statements provide loop control.

For

The **for** statement defines a block of statements that run in a loop until a specified value is exceeded. For example, the following code writes the numbers 10, 20, 30, and 40 to the standard output.

```
for (i int from 10 to 40 by 10)
    sysLib.writeStdOut(i);
end
```

The following code writes the numbers 40, 30, 20, and 10.

```
for (i int from 40 to 10 decrement by 10)
   sysLib.writeStdOut(i);
end
```

While

The **while** statement defines a block of statements that run in a loop until a test fails. The following code writes the numbers 10, 20, 30, and 40.

```
i INT = 10;
while (i <= 40)
  sysLib.writeStdOut(i);
  i = i + 10;
end
```

Continue

The **continue** statement returns control to the start of an enclosing loop in the same function. For example, the following code writes the numbers 1, 2, and 4 to the standard output.

```
for (i int from 1 to 4 by 1)
  if (i == 3)
    continue;
  end
  sysLib.writeStdOut(i);
end
```

Transfer of Control Within a Program

Function invocations and the **return** and **exit** statements transfer control within a program or handler.

Function Invocation

A function invocation runs a function and includes arguments to match the function parameters. The arguments must match the parameters in number, with some variation allowed in the data type, as specified in compatibility rules.

The next statement passes a string to a function.

```
myFunction("test this string");
```

If a function returns a value, two rules apply. First, you can code a variable to receive that value from the function, but the variable is not required. Second, you can code the function invocation inside a larger expression. For example, if the function in the next expression returns the name *Smith*, the string sent to the standard output is *Customer 23 is Smith*.

```
sysLib.writeStdOut("Customer 23 is "
                + getCustomerName(23));
```

Return

The **return** statement returns control from a function and optionally returns a value to the invoker. In the next example, the statement returns 0.

```
for (i int from 10 to 40 by 10)
    sysLib.writeStdOut(i);
end
return(0);
```

Exit

The **exit** statement ends the processing of the nearest enclosing statement of a stated kind. For example, the following code stops processing the **for** statement when the value if i is 3.

```
for (i int from 1 to 4 by 1)
   if (i == 3)
     exit for;
   end
   sysLib.writeStdOut(i);
end
```

The code writes the numbers 1 and 2 to the standard output.

Transfer of Control Out of a Program

The **call**, **forward**, and **transfer** statements transfer control to logic that's outside the program or handler.

Call

In Rich UI, the **call** statement invokes a service, as described in Chapter 6.

```
call myService.getEmployee(123)
    returning to myCallback
    onException
      serviceLib.serviceExceptionHandler;
```

Outside of Rich UI, the **call** statement transfers control to another program. The arguments must match the program parameters in number and type.

```
myCustomerNumber = 23;
myCustomerName = "Smith";
call myProgram(myCustomerNumber, myCustomerName);
```

Forward

The **forward** statement in a JSF handler transfers control; in most cases, to another Web page.

```
forward to "myWebPage";
```

The current example forwards control to the logic that the JavaServer Faces runtime identifies as *myWebPage*. In most cases, that logic is (essentially) a Web page.

Transfer

The **transfer** statement transfers control from one main program to another, ending the first program and optionally passing a record. The following code transfers control to **Program02** and passes a record named **myRecord**.

```
transfer to Program Program02 passing myRecord;
```

System Libraries

In addition to developing libraries that include variables, constants, and functions, you can access EGL system libraries such as the following ones.

- The **sysLib** library lets you write to an error log or a standard location, commit or roll back database changes, retrieve properties and messages from text files, wait for time to elapse, or run an operating-system command.

- The **strLib** library lets you format date and time variables and manipulate strings.

- The **mathLib** library lets you perform common mathematical and trigonometric operations. You can round a number in various ways and determine the maximum or minimum of two numbers.

- The **datetimeLib** library lets you retrieve the current date and time and lets you process dates, times, and intervals in various ways.

- The **serviceLib** library lets you specify a service location to be accessed at run time and, for Rich UI, processes JSON strings.

- The **lobLib** library lets EGL-generated Java code work with variables of type BLOB (binary large object) or CLOB (character large object). You can associate a file with a variable of one of those types, transfer data to and from the file, and gain access to a string that represents the data.

- The **XMLLib** library converts an XML string to or from a record.

Some libraries are specific to a runtime technology; for example:

- The **sqlLib** library lets you interact with relational database management systems; for example, to connect to a database at run time.

- The **j2eeLib** library lets you interact with a JEE-compliant application server from an EGL JSF handler.

Exception Handling

EGL-generated code can encounter an exception during the following runtime operations: a program call or transfer; access of a service or library; a function invocation; access of persistent storage; a data comparison; or a data assignment. You also can *throw*—register—an exception in response to some runtime event; for example, a user's entering an invalid customer ID at a Web browser.

To make an exception available to be *caught*—that is, to be handled—you embed business logic inside a **try** block. Here's an outline of a **try** block.

```
try
    // place your business logic here

    onException
        (exceptionRecord ExceptionType01)
        // handle the exception here

    onException
        (exceptionRecord ExceptionType02)
        // handle the exception here
end
```

The **try** block includes zero to many **onException** blocks. Each **onException** block is essentially an error handler and is similar to a function that accepts a single parameter—an exception record—and returns no value. Unlike a function, the **onException** block has no **end** statement; instead, the block ends at the start of the next **onException** block, if any, or at the bottom of the **try** block.

The use of a **try** block has a performance cost, so you may decide to embed only the most exception-prone code in such a block.

In the following example, the attempt to add content to an uninitialized array causes an exception that we describe with the phrase "**NullValueException**."

```
Program myProgram type BasicProgram
    myStringArray STRING[];
    Function main()
        try
            myStringArray.appendElement("One"); // error
            onException (exception NullValueException)
                myStringArray = new STRING[];
                sysLib.writeStdErr ("NullValueException");
            onException (exception AnyException)
                sysLib.writeStdErr ("AnyException");
        end

        sysLib.writeStdErr
            ("Size of array is " +
                myStringArray.getSize());
    end
end
```

In this example, an **onException** block catches the exception, initializes the array, and writes the name of the exception type to the standard error output. A statement outside the **try** block then writes the following string to that output: *Size of array is 0.*

In general, the exception is caught by the first **onException** block that is specific to the exception type; here, the type is NullValueException. However, if no onException block is specific to the exception type, the EGL runtime invokes the **AnyException** block, if any. The placement of the **AnyException** block in the list of **OnException** blocks is not meaningful; the **AnyException** block is invoked only as a last resort.

An **OnException** block can itself include try blocks, to any level of nesting. In the following example, a statement in a **try** block also throws a **NullValueException**.

```
Program myProgram type BasicProgram
   myStringArray STRING[];
   myStringArray02 STRING[];
   Function main()
      try
         myStringArray.appendElement("One");
         onException (e01 NullValueException)
            try
               myStringArray.appendElement("One");
               onException
                  (e02 NullValueException)
                  myStringArray = new STRING[];
                  myStringArray.appendElement("One");
            end
      end
      sysLib.writeStdErr
         ("Size of array is " +
         myStringArray.getSize());
   end
end
```

The last statement in the example writes the string *Size of array is 1*.

We say that an exception is *cleared* if the code continues running without being interrupted again by that exception. The exception is cleared in the following two cases: the exception causes invocation of an **OnException** block at the current nesting level; or the exception occurs in a **try** block that has no **OnException** handlers at all. That second case has little practical value because you probably don't want your code to continue running unless you first correct the error or at least log the details.

The function ends immediately in the following case: an exception occurs and the **try** block at the current nesting level includes **onException** blocks, but none of the blocks catches the exception.

Propagation

The next example of error handling is similar to an earlier one, but the business logic in this case invokes the function **appendToArray**, which in turn invokes the function **doAppend**.

```
Program myProgram type BasicProgram
   myStringArray STRING[];
   Function main()
      try
         appendToArray("One");
         onException (exception NullValueException)
            myStringArray = new STRING[];
            sysLib.writeStdErr ("NullValueException");
      end

      sysLib.writeStdErr
         ("Size of array is " +
            myStringArray.getSize());
   end
   Function appendToArray (theInput STRING IN)
      doAppend(theInput);
      sysLib.writeStdErr ("You won't see the message." );
   end
   Function doAppend (theString STRING IN)
      myStringArray.appendElement(theString);
      sysLib.writeStdErr ("You won't see the message." );
   end
end
```

Listing 11.1: Propagation of exception

The **NullValueException** exception now occurs in **doAppend**, but the exception is handled as before, in the **main** function.

If a function throws an error that is not cleared, the function immediately ends, and the exception *propagates*—moves its influence— to the function's invoker, which clears the error or immediately ends. An uncleared exception propagates to the immediate invoker and then to progressively higher-level invokers until the exception is cleared or the program ends (Figure 11.1).

An exception also propagates from a called program to progressively higher-level callers. However, a failed service returns

Figure 11.1: Propagation

ServiceInvocationException, regardless of the exception that caused the service failure.

Exception Fields

Two fields—**message** and **messageID**—are available in every exception record. In relation to an exception that is defined by EGL, the **message** field contains a series of messages, each with an error number, and the **messageID** field contains the error numbers alone. For example, we might have coded one of our earlier **OnException** blocks as follows.

```
onException (exception NullValueException)
   myStringArray = new STRING[];
   sysLib.writeStdErr
      ("Handled this issue: \n" + exception.message);
```

In EGL-generated Java code, the new-line character (**\n**) makes the first error message appear on a new line, as shown next.

```
Handled this issue:
EGL0098E The reference variable named myStringArray is null.
EGL0002I The error occurred in the myProgram program.
```

Our next example shows a way to throw an exception of your own. We begin with an SQL Record part and an Exception part.

```
Record MyCustomerRecord type SQLRecord
    { keyItems = [customerNumber],
      tableNames = [["Customer"]] }
    customerNumber STRING;
    creditScore INT;
end

Record CustomerException type Exception
    customerID STRING;
end
```

After we declare a record that is based on the SQL Record part, we assign a customer number and code an EGL **get** statement to retrieve details about the customer identified by that number. The logic is similar to what is shown here.

```
myCustomer MyCustomerRecord;
myCustomer.customerNumber = "A1234";
get myCustomer;
```

We ignore the need to handle an SQL exception but show how to throw an exception of your own. In the following program, the CustomerException block uses the following fields: **customerID**, which was defined explicitly in the CustomerException part, and **message**, which is of type STRING and is present in any Exception record.

```
Program myProgram type BasicProgram

    Function main()
        myCustomer MyCustomerRecord;
        myCustomer.customerNumber = "A1234";
        try
            retrieveOne(myCustomer);
            onException (exception CustomerException)
                sysLib.writeStdErr
                    ("Customer: " + exception.customerID
                    + "\nIssue: " + exception.message);
        end
    end
```

Listing 11.2: Throwing an Exception (part 1)

```
Function retrieveOne(theCustomer MyCustomerRecord)
    get theCustomer;
    if (theCustomer.creditScore < 310)
        throw new CustomerException
            { customerID = theCustomer.customerNumber,
              message = "No Credit" };
    end
  end
end
```

Listing 11.2: Throwing an Exception (part 2)

After the get statement runs, the record **theCustomer** includes the credit score for the customer whose number is A1234. If the score is less than 310, the **throw** statement creates a new record, initializing the record fields for use in the **CustomerException** block. The output is as follows.

```
Customer: A1234
Issue: No Credit
```

CHAPTER 12

Files and Relational Databases

EGL lets you access files and message queues without requiring that you know details of the access technologies. A further convenience is that you can use the same EGL file-access statements to interact with databases.

In this chapter, we list the data-access statements and give examples of their use with serial files and relational databases. We begin by describing how EGL handles an issue that affects most applications.

Logical Unit of Work

A *logical unit of work* is a set of changes to persistent storage, such that all the changes are *committed*—made permanent—or *rolled back*—revoked—as if they were a single change. For example, the transfer of money between two bank accounts is a two-stage process that subtracts a value from one account and adds a value to another. The two changes are a logical unit of work because they must occur together or not at all.

A logical unit of work applies to some kinds of persistent storage and not to others. For example, your code can roll back its changes to a relational database by invoking a single function, sysLib.rollback; but that function has no effect on a Windows-platform serial file. Your code can only compensate for an earlier change to such a file, perhaps by making a second change to the same file or by adding an entry to an error log. We say that the relational database is *recoverable* and that the serial file is *non-recoverable*.

A logical unit of work begins when your code changes a recoverable resource and ends at the point of commit or rollback. A commit occurs if your code runs sysLib.commit or if the EGL runtime causes an implicit commit; as occurs, for example, when the first program in a run unit ends successfully. A rollback occurs if your code runs sysLib.rollback or if the EGL runtime causes an implicit rollback; as occurs, for example, after an uncaught exception.

Several resources can be recoverable, including databases, VSAM files on CICS, and WebSphere MQ message queues. In your EGL code, a logical unit of work applies to all the recoverable resources that your code changes.

Data-Access Statements

Table 12-1 lists the major EGL data-access statements for files and relational databases.

Table 12-1: Kinds of EGL Data-Access Statements	
Statement Type	**Purpose**
add	To place a record in a file, message queue, or database; or to place a set of records in a database.
close	To close the file or message queue associated with a given record; to disconnect from a printer; or, in the case of an SQL record, to close the *cursor*—a list of database rows—that was made available by an EGL open or get statement.
delete	To remove a record from a file, or a row from a relational database.
execute	To run one or more SQL statements; in particular, SQL data-definition statements such as CREATE TABLE; and data-manipulation statements such as INSERT or UPDATE.
get	To retrieve a single file record or database row or to retrieve a set of database rows. The retrieval may allow for a subsequent update or delete.
forEach	To process data from each of several database rows returned from an open or get statement.
open	To select a set of rows from a relational database.
prepare	To specify an SQL PREPARE statement, which builds a database-access statement at run time
replace	To put a changed record into a file or database.

File Access

An EGL Record part can be the basis of a variable used as the source or target of an I/O operation. For example, here's a Record part used as the basis of a serial record.

```
Record MyRecordPart type SerialRecord
    { FileName="Inner" }
    PolicyID CHAR(15);
end
```

Here's a related record declaration and assignment, followed by an EGL add statement that places data from the record into a file.

```
myRecord MyRecordPart;
myRecord.PolicyID = "A1234";
try
    add myRecord;
    onException(except FileIOException)
        ;
end
```

In this case, the record myRecord is said to be the *I/O object* of the add statement.

We can retrieve data back into the same record by closing the file and writing a get statement. Here's the code.

```
try
    close myRecord;
    myRecord.PolicyID = "";
    get next myRecord;
    onException(except FileIOException)
        ;
end
sysLib.writeStdOut(myRecord.PolicyID);
```

Despite our having cleared the PolicyID field in the second line, the last line in the example displays the value *A1234*, which was retrieved from the same file as the one that received the data. But what file was acccessed?

File Names and Resource Associations

The only file name previously in our example is the setting of the FileName annotation, in the Record part MyRecordPart.

```
Record MyRecordPart type SerialRecord
   { FileName="Inner" }
   PolicyID CHAR(15);
end
```

The FileName setting is known as the *logical file name* and does not specify the name of a *physical file*, which is a storage location on the target platform.

Resource Associations Part

Before you generate EGL code, you configure a *build descriptor*, which is a build part that guides the generation process and references other definitions. If a record in your logic accesses a physical file, you are likely to reference a *resource associations part* in the build descriptor. The resource associations part can associate the logical file name with a physical file on each target platform where you intend to run your code.

In essence, the resource associations part provides a table like Table 12-2, where the phrase *System Name* refers to the physical file's system-specific name,

Table 12-2: Content for a Resource Associations Part		
File Name	**System Type**	**System Name**
Inner	win	c:\Outer.txt
	zosbatch	MYFILE

The table indicates that the logical file name *Inner* is associated with one file if the code runs on a Microsoft Windows platform, and another file if the code runs as a z/OS batch program.

The benefit of this mechanism is that, at generation time, a change to the resource associations part redirects runtime processing to a different file. In this way, you can change from a test environment to a production environment without changing your code.

In our resource associations part, the system name specified for z/OS batch was itself a logical file name. The implication is that on z/OS, a switch from one physical file to another is possible at deployment time.

ResourceAssociation Field

Your code can retrieve the value of the field resourceAssociation to determine what physical file was accessed. The field is present in every Record part whose stereotype is primarily for file I/O, as is the case for a SerialRecord part. Here's how we retrieve the file name from a record that's based on MyRecordPart.

```
sysLib.writeStdOut(myRecord.resourceAssociation);
```

We'll hereafter assuming that the code is running on a Microsoft Windows platform, where the file name is "c:\Outer.txt".

You can also redirect processing in your code—for example, in response to user input—by setting the field resourceAssociation, as shown next.

```
myRecord.resourceAssociation = "c:\\Outer02.txt";
myRecord.policyID = "Z4321";
try
    add myRecord;
    onException(exceptRecord FileIOException)
        ;
end
```

The assignment of the name c:\Outer02.txt to resourceAssociation means that the add statement writes *Z4321* to that file.

Escape Character

We'll digress briefly to clarify a point of syntax. In that last example, the two backslashes in the file name are needed because the first is the EGL *escape character*, which is not processed as other characters are processed.

An escape character allows use of a subsequent character in a context where the subsequent character would interfere with the desired behavior. For example, a quote mark within a string would end the string prematurely. You avoid that outcome by preceding the quote mark with an escape character, as in the following example.

```
quote STRING = "You might say, \"Forget about it!\"";
```

Support for Relational Databases

The basic idea of a relational database is that data is stored in persistent tables. Each table column represents a discrete unit of data such as an order ID or an order-status code, and each row represents a collection of such data. In short, a table row is equivalent to a file record.

In most cases, one or more columns in a database table are *primary keys*, which means that the values in those columns are unique to a given row. If multiple columns are primary keys, the sequence of column values must be unique to a given row.

Access to relational databases is by way of Structured Query Language (SQL). For some interactions, you don't need to know SQL at all. However, many enterprise applications use complex database queries, requiring that you have expertise with the language or that someone on your development project has such expertise.

You can interact with a relational database as follows: define a Record part whose stereotype is SQLRecord, create a variable based on that Record part, and use the variable as an I/O object in different data-access statements.

Insertion and Retrieval

Here's an example Record part.

```
Record OrderPart type sqlRecord {
        tablenames=[["ORDERS"]],
        keyItems=[orderID] }

    orderID INT
        { Column="ID" };
    orderStatus CHAR(1)
        { Column="STATUS" };
end
```

Each field in the Record part is associated with a table column, as indicated by use of the Column annotation. By associating a record field and a column, you ensure that when an SQL record is used in a data-access statement at run time, data passes from field to column or from column to field. If a Record-part field name is the same as the corresponding table-column name, you don't need to set the Column annotation.

The Record part as a whole has two annotation fields. First, the tableNames annotation field identifies a single table, but could indicate that the part provides access to a *join*, which is combination of tables. For example, a join of two tables might be necessary to access all the item details for a given order. Second, the keyItems annotation field lists the *key fields*, which are, in most cases, the Record part fields that correspond to the unique keys in the table. However, the key fields may refer to other columns, as can be useful to exploit the default behavior of EGL data-access statements in different ways.

Here's a record declaration and field assignments, along with an EGL add statement that places data from the record into the database table ORDERS.

```
myRecord OrderPart;
myRecord.orderID = 123;
myRecord.orderStatus = "1";
try
    add myRecord;
    onException(except SQLException)
        ;
end
```

To retrieve a row, you assign a value to the record field associated with the key column and then issue a get statement, as in the next example, which retrieves the row we just added.

```
myRecord.orderID = 123;
try
    get myRecord;
    onException(except SQLException)
        ;
end
```

Implicit and Explicit SQL Statements

For a given EGL statement, the generated code issues one or more SQL statements in accordance with details specified in the Record part. For example, in place of the EGL add statement, the generated code issues an SQL INSERT statement, which adds one or more rows to the table. In our current example, the INSERT statement adds a single row to the table, placing a value in every column. The SQL code includes EGL variables such as myRecord.orderID.

```
insert into ORDERS
    ( ORDERS.ID,
      ORDERS.STATUS )
values
    ( :myRecord.orderID,
      :myRecord.orderStatus )
```

You don't need to understand SQL or to see the SQL code during development. The code is implicit in the EGL statement. However, you can make the SQL code explicit, as follows: right-click on the EGL statement name in the Workbench, select **SQL Statement**, and click **Add** (meaning "add the SQL statement"). The EGL statement itself is now expressed differently.

```
add myRecord with
#sql{
    insert into ORDERS
        ( ORDERS.ID,
          ORDERS.STATUS )
    values
        ( :myRecord.orderID,
          :myRecord.orderStatus )};
```

When the SQL statement is explicit, you can revise it in your EGL code, but changes to the Record part have no effect on how the EGL statement interacts with the database. Explicit statements takes precedence over implicit ones.

If you make explicit the SQL statement that's related to the EGL get statement, the EGL statement is expressed as follows.

```
get myRecord with
#sql{
    select
      ORDERS.ID,
      ORDERS.STATUS
    from ORDERS
    where
      ORDERS.ID = :myRecord.orderID};
```

The WHERE clause in any SQL SELECT statement restricts what rows are retrieved. In this case, the SELECT statement retrieves only those rows for which the ID column equals the value specified in the EGL field orderID.

In general, the following rules apply to an EGL get statement for which an SQL record is the I/O object:

- The implicit SQL SELECT statement retrieves data into all the fields listed in the Record part.

- The implicit WHERE clause restricts the retrieved rows to those for which as many as two conditions apply: the value in each key field is found in the related column; and the *default select condition* is fulfilled, as shown in the next section.

Open and ForEach

The open statement gives you a way to identify a set of rows, and the forEach statement provides an elegant way to process them. We'll show one of many possible variations.

First, assume that the database table ORDERS has three rows, with column names and values as shown in Table 10.3.,

Table 12-3: ORDERS table	
ID	Status
123	1
456	2
789	2

Here's the Record part we used earlier, with a revision in boldface.

```
Record OrderPart type sqlRecord {
      tablenames=[["ORDERS"]],
      keyItems=[orderID],
      defaultSelectCondition=#sqlCondition{STATUS = '2'} }

   orderID INT
      { Column="ID" };
   orderStatus CHAR(1)
      { Column="STATUS" };
end
```

In our use of the open statement, the implicit SQL statement selects only the table rows that fulfill two requirements:

- The value in the ID column is greater than or equal to the value in the orderID field. The value of the annotation field keyItems sets this requirement.

- The STATUS column is equal to 2. The value of the annotation field defaultSelectCondition sets this requirement.

In this case, the annotation field keyItems also ensures that the rows are returned in ascending ID order. The field has no affect on ordering if keyItems refers to multiple key fields.

Here's the code.

```
oneOrder OrderPart;
oneOrder.ID = 400
try
   open myResultSet for oneOrder;

   forEach (oneOrder)
      sysLib.writeStdOut
         (oneOrder.orderStatus + " " +
          oneOrder.orderID);
   end

   onException (except SQLException)
      ;
end
```

The open statement identifies a name for the set of rows returned by the statement. That name—here, *myResultSet*—lets you associate the open statement with another EGL statement that acts on the result set. The name is not used in the current example, though. Instead, the forEach statement accesses each retrieved row in turn and processes it, writing the following strings to the standard output.

```
2 456
2 789
```

You can specify additional details in the open statement, for the purpose of overriding the default selection and ordering behaviors.

In passing, we'll note that the open statement is often used in *dynamic SQL*, which is a mechanism for structuring the SQL statement WHERE clause at run time so that, for example, user input can determine many aspects of a database search.

Dynamic Arrays of SQL Records

You can use dynamic arrays of SQL records to add or retrieve data from a relational database. To show this, we'll rely on our previous SQL Record part, which included the annotation field defaultSelectCondition.

First, we declare an array of records and add three rows to an otherwise empty database table.

```
myOrder OrderPart[3]{};
myOrder[1].orderID = 123;
myOrder[1].orderStatus = "1";
myOrder[2].orderID = 456;
myOrder[2].orderStatus = "2";
myOrder[3].orderID = 789;
myOrder[3].orderStatus = "2";

try
    add myOrder;
    onException (except SQLException)
        ;
end
```

As shown, the additions are fulfilled by coding a single EGL add statement.

Next, we'll use a get statement to retrieve the added rows into a dynamic array.

```
yourOrder OrderPart[]{};
try
    get yourOrder;
    onException (except SQLException)
        ;
end

arraySize int = yourOrder.getSize();

for (i int from 1 to arraySize by 1)
    sysLib.writeStdOut
        (yourOrder[i].orderStatus + " " +
         yourOrder[i].orderID);
end
```

The annotation field defaultSelectCondition causes retrieval of data only from the rows for which the STATUS column value is 2. In this case, the annotation field keyItems causes retrieval of the data in ascending ID order.

The output of the logic is as follows.

```
2 456
2 789
```

Exception Handling

One of the benefits of using an EGL record for data access is that you can use the is or not operator to test the record for an error value, as in the following examples.

```
// not end of file
if (yourRecord not endOfFile)
    ;
end

// no record found
if (myRecord is noRecordFound)
    ;
end

// wrongly tried to add an existing
//     file record or database row
if (myRecord is unique)
    ;
end
```

Where in your code do such entries belong? By default, the following conditions are *not* exceptions: first, an end-of-file condition, which is only possible when reading from a file; and second, a no-record-found condition when an EGL record is used as an I/O object—that is, when the EGL statement has content such as add mySerialRecord or get mySQLRecord. In the following example, the defaults apply.

```
try
    get mySQLRecord;
    onException (except SQLException)
        ;
end
if (mySQLRecord is noRecordFound)
    ;
end
```

If you prefer to cause the end-of-file (endOfFile) and no-record-found (noRecordFound) conditions to be treated as exceptions, set the following program or handler annotation to *yes*: ThrowNrfEofExceptions.

CHAPTER 13

Reporting

We focus now on the handlers used with BIRT reports and EGL text reporting.

Support for BIRT Reports

Your EGL program can invoke the BIRT report engine, which is software that creates graphically sophisticated output. Figure 13.1 outlines the runtime relationships.

Your code's initial access of the BIRT report engine can include the following details, among others:

- The name of a report design file, which identifies the structure of the report. You define the file in the Workbench, in the BIRT Report Designer.

- The name of an output file, as well as the output type, which may be HTML or PDF.

- The name of an EGL BIRT handler.

Figure 13.1: Support for BIRT Reports

The BIRT report engine interacts with the EGL BIRT handler, if any, and the handler in turn responds to runtime events. For example, the handler can receive displayable data from your EGL program and provide that data to the report engine as the engine prepares the report. For another example, the handler can change the color of report text in response to a value received into the report from your program or from a database or file.

Initial Access of the BIRT Report Engine

Your program accesses the report engine by creating a variable of type BIRTReport and then invoking functions that are available by way of that variable. Here's an example.

```
function CreateThisReport()

   myReport BIRTReport =
      new BIRTReport
         ("C:/MyReportDesign.rptdesign", null,
          "C:/MyFinalOutput.pdf", "pdf", null);

   myReport.createReportFromDesign();
end
```

The invocation of a function that creates the report—here, the function
createReportFromDesign—is the last interaction between your program and
the BIRT report engine. Thereafter, the report engine acts in accordance with
the input you specify.

A BIRT handler is a variable based on the EGL BIRT handler part. To make
the handler available to the report engine, you include the handler variable
when you declare the BIRT report variable, as shown next.

```
function CreateThisReport (draft Boolean)

    myHandler MyHandlerPart;

    myReport BIRTReport =
        new BIRTReport
            ("C:/MyReportDesign.rptdesign", null,
             "C:/MyFinalOutput.pdf", "pdf", myHandler);

    myReport.createReportFromDesign();
end
```

BIRT Handler

The BIRT handler is a generatable logic part that contains event handlers. For
example, consider the following report table, which lists customers and the
balance due for each.

Table 13-1: BIRT Report without Event Handling			
Last Name	**First Name**	**Account Balance**	**Remark**
Summer	Cleo	0	
Smith	Grace	42.00	
Taylor	Vlad	0	
Winter	Ben	22.00	

As the report is being prepared, the BIRT report engine invokes an event
handler in response to each row created in the table. In our example, we

ensure that if an account balance is present, the event handler updates the row. Here's the output when the event handler is in use.

Table 13-2: BIRT Report with Event Handling			
Last Name	**First Name**	**Account Balance**	**Remark**
Summer	Cleo	0	
Smith	Grace	42.00	Balance Due
Taylor	Vlad	0	
Winter	Ben	22.00	Balance Due

The following BIRT handler includes the function **onMyLabel**, which is the event hander for our example.

```
Handler MyHandlerPart type BIRTHandler

    function onMyLabel( myRemark LabelInstance,
                        myContext ReportContext )
        {  EventType = onCreate,
           ElementName = "remark" }

        myBalance float =
            myRemark.getRowData().getColumnValue("balance");
        if ( myBalance > 0 )
            myRemark.text = "Balance Due";
        end
    end
end
```

The name of any BIRT event handler is arbitrary. If the **EventType** annotation is set to **onCreate**, the event handler is invoked during creation of a specific part of the report table. In BIRT, the part we're talking about is known as the runtime instance of a report element.

Each report element is named in the BIRT design file. In this case, the element is a label named *remark*. That label identifies the fourth column in the output table. The instance—the *label instance*—is a report-table cell that is specific to the column and is created every time a row is created.

The first event-handler parameter accepts the label instance for a specific row and uses that label instance to access other data in the row. If the Account

Balance column—identified in the design file as *balance*—has a positive value, the event handler assigns the string *Balance Due* to the label instance.

Our event handler does not use the function parameter of type **ReportContext**. That parameter lets you get or set a report parameter at run time. For example, an event handler invoked early in report creation might set a report parameter so that only those customers who live in a particular city are represented in the report.

Support for EGL Text Reporting

We turn now to EGL text reporting. When you create a report with this technology, a *basic handler* starts the report in response to invocation by an EGL program. The handler then returns control to the program, which invokes additional handler functions for doing tasks such as transferring data to the handler or signaling that the input is complete. As the report is being created, a text-report engine—a variable declared in the handler—invokes other functions in the handler. Figure 13.2 illustrates the basic relationships.

Figure 13.2: EGL Text Reporting

The program-handler interaction is greater than in the case of BIRT reports, where almost all the EGL logic is in the BIRT handler.

We can best describe the handler by example. Consider the following EGL text report:

```
                                             page 1

     Name               Position

     Grace              President
     Taylor             Treasurer
```

To create the report, the following program invokes functions that reside in a basic handler named MyReportHandler.

```
Program MyProgram

    myHandler MyReportHandler{};

    Function main()
        myHandler.myInitialization();
        myHandler.myInput("Grace", "President");
        myHandler.myInput("Taylor", "Treasurer");
        myHandler.myFinish();
    end
end
```

All of those function names are arbitrary, but you are likely to divide the runtime processing as shown there: initialize the report, submit input as needed, and finish the report.

You can code handler-global variables in the basic handler so that the data your program transfers is available when output is created. To create output, the EGL text-report engine invokes handler functions.

In our example, a handler-global variable is based on the following Record part.

```
Record HandlerRecordPart
    name STRING;
    position STRING;
end
```

Here's an outline of the handler.

```
Handler MyReportHandler type BasicHandler

    textReport TextReport{};
    pageNumber INT;
    handlerRecord HandlerRecordPart;

    Function myInitialization() end
    Function myInput(name STRING, position STRING) end
    Function myHeaderFunction(myEvent textReportEvent) end
    Function myRowFunction(myEvent textReportEvent) end
    Function myFinish() end
end
```

A variable of type **TextReport** is the text-report engine. Two other handler-global variables are also available: **pageNumber**, which is an integer to store the page number; and **handlerRecord**, a record based on the Record part described earlier. Two of the functions are accessed by the text-report engine: **myHeaderFunction**, which writes header details on each output page, and **myRowFunction**, which writes a given row. Again, those function names are arbitrary.

The function names become known to the text-report engine when you register them by way of the variable **textReport**, as shown in the initialization function,

```
Function myInitialization()
    textReport.onFirstPageHeaderListener = myHeaderFunction;
    textReport.onPageHeaderListener = myHeaderFunction;
    textReport.onEveryRowListener   = myRowFunction;
    textReport.setFirstHeaderLines(5);
    textReport.startReport("D:/temp/myOutput.txt",
            null,null,null,null, 20, null);
end
```

The initialization function also sets the number of lines at the top of the first header and directs the text-report engine to start report production and to use 20 lines per output page.

The function **myInput** accepts data from the program, assigns input to a global record, and requests the text-report engine to create output; in this case, to create the following rows: a header, if the report requires one at that point in processing; and a row of data.

```
Function myInput(name STRING, position STRING)
    handlerRecord.name = name;
    handlerRecord.position = position;
    textReport.outputToReport();
end
```

The function **myHeaderFunction** reveals a simple way to specify output: by a set of statements that establish a column position, write fixed-length text, and move to the next line in the report. Here's the function, which begins by retrieving the page number from **textReport**.

```
Function myHeaderFunction(myEvent textReportEvent)
    pageNumber = textReport.getPageNumber();
    textReport.column(60);
    textReport.printText("page ");
    textReport.printText(pageNumber);
    textReport.println();
    textReport.println();
    textReport.column(5);
    textReport.printText("Name");
    textReport.column(30);
    textReport.printText("Position");
    textReport.println();
end
```

The parameter of type **textReportEvent** is characteristic of event handlers in EGL text reporting. The parameter contains the **state** field, which indicates whether the function was called because the first row is being printed, because the last row is being printed, or for neither reason. The information lets you test a condition before doing special processing at the start or end of a report.

The function **myRowFunction** inserts data from the program into the report.

```
Function myRowFunction(myEvent textReportEvent)
    textReport.column(5);
    textReport.printText(handlerRecord.name);
    textReport.column(30);
    textReport.printText(handlerRecord.position);
    textReport.println();
end
```

Last, the function **myFinish** closes the report file :

```
Function myFinish()
    myReport.finishReport();
end
```

CHAPTER 14

JavaServer Faces

In the interests of showing the range of EGL capabilities for Web development, we describe how EGL supports JavaServer Faces (JSF), and we contrast the JSF approach with that of Rich UI.

Introduction to JSF

JavaServer Faces is a *framework*—a combination of development-time shortcuts and runtime logic—for writing server-side Web applications. As noted in the Introduction, these kind of applications usually involve the download of one Web page after another (Figure 14.1).

Figure 14.1: Server-Side Processing

Even if a server-side Web application transmits a single page, the mechanism on the server for providing that page is different from the mechanism on the server for providing a client-side Web application. We're speaking of the difference between a dynamic and static Web page:

- A JEE-compliant application server can create and serve a *dynamic Web page*. That page is in the form of HTML that's built at run time and can include data known only at run time; in particular, details retrieved from databases. Dynamic Web pages can provide multimedia content and include JavaScript, but the main processing tends to occur on the server. The use of dynamic Web pages is characteristic of JavaServer Faces.

- A Web server (or application server) can retrieve and transmit a *static Web page*. That page is deployed on the server in an HTML file. The term "static" indicates that the server did not insert additional data into the HTML at run time; all the data came from the file. However, static doesn't mean "lacking capability." The use of static Web pages is characteristic of EGL Rich UI. The important point is that static Web pages don't involve a lot of initial processing on the server, as do dynamic Web pages.

A dynamic-Web-page developer who works with JavaServer Faces can ignore commonplace issues that would otherwise drain time during development. The main issue is the development effort needed to support the conversation between user and application. For example, after the JSF runtime detects a user error, the runtime software redisplays the same Web page automatically, with the user's input still on display and with the first wrong input highlighted. In the absence of a framework like JSF, the developer would need to write customized logic to cause that behavior.

JSF also offers the following benefit for server-side development: decisions about the flow—what page forwards to what other page—are not necessarily final at development time. In some cases, those decisions can be deferred until the application is deployed, with later updates possible. The ability to defer decisions adds to a company's flexibility because changes to the flow may require only a change to a configuration file on the server rather than new development.

The JSF solution has the following weaknesses:

- The repeated data exchange with the server slows the conversation between the user and application.

- A company requires additional server hardware because the server-side processing requires more resources on the server than are required when a Rich Internet Application is in use. The need for more resources is caused by two aspects of server-side processing: first, the creation of dynamic Web pages, and second, the need to store and retrieve data as the server transmits one Web page after another to the same user.

- The JSF runtime technology is complex. In the context of EGL, developers often need to understand more when they develop with JSF than when they develop with Rich UI.

EGL JSF and EGL Rich UI

Many companies that embrace EGL are likely to develop Web applications exclusively with either JSF or Rich UI. However, a company can mix the two approaches to an extent. A JSF application can include EGL-generated JavaScript in the Web page transmitted to the browser. In a more likely practice, a Rich UI application can display a hypertext link that, if clicked, opens a new browser window to provide a JSF Web application.

Data cannot be transferred easily between the two kinds of logic, because the memory areas in the case of EGL JSF are on the server, and the memory areas in the case of EGL Rich UI are on the user's local workstation,

EGL JSF Handler

To guide the user-code interaction for a specific JSF Web page, the EGL developer writes an *EGL JSF handler*, which is composed of variables and functions. At run time, the handler specifies what kind of data is transmitted to and from the page, responds to the user's button clicks, and oversees input validation.

The EGL JSF handler runs under the control of the JSF runtime. Figure 14.2 illustrates the usual one-to-one relationship between a Web page and an EGL JSF handler.

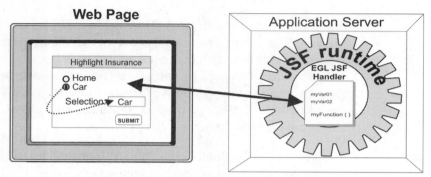

Figure 14.2: Web Page and the EGL JSF Handler

As an EGL JSF developer, you *bind* each Web-page field to a variable in the EGL JSF handler, as illustrated in Figure 14.3.

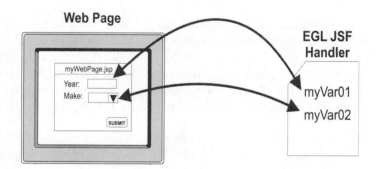

Figure 14.3: Web-Page Fields Bound to Variables in the EGL JSF Handler

The binding has two aspects. First, when the EGL JSF handler assigns a value to the variable, the JSF runtime ensures that the Web-page field receives the value. Second, when the user types data into the Web page and submits the content to the server, the JSF runtime ensures that the variable in the EGL JSF handler receives the new content from the Web-page field.

Validation is important to that second step. The JSF runtime can conduct a variety of tests on the user's input, from simple tests ("Does the value include only numeric digits?") to a range test ("Is the value between 50 and 100?"). Also possible is use of a validator function, which in this case is an EGL JSF handler function that determines whether a value conforms to a complex set of business rules. ("Is the user's payment up to date? If not, is the user's credit good enough to justify our sending the requested product?") In most cases, a failure of any of the tests causes a re-display of the same Web page, with an error message.

The EGL JSF handler oversees the interaction between user and code in another way. A Web-page button can be bound to a function in the EGL JSF handler. This binding means that at run time, when the user clicks that button, the function acts as an event handler, responding to the values received from the Web page into the variables, as illustrated in Figure 14.4.

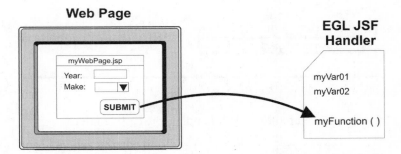

Figure 14.4: Web-Page Button Bound to a Function in the EGL JSF Handler

Similarly, a hypertext link in the Web page can be bound to a function in the EGL JSF handler, in which case a user's click of that link causes the function to be invoked.

Development Example

We'll offer a example of EGL JSF application development and later describe a way to think about EGL JSF in a larger, runtime context.

Consider the Web page shown in Figure 14.5.

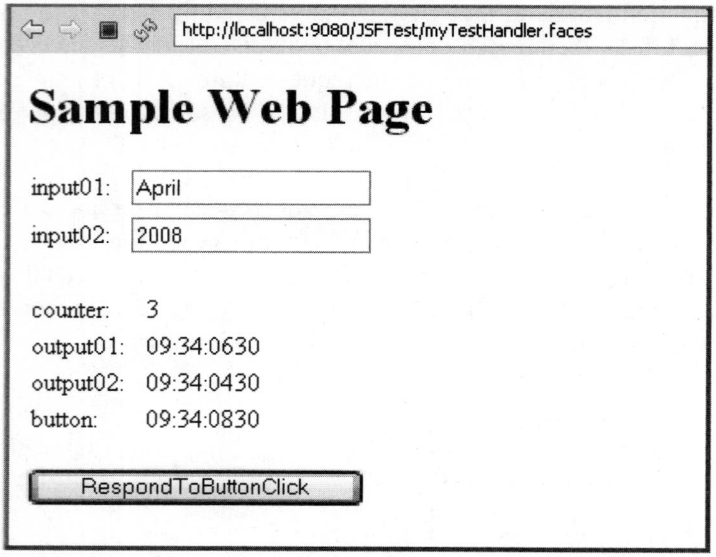

Figure 14.5: Sample Web Page

Here's the related EGL JSF handler, myTestHandler.

```
Handler myTestHandler type JSFHandler
   { onConstructionFunction = onConstruction,
     onPrerenderFunction = onPrerender,
     scope = session,
     view = "myTestHandler.jsp" }

myInput01 InputType
   { ValidatorFunction = validate01, ValidationOrder = 2 };
myInput02 InputType
   { ValidatorFunction = validate02, ValidationOrder = 1 };
myTimestamp STRING;
const MASK STRING = "mm:ss:SSSS";
counter INT;
myOutput01, myOutput02, myOutput03 OutputType;

Function onConstruction()
   counter = 0;
end

Function onPrerender()
   counter = counter + 1;
end
```

Listing 14.1: EGL JSF Handler (part 1)

```
Function validate01()
   wait(.02);
   myTimestamp = StrLib.formatTimeStamp
      (DateTimeLib.currentTimestamp(), MASK);
   myOutput01 = myTimestamp;
end

Function validate02()
   wait(.02);
   myTimestamp = StrLib.formatTimeStamp
      (DateTimeLib.currentTimestamp(), MASK);
   myOutput02 = myTimestamp;
end

Function respondToButtonClick()
   wait(.02);
   myTimestamp = StrLib.formatTimeStamp
      (DateTimeLib.currentTimestamp(), MASK);
   myOutput03 = myTimestamp;
end
```

Listing 14.1: EGL JSF Handler (part 2)

We'll describe the handler's data and then the structure and logic.

Data in myTestHandler

In one of several scenarios for creating the page and handler, we define two data items named **InputType** and **OutputType**.

```
dataItem InputType STRING
   {DisplayUse = input, DisplayName = "input: "}
end

dataItem OutputType STRING
   {DisplayUse = output, DisplayName = "output: "}
end
```

The annotation **DisplayUse** specifies the kind of Web-page control that will be bound to the variable by default. The annotation **DisplayName** specifies a default label for that control. Our intent is to create a binding between an input text box and a variable of type **InputType**; and to create a binding between a read-only text box and a variable of type **OutputType**.

In the JSF handler, the variables of type **InputType** have annotations beyond those provided in the related data item. **ValidatorFunction** identifies a function that determines whether the user input in a bound Web-page field is valid. **ValidationOrder** indicates that the first Web-page field to be validated is the field to which **myInput02** is bound.

```
myInput01 InputType
    { ValidatorFunction = validate01, ValidationOrder = 2 };

myInput02 InputType
    { ValidatorFunction = validate02, ValidationOrder = 1 };
```

The variable **myTimestamp** and the constant **MASK** will help us show a timestamp. The purpose is to demonstrate when different functions run.

```
myTimestamp STRING;
const MASK STRING = "mm:ss:SSSS";
```

The variable **counter** identifies how many times the handler transmits data to a given user; and the variables of type **OutputType** display the value in **myTimestamp** at a given time.

```
counter INT;
myOutput01, myOutput02, myOutput03 OutputType;
```

Structure and Logic of myTestHandler

The EGL JSF handler annotations provide details that we'll explain only briefly for now: the **onConstruction** function runs when the user first requests the Web page; the **onPrerender** function runs every time that the user requests the Web page; the **Scope** annotation indicates how long the EGL JSF handler stays in memory on the application server; and the **View** annotation identifies (in essence) the Web page that runs under the handler's control.

Now we'll outline the runtime events, assuming that the Web-page fields are bound to the appropriate variables and that the Web-page button is bound to the function **respondToButtonClick**. We'll describe the binding process soon.

When the handler first runs for a given user, the **onConstruction** function runs, setting counter to 0; and the **onPrerender** function runs, setting counter to 1. A Web page is displayed with the number 1 in the field that's bound to the counter variable. Here's the code.

```
Function onConstruction()
    counter = 0;
end

Function onPrerender()
    counter = counter + 1;
end
```

On seeing the Web page, the user may type data in one or both input fields, but the handler receives the input only when the user presses the button. For example, if the user changes no input fields and clicks the button, the following code runs immediately.

```
Function respondToButtonClick()
    wait(.02);
    myTimestamp = StrLib.formatTimeStamp
        (DateTimeLib.currentTimestamp(), MASK);
    myOutput03 = myTimestamp;
end
```

The effect of **respondToButtonClick** is to wait for .02 seconds, as necessary to ensure that the handler provides different values for different timestamps. The handler then sets **myOutput03** with the current timestamp, which is formatted in accordance with the value of **MASK**. The onPrerender function runs, and the timestamp and counter value (now 2) are displayed.

Next, if the user types a value into the first and second input field and clicks the button, the validator functions run in the order specified in the

ValidationOrder annotations. Here are the validator functions.

```
Function validate01()
    wait(.02);
    myTimestamp = StrLib.formatTimeStamp
        (DateTimeLib.currentTimestamp(), MASK);
    myOutput01 = myTimestamp;
end

Function validate02()
    wait(.02);
    myTimestamp = StrLib.formatTimeStamp
        (DateTimeLib.currentTimestamp(), MASK);
    myOutput02 = myTimestamp;
end
```

In general, the field-specific validator functions runs for all fields that the user changed, even if a specific validation fails. A validation fails if a validator function runs **sysLib.setError**; however, that function is not invoked in **myTestHandler**, and all validations succeed.

In general, validator functions run before event handlers; and in our scenario, functions run in the following order: **validate02, validate01, respondToButtonClick**, and **onPrerender**.

The timestamp values provided to the user demonstrate the behavior.

Generation Outputs

The effect of generating the EGL JSF handler is to create several outputs, including these: first, the Java equivalent of the EGL JSF handler; second, a formatted but largely empty Web page, if the page doesn't already exist; and third, a set of entries in an onscreen area named the Page Data view.

The Page Data view makes data and function binding possible, including one entry for each global variable in the EGL JSF handler and one entry for each handler function, with a few exceptions. In our example, an entry is provided for seven variables and for the functions **respondToButtonClick, validate01**, and **validate02** (Figure 14.6).

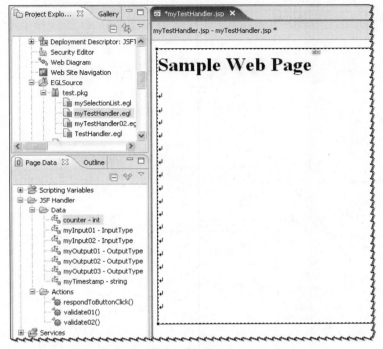

Figure 14.6: Page Data View Before Binding

Binding a Web-Page Field to a Variable or Function

The basic process for binding a Web-page field is that you drag an entry from the Page Data view and drop the entry on the Web-page surface (Figure 14.7). For data, the entry includes visual detail such as the type of control that you intended, as well as a default label. For actions—functions that you're providing—the entry lets you create a button that's bound to the specified function.

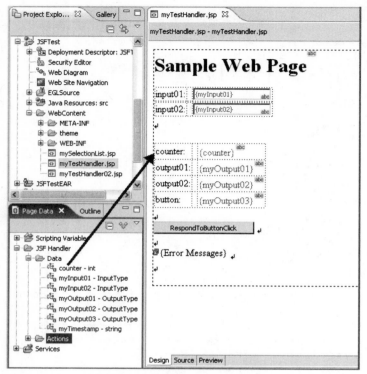

Figure 14.7: Page Data View After Binding

The importance of having up-to-date entries in the Page Data view explains why—by default—the product Workbench generates an EGL JSF handler as soon as the handler is saved. However, immediate update of the Page Data view isn't necessary for everyone. You might send your work to a Web-page designer, who would use the entries in the Page Data view to format the Web page.

The person who binds a Web-page field to a variable can accept or overwrite details that were specified in the EGL JSF handler.

EGL JSF in Context

As noted in our review of Rich UI, a *tier* is software that fulfills a large and distinct purpose at run time. Our focus now is on the processing that occurs in a JEE-compliant application server (Figure 14.8).

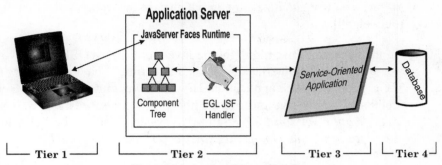

Figure 14.8: Logical Tiers at Run Time

As before, we describe the Model View Controller (MVC) relationships by referencing the multiple tiers. In the case of JSF, the browser and to some extent the application server are the View. and the services that access the databases—along with the databases themselves—are the Model. The Controller is on the application server, primarily.

Frameworks

A *framework* is a combination of runtime logic and a set of configuration files that affect the runtime behavior, along with constructs that are used at development time. An example of such a construct are the controls that a Web designers drags from a palette and drops on a Web-page surface.

A framework can offer several benefits. First, it lets you write fewer lines of code. The framework handles the runtime situations that are common in most applications. Like other advances in software technology, the framework shields business developers from the complexity of runtime systems.

The framework also simplifies application update. To customize some behaviors of your application, you don't alter and recompile your code; instead, you customize text files for the framework, either in a text editor or by setting values in a graphical environment. We describe the situation by saying that the framework *externalizes content*. We've seen this idea before, in regard to using a configuration file that has details on service location.

A framework's creators decide what the framework accomplishes, what application behavior is predetermined, and what application behavior is externalized. The cost of relying on their work is that you lose the ability to control some of the behavior yourself. However, a well-designed framework allows you to customize a lot, in which case the framework's benefits outweigh the cost.

In the next pages, we highlight the JavaServer Faces (JSF) framework. Our review of the JSF internals explains the runtime behavior of a server-centric, EGL-generated Web application. However, we omit some of the technical details of the JSF runtime. For the non-EGL details, see the *JavaServer Faces Specification Version 1.1* by Sun Microsystems, Inc., at the following Web site: *http://java.sun.com/javaee/javaserverfaces/download.html*.

Controller

The JavaServer Faces runtime controls a set of applications, including those provided by one or more EGL JSF handlers. You customize the JSF runtime largely by relying on the Workbench, which automatically updates a configuration file being deployed with your application. The update involves two details that help to clarify how your EGL code interacts with the JSF runtime.

First, the configuration file identifies the runtime Java handler as a *managed bean*, which means that the JSF runtime can access your code as needed. Second, the configuration file includes navigation rules to specify what logic will be accessed when the JSF runtime receives a request. One request might be from a JSF handler function that issues an EGL forward statement to navigate to a new page. The forward statement might specify an outcome value such as success or failure, in which case the JSF runtime reviews the navigation rules and then invokes the runtime logic that you associated with the specified outcome value.

In your first work with EGL JSF handlers, you are likely to specify an outcome value that's identical to the name of the Web page you wish to invoke. If you follow that convention, you don't need to update the JSF configuration file by hand.

View

You build a JSF-compliant Web page. The page includes tags that correspond to controls such as text boxes and buttons. The JSF runtime uses the information in those tags to structure the HTML transmitted to the browser.

When you work with a JSP file in the product Page Designer, you can see the tags if you click on the Source tab. The tags are organized in a hierarchy. For example, a form tag (starting with <h:form>) might include an input tag (starting with <h:inputText>) and a button tag (starting with <hx:commandExButton>).

Consider the following input tag.

```
<h:inputText
    id="textMyInput011"
    value="#{myTestHandler.myInput01}"
    binding="#{myTestHandler.myInput01_Ref}"
    styleClass="inputText">
</h:inputText>
```

The id property holds the component ID, which is used in some EGL functions. The value property holds a JSF *value-binding expression*, which indicates that the Web-page field represented by the tag is bound to the handler field specified in curly braces. In this case, the managed-bean name in the JSF configuration file is myTestHandler; and the variable name in the JSF handler is myInput01. The binding property also includes a value-binding expression; but in this case, the property is solely for use by EGL system code. The styleClass property causes the Web-page field to have the visual characteristics of a text box used for input.

Another tag property of interest is the action property, which in many cases identifies an EGL JSF handler function. The action value identifies what logic to run in response to the user's click. The following action property results in the runtime invocation of the handler function respondToButtonClick.

```
action="#{myTestHandler.respondToButtonClick}"
```

The JSF runtime creates server-side *components*—Java objects in memory—that correspond to the JSF tags for a given Web page. A component includes tag-specific detail. A runtime hierarchy of components—the *JSF component tree*—corresponds to the tag hierarchy that you see at development time. The tree is illustrated in Figure 14.9.

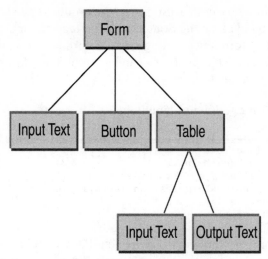

Figure 14.9: JSF Component Tree

An EGL JSF handler can update aspects of the components in response to user input or back-end processing. For example, the handler can do any of the following tasks: change the style of a textbox; change the target of a hypertext link; enable or disable a control; change the size of an image; assign different colors to alternate rows in an onscreen table; or add JavaScript to a button so that a user click causes processing in the browser.

The JSF runtime *renders* the component tree; in other words, creates HTML that represents the content of the tree. The JSF runtime then transmits the HTML to the user.

The component tree and the rendered HTML are the View.

Model

In relation to JavaServer Faces, the Model is the global data in the EGL JSF handler. A managed bean—the EGL JSF handler—is created, updated, or destroyed in accordance with a set of rules that we describe later.

The JSF runtime assigns the EGL JSF handler to one of three *scopes*, each of which defines the lifetime of a managed bean. The scopes correspond to the three possible values of the Scope annotation: *request*, *session*, and *application*. The three scopes are available to you, as well, allowing for temporary storage as you transfer data from one function to another in the same or a different EGL JSF handler. We speak of running an EGL JSF handler or storing data "in scope":

- Data in *request scope* is available from the time that the JSF runtime receives a request from the user until your code responds to that user. An EGL JSF handler in request scope might provide the status of a specific order in response to a user request. You can store data in request scope regardless of the Scope annotation.

- Data in *session scope* is available from the time that the JSF runtime receives data from the user and lasts through multiple user-code interactions until the server session is made invalid. The server session is made invalid in several ways: for example, by a session timeout or because the EGL JSF handler is *restarted*—reinitialized—in the application server. A handler in session scope might hold an order number required for a series of interactions. You can store data in session scope when the Scope annotation is *session* or *application*.

- Data in *application scope* is in a multiple-user scope and is available from the time a Web application starts for any user and lasts until the application is terminated. An EGL JSF handler in application scope might hold the next available order number. You can store data in application scope when the Scope annotation is *application*. Use of application scope is an advanced subject, and we'll not consider the issue again.

JSF Life Cycle

When a user requests a page or submits form data, or when some logic forwards control to a JSF handler, the initial phase of the JSF life cycle begins.

Figure 14.10 illustrates the JSF life cycle and reflects EGL-specific behaviors.

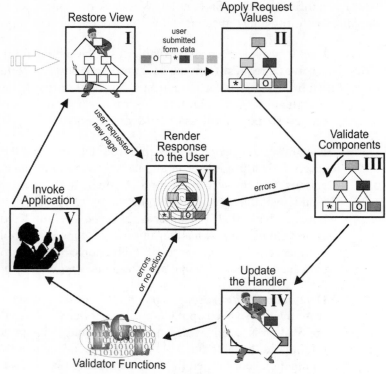

Restore View

Apply Request Values

user submitted form data

Render Response to the User

Validate Components

Invoke Application

errors

user requested new page

errors or no action

Update the Handler

Validator Functions

Figure 14.10: JSF Life Cycle with EGL

Overview

The JSF runtime creates the component tree; analyzes whether the user's form data, if any, is valid; and acts in one of two ways. If the user submitted invalid form data, the JSF runtime renders the component tree and displays the page again so that the user can correct and resubmit the input. Alternatively, if the user's input is valid, the JSF runtime updates the Model—the data values in the EGL JSF handler—and continues processing in accordance with the intended application flow, possibly forwarding control to another Web page.

JSF Life-Cycle Phases

We now consider the JSF life-cycle phases.

Phase I: Restore View. The JSF runtime creates the component tree and determines whether the EGL JSF handler exists. At this point, a handler intended for request scope cannot exist, and a handler intended for session scope may or may not exist, depending on what events preceded Phase I.

If the handler does not exist, the JSF runtime creates the handler, places it in the scope specified in the JSF configuration file, and runs the onConstruction function to provide data to the component tree.

If the user requested the page and did not submit form data, or if the page received control from other logic such as another EGL JSF handler, processing continues at Phase VI: Render Response. Alternatively, if the user submitted form data, processing continues at Phase II.

In later phases, the EGL JSF handler may be removed from scope. The effect of removing a handler from scope is that the handler will be destroyed, and a later use of the same handler will display fresh data to the user.

Phase II: Apply Request Values. Each component receives whatever data was provided by the page control that corresponds to the component.

Phase III: Validate Components. The JSF runtime converts the input strings to the Java data types that are required by the EGL JSF handler. Then, for each component in turn, the JSF runtime handles both EGL and JSF validations.

Validate Components is when most validations occur for each component. You specify the JSF validations, if any, when you work on the JSP file in the Page Designer. You specify the EGL validations when you write the EGL JSF handler.

All components are validated. For a given component, the conversions and validations occur until one of them fails. You cannot specify the order of component validations in Phase III.

The EGL component-specific validations include elementary edits such as minimum input; type-based edits such as digits only; and comparisons against data-table values. After the EGL and JSF validations run for a specific component, the EGL onValueChange function runs for the same component. Other EGL validator functions run in a later phase.

If a conversion or validation fails during Phase III, as occurs if an onValueChange function issues sysLib.setError, processing continues at Phase VI: Render Response. Otherwise, processing continues at Phase IV.

Phase IV: Update the Handler. The JSF runtime updates the EGL JSF handler with the validated data. The JSF specification refers to this phase as **Update Model Values**.

Phase V: Invoke Application. During this phase, the JSF runtime responds to the action requested by the user. From the perspective of JavaServer Faces, the code that's executed is "the application" because phase V is when business logic runs.

Before the JSF runtime fulfills the action specified by the user, the JSF runtime runs all the component-specific EGL validator functions, even if some fail.

The default order of validator-function execution is based on the position of tags on the Web page: left to right, primarily, and top to bottom. You can override that order by specifying the EGL ValidationOrder annotation for some or all components.

If all validations succeed, the JSF runtime runs the EGL validator function for the handler as a whole.

If a validation function runs sysLib.setError or if the user specified no action value, processing continues at Phase VI. However, if all validations succeed, the JSF runtime responds to the binding expression in the action property of the SUBMIT button, as found in the JSP file that represents the Web page. In most cases, the binding expression specifies a handler function, which can update the component tree, forward control to another Web page, or do other work.

An EGL forward statement ends processing in the handler. If the handler is in request scope, the handler is removed from that scope. If the handler is in session scope, the handler is removed from that scope only if the annotation cancelOnPageTransition was set to true and only if the forward statement directs processing to a handler other than the current handler.

Phase VI: Render Response to the User. The JSF runtime runs the onPrerender function, renders the component tree, transmits the response, and runs the handler's onPostrender function. Any change to the component tree in the onPostrender function affects the user only if the same page is rerendered later.

If the handler is in request scope, the JSF runtime has already removed the handler from request scope; and any change to the component tree in the onPostrender function has no effect.

Sources of Information

Several sources of information are available on EGL and the technologies featured in this book.

EGL and Rich UI

The primary Web site for the language is the EGL Cafe:

www.ibm.com/rational/eglcafe; click **EGL Cafe** at the left

Among the subjects covered there:

- EGL Rich UI. Click **Hubs > Rich UI**.

- Products, most of which offer free trials. Click **Products**.

- Details on customer experience:

    http://www.ibm.com/rational/eglcafe/docs/DOC-2701

MC Press

The MC Press site may include additional details on this book:

http://www.mc-store.com/5107.html

Eclipse and BIRT

The products that feature EGL are built on Eclipse. You don't need to download Eclipse separately from a product, but might want to learn more about the development platform:

http://www.eclipse.org

Also on that site is information on Business Intelligence and Reporting Tools (BIRT), including a tutorial:

http://www.eclipse.org/birt/phoenix/

JavaServer Faces

JavaServer Faces Specification Version 1.1 by Sun Microsystems, Inc., is at the following Web site:

http://java.sun.com/javaee/javaserverfaces/download.html

EGL Rich UI Widgets

We offer details on the Rich UI widgets, starting with an overview of styles and ending with a list of fields available for most widgets.

Styles

Rich UI projects are likely to be most successful if your company divides the responsibility for two tasks: laying out the user interface, as handled by an EGL developer, and creating the interface look and feel, as handled by a Web designer. To make this division of labor possible, we recommend that you use *cascading style sheet*s (CSS files). A CSS file sets the display characteristics of an individual widget or of a category of widgets.

The Workbench provides facilities for working with cascading style sheets. Here's an example file.

```
.EglRuiGridTable
{ border: 3px solid black; }

.EglRuiGridHeader
{ color:yellow;
  background-color:red; }

.EglRuiGridCell
{ color:black;
  background-color:aqua; }
```

Each of the dotted symbols such as .EglRuiGridTable can be referenced in a widget declaration or in the custom definition of a new type of widget.

Here are the main rules for handling styles:

- Every Rich UI application accesses a system CSS file in the **WebContent** folder. Leave the file alone; your updates are likely to be lost when you upgrade to a new version of the Workbench.

- You can override and supplement the provided styles by maintaining your own CSS file. You make it available to the Rich UI handler by setting the handler field cssFile, as shown here.

```
Handler ButtonTest Type RUIHandler
{ children = [ui], cssFile = "buttontest/coolblue.css" }
```

The value of cssFile is relative to the WebContent folder.

- Each widget type provided in Rich UI names a style class that you can include in a CSS file. The class name has the following pattern, where *WidgetTypeName* is the widget-type name such as TextArea.

```
EglRuiWidgetTypeName
```

Some widgets (which are described later) reference additional class names:

- The grid widget includes children that reference the style classes EglRuiGridTable, for setting the border style of the grid as a whole; EglRuiGridHeader, for setting characteristics of header cells; and EglRuiGridCell, for setting characteristics of body cells

- If a textField widget is read only, the widget references the style class EglRuiTextFieldReadOnly

- If a passwordTextField widget is read only, the widget references the style class EglRuiPasswordTextFieldReadOnly

- You can override a style class by setting class,

```
loginBox Box { numColumns=2, class="NormalBoxStyle" };
```

Here is an example of the related content in a CSS file.

```
.NormalBoxStyle
{ color:black;
  background-color:aqua; }
```

- You can specify a set of styles by using the syntax of CSS files when you declare a widget.

```
loginBox Box
{ numColumns=2,
  style="background-color:lightgreen;
         border-style:solid;"};
```

All the CSS styles are available if you use style as shown. However, for most purposes you assign values to individual style-related fields. The following declaration is equivalent to the previous one and does not involve CSS syntax.

```
loginBox Box
{ numColumns=2,
  backgroundColor="lightgreen",
  borderStyle="solid" };
```

Widget Types by Category

Table B-1 lists the widget types by category.

Category	Type	Purpose
Container	Box	To define a box that embeds other widgets
	Div	To define a rectangular section that is, in most cases, below all previous content
	FloatLeft	To define a div that includes the CSS element float:left
	FloatRight	To define a div that includes the CSS element float:right
	Grouping	To display a set of widgets, with text at the top left border of an enclosing box.
Information	Grid	To display a set of values in a table
	HTML	To present an HTML-formatted segment; for example, from a Web site or Web service
	Image	To display a graphic
	Shadow	To create a shadow to a specified div
	Span	To display a read-only string, possibly including an HTML-formatted segment
	TextLabel	To display a read-only string, possibly including HTML tags, which are displayed as tags
	Tree	To define a tree of displayable nodes
Interactive	BidiTextArea	To define a rectangle containing one or more lines of bidirectional text
	BidiTextField	To define a text box containing a single line of bidirectional text
	Button	To define a button, which elicits a user click and can respond by invoking a function
	CheckBox	To define a check box, which displays a true-false option and can respond to input by invoking a function

Table B-1: Supported Widgets by Category

Table B-1: Supported Widgets by Category		
Category	**Type**	**Purpose**
Interactive (continued)	Combo	To define a combo box, which presents one of several selectable options and lets the user open a dropdown list to select a different option
	Hyperlink	To define a Web page link that, if clicked, displays the page in the same or different browser
	List	To define a list box from which the user can select a single entry
	ListMulti	To define a list box from which the user can select multiple entries
	Menu	To define a menu bar entry
	PasswordTextField	To define an input text field whose value is displayed as bullets, as appropriate when the user types a password
	RadioGroup	To define a set of radio buttons, each of which responds to a click by deselecting the other radio button in the same group
	TextArea	To define a rectangle containing one or more lines of text
	TextField	To define a text box containing a single line of text
Hover	GridTooltip	To define a hover help; that is, one or more widgets that are displayed when the user hovers over a grid cell
	Tooltip	To define a hover help that is displayed when the user hovers over a widget
	TreeTooltip	To define a hover help that is displayed when the user hovers over a tree node

We describe the widgets by category.

Container Widgets

Widgets of the following types embed other widgets: Box, Div, FloatLeft, FloatRight, and Grouping.

Common Fields

children   An array of subordinate widgets

Box

A box contains widgets in columns. The width of each column is defined by the widest widget in the column:

- If the number of embedded widgets is less than the number of columns, the number of columns equals the number of widgets

- If the number of embedded widgets is greater than the number of columns, the first widget whose position exceeds the number of columns is placed in the next row.

Fields

alignment   Indicates how the content is aligned horizontally in its column.

            Integer. 0 = left (the default), 1 = center, 2 = right.

columns   Number of columns in the box.

            Integer. Default is 1.

Graphic and Code

This text is centered inside a box

Figure B.1: A Three-Column Box with One Child

```
txtLbl TextLabel{
        text = "This text is centered inside a Box"};

myBox Box{alignment = 1, columns=3, children=[txtLbl],
        borderstyle= "solid", borderWidth = 2,
        borderColor = "black"};
```

Div

A div defines a rectangular section that is, in most cases, below all earlier content. The contained widgets are left justified by default (Figure B.2).

A div preceded by a floatRight or floatLeft is on the same line as the other widget, if space permits. If the space is insufficient, the div goes below the earlier content (Figure B.3).

Graphic and Code

Figure B.2: Div Widget

```
tf TextField {width = 200,
             text = "Text field with a Width of 200"};
d2 Div {backgroundColor = "gray", width = 40, textLayout = "",
        innerHTML = "<br><br>Div", color = "yellow"};

d Div  {children =[tf, d2], width = 450, borderWidth = 1,
        borderstyle= "solid", borderColor = "black"};
```

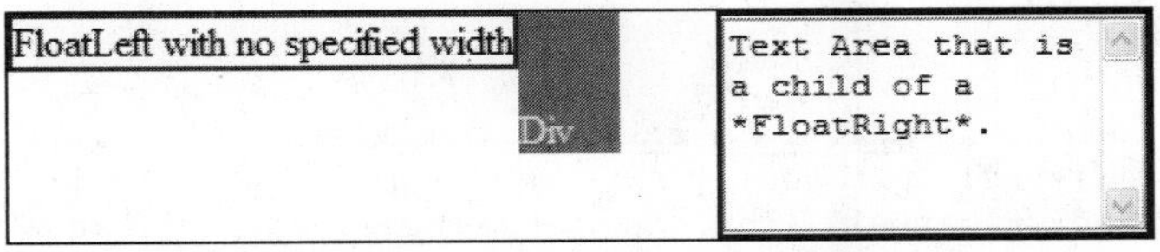

Figure B.3: Div Widget with Floats

```
fl1 FloatLeft {innerText = "FloatLeft with no specified width",
              borderstyle= "solid", borderWidth = 2,
              borderColor = "red"};
ta3 TextArea {numRows = 5, numColumns = 18,
            text="Text Area that is a child of a *FloatRight*."};
d3 FloatRight {children = [ta3], borderstyle= "solid",
              borderWidth = 2, borderColor = "black"};
d2 Div {backgroundColor = "gray", width = 40, textLayout = "",
        innerHTML = "<br><br>Div", color = "yellow"};

d Div {children =[fl1, d3, d2], width = 450, borderWidth = 1,
       borderstyle= "solid", borderColor = "black"};
```

FloatLeft

A floatLeft defines a rectangular section that includes the CSS element float:left.

In most cases, a floatLeft is below its previous siblings and is left justified in its container. The exception occurs when a previous sibling is a floatLeft or floatRight:

- If a previous sibling is a floatLeft, the sides of the floatLeft widgets touch (Figure B.4)

- If a previous sibling is a floatRight, the floatRight is displayed on the right of the floatLeft, as far right as possible (Figure B.5)

If the space is insufficient to display the floatLeft, the floatLeft is displayed on the left of the first subsequent container line where space is available (Figure B.6).

Graphic and Code

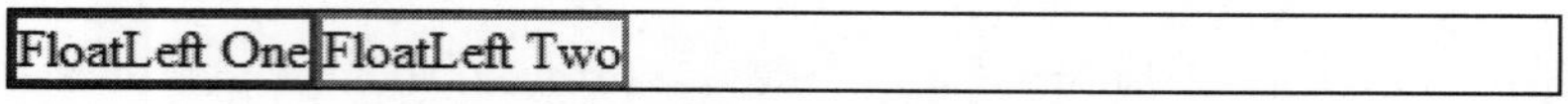

Figure B.4: FloatLeft Widget Followed by FloatLeft Widget

```
txtLbl TextLabel {text = "FloatLeft Two"};
d1 FloatLeft {children = [txtLbl], borderstyle= "solid",
             borderWidth = 2, borderColor = "gray"};
fl1 FloatLeft {innerText = "FloatLeft One", borderWidth = 2,
              borderstyle= "solid", borderColor = "red"};

d Div {children =[fl1,d1], width = 450, borderWidth = 1,
      borderstyle= "solid", borderColor = "black"};
```

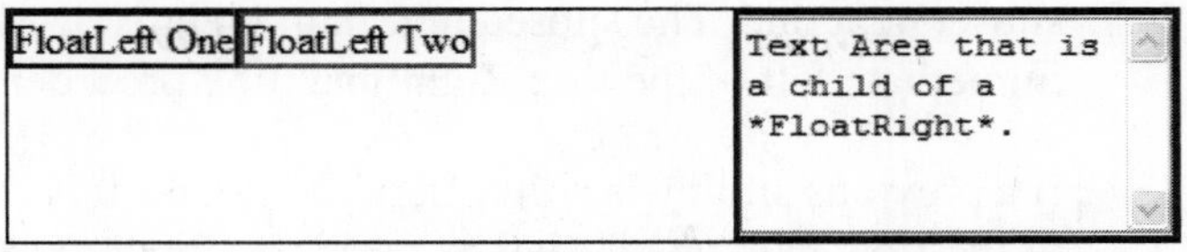

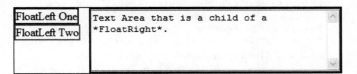

Figure B.5: FloatLeft Widgets Preceded by a FloatRight

```
ta3 TextArea {numRows = 5, numColumns = 18,
        text="Text Area that is a child of a *FloatRight*."};
d3 FloatRight {children = [ta3], borderstyle= "solid",
            borderWidth = 2, borderColor = "black"};
txtLbl TextLabel {text = "FloatLeft Two"};
d1 FloatLeft {children = [txtLbl], borderstyle= "solid",
            borderWidth = 2, borderColor = "gray"};
fl1 FloatLeft {innerText = "FloatLeft One", borderWidth = 2,
            borderstyle= "solid", borderColor = "red"};

d Div {children =[d3, fl1,d1], width = 450, borderWidth = 1,
        borderstyle= "solid", borderColor = "black"};
```

Notice the difference when we set the numColumns field in the TextArea to 40.

Figure B.6: FloatLeft Widgets Preceded by a Wide FloatRight

```
ta3 TextArea {numRows = 5, numColumns = 40,
        text="Text Area that is a child of a *FloatRight*."};
```

FloatRight

A floatRight defines a section (HTML DIV tag) that includes the CSS element float:right.

In most cases, a floatRight is below its previous siblings and is right justified in its container. The exception occurs when a previous sibling is a floatLeft, or a floatRight:

- If a previous sibling is a floatRight, that widget touches the right side of the container; that is, the first floatRight takes precedence over the subsequent one. The subsequent floatRight is displayed to the immediate left of the floatRight that took precedence (Figure B.7)

- If a previous sibling is a floatLeft, the floatLeft is displayed on the left of the floatRight, as far left as possible (Figure B.8)

If the space is insufficient to display the floatRight, the floatRight is displayed on the right of the first subsequent container line where space is available.

A floatRight can be on the right of its later siblings, but only if they can fit on the same plane.(Figure B.9)

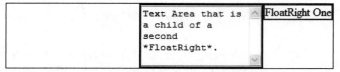

Figure B.7: FloatRight Widget Preceded by a FloatRight Widget

```
fr1 FloatRight {innerText = "FloatRight One", borderWidth = 2,
            borderstyle= "solid", borderColor = "green"};
ta3 TextArea {numRows = 5, numColumns = 18,
    text="Text Area that is a child of a second *FloatRight*."};
d3 FloatRight {children = [ta3], borderstyle= "solid",
            borderWidth = 2, borderColor = "black"};

d Div {children =[fr1, d3], width = 450, borderWidth = 1,
        borderstyle= "solid", borderColor = "black"};
```

FloatLeft	FloatRight

Figure B.8: FloatRight Widget Preceded by a FloatLeft

```
fl1 FloatLeft {innerText = "FloatLeft", borderWidth = 2,
            borderstyle= "solid", borderColor = "red"};
fr1 FloatRight {innerText = "FloatRight", borderWidth = 2,
            borderstyle= "solid", borderColor = "green"};

d Div {children =[fl1, fr1], width = 450, borderWidth = 1,
        borderstyle= "solid", borderColor = "black"};
```

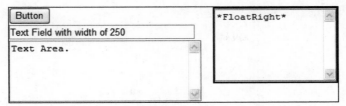

Figure B.9: FloatRight Widget with Later Siblings

```
ta3 TextArea {text="*FloatRight*",
              numRows = 6, numColumns = 18};
d3 FloatRight {children = [ta3], borderWidth = 2,
               borderstyle= "solid", borderColor = "black"};
btn Button {text = "Button"};
ft1 TextField {width = 250,
               text = "Text Field with width of 250"};
ta2 TextArea {text="Text Area.", numRows = 5, numColumns = 30};

d Div {children =[d3, btn, ft1, ta2], width = 450, borderWidth = 1,
       borderstyle= "solid", borderColor = "black"};
```

Grouping

A grouping displays a set of widgets, with text at the top left border of an enclosing box.

Fields

text   Text shown in the border.

       String. default is " ".

width   Width in pixels.

       Integer. Default is 100%.

Graphic and Code

Figure B.10: Grouping Widget

```
btn1 Button {text = "Button1"};
btn2 Button {text = "Button II"};
txtLbl TextLabel {text = "a Text Label", padding = 20};

gr Grouping {text = "My first group",
             children = [txtLbl, btn1, btn2], width = 200};
```

Information Widgets

Widgets of the following types are primarily to display output: Grid, HTML, Image, Shadow, Span, Textlabel, and Tree.

Grid

A grid displays a set of values in a table.

Fields

behaviors   Array of functions that describe the behavior of the non-header rows in the grid.

Function name. Can be custom or provided by the Workbench.

columns	Array of records of type GridColumn, each of which represents a column in the grid.

GridColumn:
```
Record GridColumn
    displayName String;  // the column header to display
    name        String; // name of the data field
    width       Int;    // number of pixels in a column
end
```

data	Array of developer-defined records.

Any.

header Behaviors	Array of functions that describe the behavior of the header rows in the grid.

Function name. Can be custom or provided by the Workbench.

totalRows	Number of rows in the grid.

Integer. Read only.

Graphic and Code

Plant Name ▲	Month Bloom	Year Planted
Hosta	May-June	2003
Camillia	March	2006
Gardenia	August	2007
Azelia	April	1992
Rose	April-June	2005
Ajuga	September	1996

Figure B.11: Grid Widget

```
myPlants Plant[]{}; //array of customized records, with values
gridSort GridSorter {sortByName = "plantName"};
gridSel GridSelector {color = "lightgreen"};

PlantsGrid Grid {
    headerBehaviors = [GridBehaviors.grayCells,
                        gridSort.columnSorter],
    behaviors = [gridSel.enableSelection,
                  GridBehaviors.alternatingColor],
    columns = [
       new GridColumn {name = "plantName",
                        displayName = "Plant Name", width = 100},
       new GridColumn {name = "bloom",
                        displayName = "Month Bloom", width = 100},
       new GridColumn {name = "Planted",
                        displayName = "Year Planted", width = 100}],
    data = myPlants as any[]
};
```

Delegates

The delegate CellBehavior gives the prototype for each function referenced by the behaviors array in a grid.

```
Delegate CellBehavior(grid Grid in, cell Widget in, row any in,
                       rowNumber int in, column GridColumn in) end
```

grid	Grid passed to the function.
cell	Internal widget that represents the grid cell and is based on the HTML TD tag.
row	Record that represents the row data.
rowNumber	Row number that is affected by the behavior.
column	Record that represents the column description.

HTML

An HTML widget presents an HTML-formatted segment; for example, from a Web site or Web service.

Fields

height   Maximum height in pixels.
Integer. Default is the height of the displayed HTML.

src   Web site address of the source for the text field.
String.

text   Text that is displayed at the top left border of an enclosing box.
String.

width   Width in pixels.
Integer. Default is 100%.

Graphic and Code

First is an HTML widget that uses the text field (Figure B.12).

Figure B.12: HTML Widget that Uses the Text *Field*

```
myHtml HTML {text = "<div align='right'>" +
    "<table border='1' cellpadding='14' " +
    "style='border-collapse: collapse'" +
    "bordercolor='#111111' width='25%' height='100'" +
    "align='right' bgcolor='#3366FF' cellspacing='8'>"+
    "<tr> <td width='100%' height='48'>"+
    "<p align='center'><b><font face='Verdana' size='2'>" +
    "<font color='#FFFFFF'>Already have the book?<br>"+
    "</font> <a href='http://www.mcpressonline.com/forums/"+
    "276-ibm-rational-business-developer-with-egl/'>"+
    "<font color='#FFFFFF'>Click here</font></a><br>"+
    "<font color='#FFFFFF'> for tutorial download."+
    "</font></font></b></td></tr></table></div>"};
```

Second is an HTML widget that uses the src field (Figure B.13).

38.898748,-77.037684,1600 Pennsylvania Ave NW,Washington,DC,20502

Figure B.13: HTML Widget that Uses the Src Field

```
html HTML{src =
    "http://geocoder.us/service/csv/geocode?address=1600"+
    " Pennsylvania Ave Washington DC"};
```

Image

An image widget displays a graphic.

Fields

height   Height in pixels

Integer. Default is the original height of the image.

src   Address of the image on disk or on the Web.

String.

text   Text shown in browsers that cannot show graphics or the hover text.

String. Default is " ".

width   Width in pixels

Integer. Default is the original height of the image.

Graphic and Code

Figure B.14: Image Widget with Hover Text

```
myImage Image{height="50", text="logo created in 1972",
               src="http://www.ibm.com/i/v16/t/ibm-logo.gif",
               width="110", backgroundColor = "black"};
```

Shadow

A shadow widget adds a shadow to a specified div.

Fields

div   Div widget to which the shadow applies.

Graphic and Code

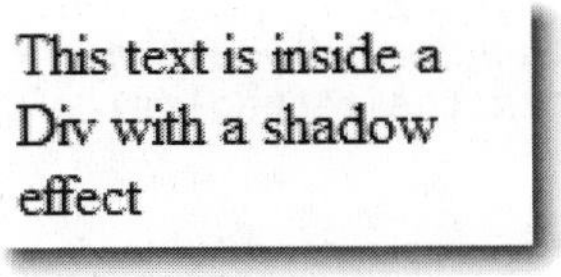

This text is inside a
Div with a shadow
effect

Figure B.15: Shadow Widget

```
txtLbl TextLabel{
    text = "This text is inside a Div with a shadow effect"};
myShadow Shadow{width=150, div=new Div {padding=5,
                                        children=[txtLbl]}};
```

Span

A span displays a read-only string, possibly including an HTML-formatted segment.

Fields

text   HTML fragment.

        String.

Graphic and Code

- Gives an overview
- Describes the main constructs
- Demonstrates
- Gives you practical experience
- Introduces the technology

Figure B.16: Span Widget

```
mySpan Span{text = "<BR><ul><li>Gives an overview"+
"<li>Describes the main constructs"+
"<li>Demonstrates"+
"<li>Gives you practical experience"+
"<li>Introduces the technology </ul><BR>"};
```

TextLabel

A text label displays a read-only string, possibly including HTML tags, which are displayed as tags.

Fields

text   Text to display
String.

Graphic and Code

This is an example of a TextLabel widget

Figure B.17: TextLabel Widget

```
myTxtLbl TextLabel{
        text = "This is an example of a TextLabel widget"};
```

Tree

A tree widget displays a tree of displayable nodes.

Fields

behaviors   Array of functions that describe the behavior of the nodes in the tree.

Function name. Can be custom or provided by the Workbench.

children   Array of subordinate TreeNode widgets.

A TreeNode represents a node in the tree and has the following fields:
    children. Array of subordinate TreeNode widgets.
    text. Value displayed for a node.
The String can have HTML tags.

Graphic and Code

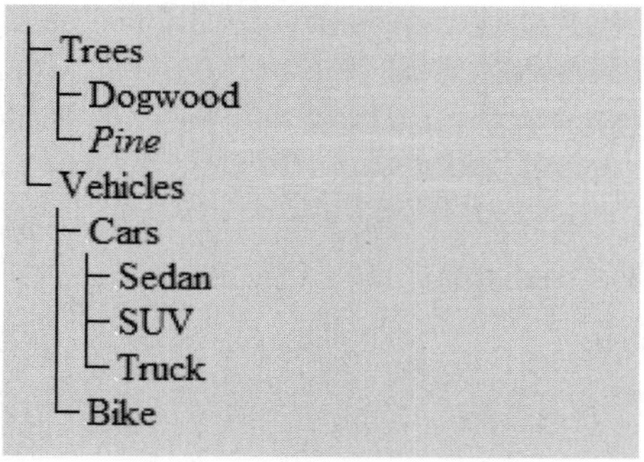

Figure B.18: Tree Widget

```
tr Tree {backgroundColor="#ddd", width=240, padding=9,
         behaviors = [TreeBehaviors.pointer,clickBehavior],
         children = [child1, child2]};

child1 TreeNode {text = "Trees",
                 children = [grandchild1,grandchild2]};
grandchild1 TreeNode {text = "Dogwood"};
grandchild2 TreeNode {text = "<i>Pine</i>"};

child2 TreeNode {text = "Vehicles",
                 children = [grandchild3, grandchild4]};
grandchild3 TreeNode {text = "Cars",
                      children = [ggc1, ggc2, ggc3]};
ggc1 TreeNode {text = "Sedan"};
ggc2 TreeNode {text = "SUV"};
ggc3 TreeNode {text = "Truck"};
grandchild4 TreeNode {text = "Bike"};
// Define a behavior for the nodes of the tree
function clickBehavior (node TreeNode in)
    node.onClick ::= click;
end
function click (e Event in)
    n INT = (e.widget as TreeNode).children.getSize();
    if( n  )
        myTextLable.text = "This is a Parent node. " +
                           "Number of children is: " + n;
    else
        myTextLable.text = "This is NOT a parent Node!!!";
    end
end
```

Listing B.1: Tree Widget Code

Delegates

The delegate TreeNodeBehavior gives the prototype for each function referenced by the behaviors array.

```
Delegate TreeNodeBehavior(node TreeNode) end
```

Interactive Widgets

Widgets of the following type are used for most user-code interaction: BidiTextArea, BidiTextField, Button, Checkbox, Combo, Hyperlink, List, ListMulti, Menu, PasswordTextField, RadioGroup, TextArea, and TextField.

BidiTextArea

A bidi text area widget defines a rectangle containing one or more lines of bidirectional text. For details, see the entry for TextArea.

BidiTextField

A bidi text field widget defines a rectangle containing a single line of bidirectional text. For details, see the entry for TextField.

Button

A button elicits a user click and can respond by invoking a function.

Fields

text   Text to display on the button.

           String.

Graphic and Code

click this

Figure B.19: Button Widget

```
myButton Button{text = "click this",
                onClick ::= myButtonClicked};

function myButtonClicked(e Event in)
   myButton.text = "click again";
end
```

CheckBox

A check box displays a true-false option and can respond to input by invoking a function.

Fields

text   Text to display to the right of the check box. Can be an HTML fragment

                String.

selected   Indicates whether the box is checked.

                Boolean. Default is false; the check box is not selected.

Graphic and Code

☐Box **Unchecked**

Figure B.20: CheckBox Widget

```
myCheckBox CheckBox{text="Box <b>Unchecked</b>",
                    onClick ::= checkBoxClicked};

function checkBoxClicked (e Event in)
   if (myCheckBox.selected)
      myCheckBox.text = "Box is Checked";
   else
      myCheckBox.text = "Box is Unchecked";
   end
end
```

Combo

A combo presents one of several selectable options and lets the user open a dropdown list to select a different option.

Fields

values   Items to display in the list.

Array of strings.

selection   Position of the selected string in the array.

Integer. Default is 1, which refers to the first string in the list.

Graphic and Code

Figure B.21: Combo Widget

```
myCombo Combo {
      values=["silver","gray","pink","salmon","yellow","orange"],
      selection = 4, onChange ::= myComboChanged};

function myComboChanged (e Event in)
   sel int = myCombo.getSelection();
   myCombo.backgroundColor = myCombo.getValues()[sel];
end
```

Hyperlink

A Web page link that, if clicked, displays the page in the same or different browser.

Fields

href   Location of the link document.

        String.

target   Specifies the window in which to open the document.

        One of the following strings:
           "_top"; use the current window (the default).
           "_blank"; use a new window.

text   Text to elicit the user's click. Can be an HTML fragment.

        String.

Graphic and Code

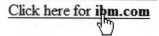

Figure B.22: Hyperlink Widget

```
myHyperlink HyperLink {
            text = "Click here for <b>ibm.com</b>",
            href = "http://www.ibm.com", target = "_blank" };
```

List

A list defines a list box from which the user can select a single entry.

Fields

selection	Position of the selected string in the array.
	Integer. Default is 1, which refers to the first string in the list.
size	the number of items to display without scrolling.
	Integer. Default is all items.
values	Items to display in the list.
	Array of strings.

Graphic and Code

Figure B.23: List Widget

```
myList List {
     values=["silver","gray","pink","salmon","yellow","orange"],
     size = 4, onChange ::= myListChanged};
div Div {width = 100, height = 100, children = [myList]};

function myListChanged (e Event in)
   sel int = myList.getSelection();
   div.backgroundColor = myList.getValues()[sel];
end
```

ListMulti

A listMulti widget defines a list box from which the user can select multiple entries.

Fields

selection   Position of the selected string in the array.

Array of integers. Default is none.

size   Number of items to display without scrolling.

Integer. Default is all items.

values   Items to display in the list.

Array of strings

Graphic and Code

Select colors from the list.

Hold the Ctrl key down to select more than one color

silver red yellow green

Figure B.24: ListMulti Widget

```
myTextLabel TextLabel {text = "Select colors from the list."};
myTextLabel2 TextLabel {
  text = "Hold the Ctrl key down to select more than one color"};
myListMulti ListMulti {
    values=["silver","gray","pink","salmon","yellow","orange"],
    onChange ::= myListMultiChanged};
resultSpan Span {};

function myListMultiChanged (e Event in)
   strColor String;
   sel int[] = myListMulti.getSelection();
   resultSpan.text = "";
   for (index int from 1 to sel.getSize() by 1)
     strColor =
             myListMulti.values[myListMulti.selection[index]];
     resultSpan.text = resultSpan.text + "  <font color=" +
                       strColor+ ">" + strColor +"</font>";
   end
end
```

Menu

A menu defines a menu bar entry such as **File**, which we'll use as an example. The **File** entry has an array of menuItems, which must be declared before the menu itself is declared. Each menuItem identifies an entry in the File menu and has the following characteristics:

- An optional *ID* for accessing a CSS style.

- A required *item*, which is a string, a widget, or an array of subordinate menuItems. That last possibility is to display a submenu name, along with an arrow for the user to click.

- A required *item-type function*, which is invoked when the menuItem is being readied for display.

- A sometimes-required *item-action function*, which responds to the user who selects the menu item. You do not specify this function in two cases; first, if you are creating a submenu; and second, if you are creating a widget such as a checkbox, which handles a user action.

The example that follows shows the creation of a single Menu widget. If you want to create a Menu bar, create a series of Menu widgets and assign them as children of the same box. You can also create a context menu in a box, as noted in the detail that follows.

Fields

menuBehaviors   Reference to an array of functions that are used to apply certain styles and events to the menu. Use the append operator (::=) to add any of the following:

basicMenu. A menu like **File**, in our example.
contextMenu. A standalone context menu.

onMenuOpen   Reference to a function that runs when the user clicks the menu; for example, to close other menus. That function is described by the delegate `MenuOpenAction`.

options	Array of items of type MenuItem.

MenuItem is as follows:

```
Record MenuItem
  ID String; // ID in a CSS file.
  item Any; // String, widget, or array of MenuItems.
  itemType menuItemType;
          // MenuBehaviors.simpleText for string
          // MenuBehaviors.widgetItem for widget
          // MenuBehaviors.subMenu for an array
  itemAction menuItemSelection; // the item-action
                                    // function
end
```

title	Text to display. Can be an HTML fragment. String.

Graphic and Code

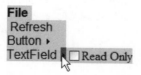

Figure B.25: Menu Widget

```
// define menu items first
fileItems menuItem[] = [
  new MenuItem {
    item = "Refresh",
    itemType = MenuBehaviors.simpleText,
    itemAction = fileCommand},
  new MenuItem {
    item = [ "Button", [
            new MenuItem {
                item = "Change Text",
                itemType = MenuBehaviors.simpleText,
                itemAction = changeText }]],
    itemType = MenuBehaviors.subMenu},
```

Listing B.2: Menu Widget Code (Part 1)

```
new MenuItem {
  item = ["TextField", [
            new MenuItem {
              item = myCheck,
              itemType = MenuBehaviors.widgetItem }] ],
  itemType = MenuBehaviors.subMenu }];

fileMenu Menu {
  menubehaviors ::= MenuBehaviors.BasicMenu,
  title = "<i>File</i>",
  options = fileItems,
  onMenuOpen = closeMenu // See MenuOpenAction delegate next};
menuBar Box{ font = "Arial", children = [fileMenu]};

myCheck CheckBox{Text = "Read Only", onChange ::= setReadOnly};
textField TextField {text = "Textfield"};
function closeMenu(keepOpen Menu in)...
function fileCommand(parentMenu Menu, item any in)...
function setReadOnly(e Event in)...
function changeText(parentMenu Menu, item any in)...
```

Listing B.3: Menu Widget Code (Part 2)

Delegates

The delegate MenuItemSelection gives the prototype for the item-action function that you code.

```
Delegate MenuItemSelection(parentMenu Menu in, Item any in) end
```

Item   The value of the string that the user clicked. That string was defined in the menuItem.

parentMenu The menu that contains the menuItem.

The delegate MenuOpenAction gives the prototype for the function that you code to respond to a menu open at run time.

```
Delegate MenuOpenAction(menu Menu in) end
```

menu   The menu being opened.

PasswordTextField

A password text field is an input field whose value is displayed as bullets, as appropriate when the user types a password.

Fields

readOnly   Indicates whether the text area is protected from user input.
Boolean. Default is false.

text   Text that is displayed as bullets in the field.
String.

Graphic and Code

Enter Password: ●●●●●●●●

Figure B.26: PasswordTextField Widget

```
PasswordPrompt span {text="Enter Password: "};
pswd PasswordTextField {readOnly=0, width=120,text="password"};
```

RadioGroup

A radio group is a set of radio buttons, each of which responds to a click by deselecting the other radio button in the same group.

Fields

groupName   Name of the group. Required for the group to exist.
String.

options   Text of a set of radio buttons.
Array of strings, one per button.

selected   Indicates which radio button is selected
String, One of the strings in the options array. Default is "".

Graphic and Code

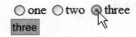

Figure B.27: RadioGroup Widget

```
result TextField {width = 30, readOnly = 1};
radioGrp RadioGroup {groupName = "radio", selected = "two",
                     options = ["one", "two", "three"],
                     onClick ::= radioGroupClicked};

function radioGroupClicked (e Event in)
    result.text = radioGrp.selected;
end
```

TextArea

A text area is a rectangle containing one or more lines of text.

Fields

numColumns	Number of columns (characters) in the rectangular area.
	Integer. Default is 20.
numRows	Number of rows to display without requiring the user to scroll.
	Integer. Default is 2.
readOnly	Indicates whether the text area is protected from user input.
	Boolean. Default is false.
text	String to display in the rectangle.
	String.

Two functions are available for this widget, neither returns a value:

- append adds content to what is already in the text area.

- setRedraw redraws the text area, as is required after you append text.

Graphic and Code

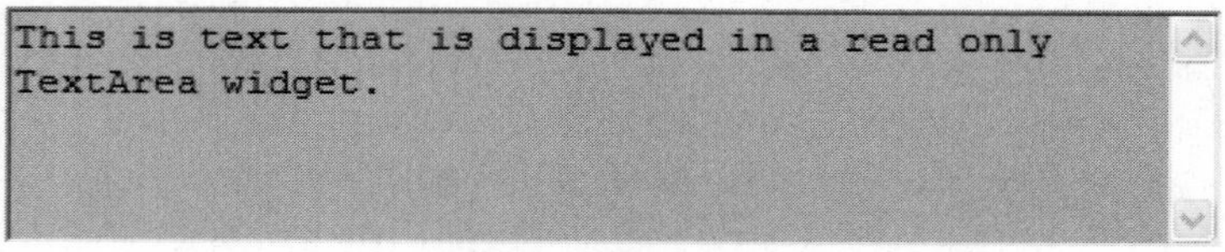

```
This is text that is displayed in a read only
TextArea widget.
```

Figure B.28: TextArea Widget

```
myTxtAtrea TextArea {numColumns = 50, numRows = 5, readOnly = 1,
                text ="This This is text that is displayed " +
                        "in a read only TextArea widget."};

function...
   myTxtArea.append ("This is some appended text");
   myTxtArea.setRedraw (true);
end
```

TextField

A text field is a text box containing a single line of text within a rectangle.

Fields

readOnly   Indicates whether the text area is protected from user input.
            Boolean. Default is false.

text   String to display.
            String.

Graphic and Code

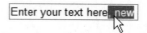

Figure B.29: TextField Widget

```
myTextField TextField {text = "Enter your text here"};
```

Hover Widgets

Widgets of the following types define a hover help; that is, a rectangle with help information, as displayed when the user hovers the mouse pointer over a widget: GridToolTip, ToolTip, and TreeToolTip.

GridTooltip

The grid tooltip defines the help displayed when the user hovers the mouse pointer over a grid cell.

Fields

provider   References a function that identifies the grid cell and returns a box for display to the user.

Name of function of type GridTooltipTextProvider.

Graphic and Code

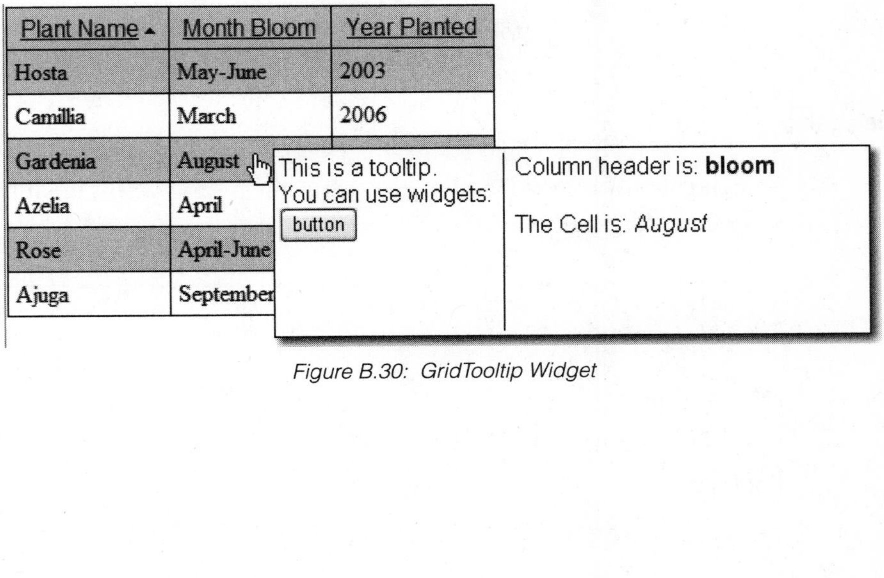

Figure B.30: GridTooltip Widget

```
myGridTooltip GridTooltip {provider = tooltipProvider,
                           tooltip.delay = 400};
PlantsGrid Grid {
  behaviors = [gridSel.enableSelection, myGridTooltip.setTooltips,
               GridBehaviors.whiteCells,
               GridBehaviors.alternatingColor],...

tooltipHTML HTML  {width=220, height=120,
                   borderLeftStyle="solid", borderLeftWidth=1,
                   paddingLeft=7, marginLeft=7 };
function tooltipProvider(row any in, fieldName String in, td Widget in)
                                                          returns(Box)
  tooltipHTML.text = "Column header is: <b>" +fieldName + "</b>"+
                     "<p> The Cell is: <i>" + td.innerText +"</i>";
  return (tooltipBox);
end

tooltipBox Box { columns=2, width=400, children = [
                new Box { columns=1, children=[
                new TextLabel { text = "This is a tooltip." },
                new TextLabel { text = "You can use widgets:" },
                new Box { columns=3, children=[
                new Button { text="button"}]}
                ]},tooltipHTML]};
```

Delegates

The delegate GridTooltipTextProvider gives the prototype for the function that you code to respond to the user's hover.

```
Delegate GridTooltipTextProvider(row any in,
                                 fieldName String in,
                                 td TD in) returns (Box)
end
```

row	Row the user is hovering over.
fieldName	Name of the column.
td	Internal widget that represents the grid cell.

To enable tooltips for a header row of the grid, use a regular tooltip. You can use a different tooltip for different header cells, or even provide different text to the same tooltip; but we offer a simple example.

Graphic and Code

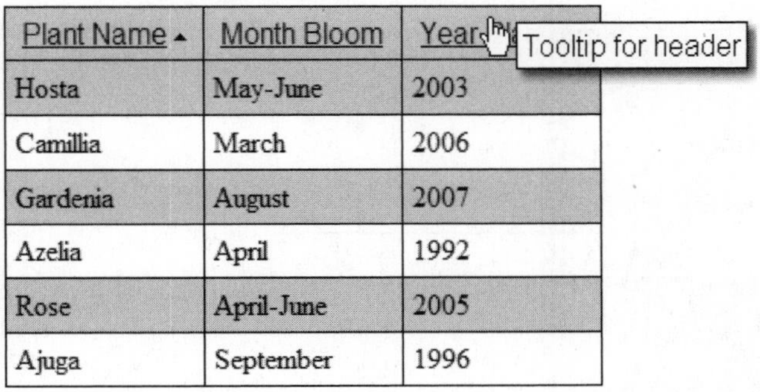

Figure B.31: Grid Widget with Header Tooltip

```
PlantsGrid Grid  {headerBehaviors = [GridBehaviors.grayCells,
                    gridSort.columnSorter, headerTooltips]...

headerTooltip Tooltip {text ="Tooltip for header"};

function headerTooltips (grid Grid in, td Widget in, row any in,
                  ignoreRowNumber int in, column GridColumn in)
    headerTooltip.enable(td);
end
```

Tooltip

A tooltip defines the help displayed when the user hovers over a widget.

Fields

text   Text to display.

            String. Default is " ".

délay   Number of milliseconds between the start of the user's hover and the display of the tip.

Integer. Default is 400.

provider   References a function that returns a box for display to the user.

Name of function of type TooltipTextProvider.

Graphic and Code

Figure B.32: Tooltip Widgets

```
myListToolTip Tooltip {Text = "list of colors", delay = 600};
myListMulti ListMulti{onChange ::= myListMultiChanged,
              values=["silver", "gray", "pink", "red", "yellow", "green"],};

function listTTprovider (widget any in) returns(Box)
  myTTspan Span {text = "Colors Selected "};
  strColor String;
  sel int[] = myListMulti.getSelection();
  for (index int from 1 to sel.getSize() by 1)
    strColor = myListMulti.values[myListMulti.selection[index]];
    myTTspan.text = myTTspan.text + "  <font color=" +strColor+
                   ">" + strColor +"</font>";
  end
  myBox Box{children = [myTTspan]};
  return (myBox);
end

function myListMultiChanged (e Event in)
  myListToolTip.provider = listTTprovider;
end

function initiallization()
  myListToolTip.enable(myListMulti);
end
```

Delegates

The delegate TooltipTextProvider gives the prototype for the function that you code to respond to the user's hover.

```
Delegate TooltipTextProvider(Widget any in) returns (Box)
end
```

Widget   Widget that the user is hovering over.

TreeTooltip

A tree tooltip defines the help displayed when the user hovers over a tree node.

Fields

provider   References a function that returns a box for display to the user. Name of function of type TreeTooltipTextProvider.

Graphic and Code

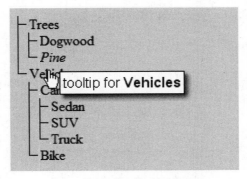

Figure B.33: TreeTooltip Widget

```
myTreeTooltip TreeTooltip {provider= showTooltip};
tr Tree {backgroundColor="#ddd", width=240, padding=9,
        behaviors = [TreeBehaviors.pointer,
                    myTreeTooltip.setTooltips,clickBehavior
                    ], children = [child1, child2]};
...
function showTooltip (node TreeNode) returns (Box)
    tooltipSpan Span {};
    tooltipBox Box {children = [tooltipSpan]};
    tooltipSpan.text = "tooltip for <b> " + node.text + "</b>";
    return (tooltipBox);
end
```

Delegates

The delegate TreeTooltipTextProvider gives the prototype for the function that you code to respond to the user's hover.

```
Delegate TreeTooltipTextProvider(node TreeNode) returns(Box)
end
```

node   Tree node that the user is hovering over.

Fields Available in Most Widgets

The following fields are available in most widgets:

ariaLive   Indicates the level of support provided for assistive technology; that is, for screen readers that are able to notify users of updates to screen regions.

ariaRole   Indicates the role specified for the widget, as used for assistive technology.

class   Identifies a CSS class used when displaying the widget.

disabled   Takes a Boolean that indicates whether the widget is disabled. A disabled widget cannot respond to events and, on most browsers, its text appears in grey.

id

Takes a string used to assign or retrieve an ID for a specific widget. You can use the ID in a cascading style sheet (CSS) to identify a specific widget.

innerHTML

Assigns or retrieves the HTML within a container; in particular, for a div, floatLeft, or floatRight.

innerText

Assigns or retrieves text within a container. You can use innerText to provide a text property that is specific to the type.

logicalParent

Is used for developing Widget types that are containers. When writing the code that adds children to the container, you set the logicalParent property so that it refers to the appropriate parent DOM element.

position

Specifies the meaning of the widget's x and y coordinates and takes one of the following values:

static

The widget's x and y coordinates are ignored, as is the default behavior. The displayed position changes if you first set the x and y values when the position value is static and then change the position value.

absolute

The widget's x and y coordinates are relative to the top left of the browser window.

relative

The widget's x and y coordinates are relative to the top left of the parent. If the widget's parent is the document element, the coordinates are relative to the top left of the viewable area of the browser.

readOnly

Takes a Boolean that indicates whether the user can change the content of a text field or text area.

tabIndex

Takes an integer that identifies the widget's placement in a tab order. The default tab order is browser specific.

x and y

Take integers that refer to the x-y coordinate of the widget. The meaning of that coordinate varies in accordance with the value of the position property.

zIndex   Takes an integer that identifies the widget's position—its
                  nearness to the front—in relation to other widgets at the
                  same x and y location. A widget with a relatively large
                  zIndex value (for example, 4) is closer to the front than a
                  widget with a relatively small zIndex value (for example,
                  2). The zIndex value has no effect when the value of
                  position is static.

Endnotes

Preface

1. N.G. Carr, "IT Doesn't Matter," *Harvard Business Review* (May 2003), 41-49.

2. Ibid., 43.

3. Ibid., 43.

Introduction

1. R. Nolan and F.W. McFarlan, "Information Technologies and the Board of Directors," *Harvard Business Review* (October 2005), 96-106.

2. Ibid., 98.

3. Ibid., 100.

4. Ibid., 100.

5. Ibid., 101.

6. Ibid., 100-101.

7. Ibid., 101.

8. N.G. Carr, "IT Doesn't Matter," *Harvard Business Review*, (May 2003), 42.

9. Ibid., 48.

10. John Seely Brown and John Hagel III, letter to the editor published in "Does IT Matter, An HBR Debate," *Harvard Business Review* (June 2003).

11. Ibid.

12. Neilsen Online, "Press Center: Free Data," http://www.nielsen-online.com (accessed February 20, 2009).

13. Jesse Alpert & Nissan Hajaj, "We knew the web was big...", The Official Google Blog, comment posted July 25, 2008, http://googleblog.blogspot.com/2008/07/ we-knew-web-was-big.html.

14. Robert Cailliau, "A Little History of the World Wide Web," World Wide Web Consortium, 1995, http://www.w3.org/History.html.

15. The term *Web 2.0* was coined by O'Reilly Media Vice President Dale Doherty during preparations for the 2004 Web 2.0 Conference. For details, see Tim O'Reilly, "What is Web 2.0", O'Reilly Media website, comment posted September 30, 2005, http://www.oreillynet.com/ pub/a/oreilly/tim/news/2005/09/30/what-is-web-20.html.

16. This section includes material first published in Ben Margolis with Joseph L. Sharpe, *SOA for the Business Developer* (Lewisville: MC Press, 2007).

17. Roger Smith, "InformationWeek Analytics: State of SOA," Information Week, February 12, 2009, http://www.informationweek.com/ showArticle.jhtml?articleID=214501922.

18. "SOA Adoption Surges," Computer Economics (January 2009), http://www.computereconomics.com/article.cfm?id=1423.

19. Gartner Group, "Cloud Computing: Defining and Describing an Emerging Phenomenon," June 17, 2008, ID number G00156220.

20. Stephen Baker. "Google and the Wisdom of Clouds," Business Week, December 13, 2007, http://www.businessweek.com/magazine/ content/07_52/b4064048925836.htm.

21. Randy H. Katz, "Tech Titans Building Boom," IEEE Spectrum Online (February 2009), http://www.spectrum.ieee.org/feb09/7327.

22. Frederick P. Brooks, "No Silver Bullet: Essence and Accidents of Software Engineering," *Computer*. 20, no. 4 (April 1987), 10-19.

23. Scott W. Ambler and Per Kroll, "Best practices for lean development governance, Part I: Principles and organization," IBM DeveloperWorks, June 2007. http://www.ibm.com/developerworks/rational/library/jun07/kroll/.

24. For example, see VersionOne, "State of Agile Development Survey," August 2008, http://www.versionone.com/agilesurvey; Scott Ambler, "IT Project Success Rates Survey," August 2007, http://www.ambysoft.com/surveys/success2007.html; and Shine Technologies, "Agile Methodologies Survey Results," January 2003, http://www.agilealliance.com/show/1121.

25. Frederick P. Brooks, "No Silver Bullet: Essence and Accidents of Software Engineering," *Computer*. 20, no. 4 (April 1987), 10-19.

26. Umesh Ballur, "Lecture 26." YouTube, http://www.youtube.com/watch?v=jRs-aFETAXY.

27. Much of the material in the sections on machine, assembly, and third-generation languages is based on David S. Frankel, *Model Driven Architecture* (Indianapolis: Wiley Publishing, 2003), 3-30.

28. Ibid., 7.

29. Frederick P. Brooks, "No Silver Bullet: Essence and Accidents of Software Engineering," *Computer*. 20, no. 4 (April 1987), 10-19.

30. David S. Frankel, *Model Driven Architecture* (Indianapolis: Wiley Publishing, 2003), 13.

31. Frederick P. Brooks, Jr., *The Mythical Man-Month* (Addison-Wesley Publishing Company, 1982 reprint), 118.

32. Ibid.

33. At this writing, you can hear Johnny Mercer or others perform the work by going to the following Web site and searching for the title "Ac-cent": http://ww.mplcommunications.com/search.asp.

34. Frederick P. Brooks, "No Silver Bullet: Essence and Accidents of Software Engineering," Computer, Vol. 20, no. 4 (April 1987), 10-19.

35. Ibid.

36. Monuments to Stubbornness," Time Magazine, July 9, 1965, http://www.time.com/time/magazine/article/ 0,9171,833932,00.html?promoid=googlep.

Web 2.0 and Network Effects

1. Social Networking's New Global Footprint," Nielsen Wire blog, March 9, 2009, http://blog.nielsen.com/nielsenwire/global/ social-networking-new-global-footprint/.

2. For an overview, see M. E. J. Newman, "The Structure and Function of Complex Networks," SIAM Review 45 (2003), 167-256, http://arxiv.org/abs/cond-mat/0303516.

3. W. Brian Arthur, "Myths and Realities of the High Tech Economy," Talk given at Credit Suisse First Boston Thought Leader Forum, September 10, 2000, http://www.santafe.edu/~wbarthur/Papers/Papers.html.

4. Michael J. Mauboussin, "Exploring Network Economics," October 11, 2004, Mauboussin on Strategy, http://www.lmcm.com/pdf/ ExploringNetworkEconomicsRevised.pdf. See also Simeon Simeonov, "Metcalfe's Law: More Misunderstood than Wrong," HighContrast blog, comment posted July 26, 2006, http://simeons.wordpress.com/2006/07/26/ metcalfes-law-more-misunderstood-than-wrong.

5. David P. Reed, "That Sneaky Exponential—Beyond Metcalfe's Law to the Power of Community Building," Web papers, http://www.reed.com/gfn/docs/reedslaw.html.

6. James Hendler and Jennifer Golbeck. "Metcalfe's Law, Web 2.0, and the Semantic Web," Journal of Web Semantics 6, no. 1 (February 2008), 14-20, http://portal.acm.org/citation.cfm?id=1346698.

7. Shivaram Rajgopal, Mohan Venkatachalam, and Suresh Kotha, "The Value Relevance of Network Advantages: The Case of E-Commerce Firms," Journal of Accounting Research, 41, no. 1 (March 2003), 136-137.

8. W. Brian Arthur, "Myths and Realities of the High Tech Economy," Talk given at Credit Suisse First Boston Thought Leader Forum, September 10, 2000, 2, http://www.santafe.edu/~wbarthur/Papers/Papers.html.

9. Ibid., 1.

10. Michael J. Mauboussin, "Exploring Network Economics," Mauboussin on Strategy, October 11, 2004, http://www.lmcm.com/pdf/ ExploringNetworkEconomicsRevised.pdf.

11. Ibid., 6.

12. Ibid, 11.

13. This list relies on David Tebbutt, "CIO Technology Analysis: The business value of collaboration software", CIO, February 16, 2009, http://www.cio.co.uk/concern/change/features/ index.cfm?articleid=804. Tebbutt interviewed Luis Suarez, a social-computing expert at IBM.

14. Jeff Howe, "Crowdsourcing Trailer," YouTube, http://www.youtube.com/watch?v=TCM7w11Ultk. Howe introduced the word in "The Rise of Crowdsourcing," Wired, June 2006.

15. Christopher Koch, "IT's Role in Collaboration and Innovation at Procter & Gamble", CIO, February 1, 2007, http://www.cio.com/article/print/28499.

16. Amy Shuen, *Web 2.0: A Strategy Guide*, (Sebastopol: O'Reilly Media, 2008), xiii. See also the Innocentive Web site: http://www.innocentive.com/servlets/project/ProjectInfo.po.

17. John K. Borchardt, "Outside Help," Mechanical Engineering, February 2009, http://memagazine.asme.org/Articles/2009/February/ Outside_Help.cfm.

18. Tom Funk, *Web 2.0 and Beyond* (Westport: Praeger Publishers, 2009), 65-71.

19. Jeremiah Owyang, "Web Strategy: How to Evolve Your Irrelevant Corporate Website," Web Strategy by Jeremiah Owyang blog, comment posted May 29, 2007, http://www.web-strategist.com/blog/2007/05/29/web-strategy- how-to-evolve-your-irrelevant-corporate-website/

20. Tom Funk, *Web 2.0 and Beyond* (Westport: Praeger Publishers, 2009), 93-102.

21. The term *freememium* was introduced in a response to Fred Wilson, "My Favorite Business Model," A VC blog, comment posted May 23, 2006, http://www.avc.com/a_vc/2006/03/my_favorite_bus.html.

22. Tom Funk, *Web 2.0 and Beyond* (Westport: Praeger Publishers, 2009), 84-85.

23. Ibid., 60. See also "What is CPM-based Advertising?," All Business, http://www.allbusiness.com/marketing/advertising- internet-advertising/2646-1.html.

24. John K. Borchardt, "Outside Help," Mechanical Engineering, February 2009, http://memagazine.asme.org/Articles/2009/February/ Outside_Help.cfm.

25. Chris Anderson, *The Long Tail* (New York: Hyperion, 2008).

26. Ibid., 23.

27. Tim O'Reilly, "What is Web 2.0", O'Reilly Media website, comment posted September 30, 2005, http://www.oreillynet.com/pub/a/oreilly/tim/news/2005/09/30/what-is-web-20.html.

28. For details on Creative Commons, see http://www.creativecommons.org. The quote is from the organization's About page: http://www.creativecommons.org/about.

Introduction to Web Security

1. "IBM Internet Security Systems XForce® 2008 Trend & Risk Report" (IBM Global Technology Services, January 2009), http://www.ibm.com/services/us/iss/xforce/trendreports/xforce-2008-annual-report.pdf.

2. Steve Christey and Robert A. Martin, "Vulnerability Type Distributions in CVE" (The Mitre Corporation, May 22, 2007), http://www.cve.mitre.org/docs/vuln-trends/index.html.

3. "Stung by Cyber Warfare, Estonia, NATO Allies to Sign Deal on Cyber Defense Center," International Herald Tribune, May 14, 2008, http://www.iht.com/articles/ap/2008/05/14/europe/EU-GEN-Estonia-NATO-Cyberterrorism.php. Also see "Kremlin Loyalist Says Launch Estonia Cyber Attack", Javno, March 12. 2009, http://www.javno.com/en-world/kremlin-loyalist-says-launch-estonia-cyber-attack_242190.

4. Open Web Application Security Project, "OWASP Security Spending Benchmarks Report," March 2009, http://www.owasp.org/images/b/b2/OWASP_SSB_Project_Report_March_2009.pdf.

5. Michael Howard and David LeBlanc, *Writing Secure Code* (Redmond: Microsoft Press, 2003), 83-86.

6. T. Dierks and E. Rescorla, "The Transport Layer Security (TLS) Protocol Version 1.2" (The Internet Engineering Task Force, August 2008), http://www.rfc-editor.org/rfc/rfc5246.txt.

7. Section of Science and Technology, American Bar Association, "Digital Signature Guidelines Tutorial," undated, http://www.abanet.org/scitech/ec/isc/dsg-tutorial.html.

8. Ibid.

9. For an example of beneficial code injection, see Jeff Rudesyle, "Greasemonkey: Code Injection is Bliss," Digital Web Magazine, February 12, 2008, http://www.digital-web.com/articles/ greasemonkey_code_interjection.

10. Michael Howard and David LeBlanc, *Writing Secure Code* (Redmond: Microsoft Press, 2003), 93-95.

11. Robert Hurlbut, "DREAD is dead", Robert Hurlbut's .NET Blog, comment posted November 15, 2005, http://weblogs.asp.net/rhurlbut/archive/2005/11/15/430662.aspx. See also David LeBlanc, "DREADful", David LeBlanc's Web Log, comment posted August 13, 2007, http://blogs.msdn.com/ david_leblanc/archive/2007/08/13/dreadful.aspx.

Service-Oriented Architecture

1. This chapter includes material first published in Ben Margolis with Joseph L. Sharpe, *SOA for the Business Developer* (Lewisville: MC Press, 2007).

2. Leonard Richardson and Sam Ruby, *Restful Web Services* (Sebastopol: O'Reilly Media, 2007), 5.

3. For a review of these styles, see Leonard Richardson and Sam Ruby, *Restful Web Services* (Sebastopol: O'Reilly Media, 2007), 13-18.

4. REST services conform to a set of principles detailed in the following source: Roy Thomas Fielding, "Architectural Styles and the Design of Network-Based Software Architectures" (PhD diss., University of California, Irvine, 2000), http://www.ics.uci.edu/ ~fielding/pubs/dissertation/top.htm. In particular, see Chapter 5.

5. Leonard Richardson and Sam Ruby, *Restful Web Services*, (Sebastopol: O'Reilly Media, 2007), 299-314.

Overview of Generation

1. Clarke, Arthur C., *Profiles of the Future* (London: Pan, 1962).

Index

A

Abstraction, 18–24
Accentuate the Positive, 25
Add statement, 226, 227, 231
Advertising revenue, 37
Agile development, 16–17
AJAX, 11
Alias, 170
Allocation, 184
And operator, 200
Annotation fields
  bindingKey, 165
  defaultSelectCondition, 234, 235
  keyItems, 231
  tableNames, 231
Annotations
  Alias, 170
  BindService, 165
  Column, 231
  defined, 151
  DisplayName, 171, 255
  DisplayUse, 255
  field level, 171
  FileName, 228
  InputRequired, 171
  MaxSize, 187
  overview, 170–173
  syntax, 171–172
  ThrowNrfEofExceptions, 237
  ValidationOrder, 256
  ValidatorFunction, 256
Apache
  Derby, 88
AppendElement, 186, 198, 199
Application scope, 265
Application server
  defined, 61
Arrays
  dynamic, 186–187, 235–236
  literals, 186
  overview, 186–188
  structure field, 188
Assignment, 189–199
  array of records, 197–199
  compatibility, 202
  record with reference variable, 196–197
  reference variable to reference variable, 191–194
  reference variable to value variable, 194–195
  value variable to reference variable, 189–191
  value variable to value variable, 189
Asymmetric cryptosystem, 51–52
Authentication
  basic, 62, 62
  defined, 60
  form based, 62, 62
authorization, 60

B

Base URI, 139–141

Basic authentication, 62
BasicRecord stereotype, 153
BasicTable stereotype, 158
Batch Message Processing program (BMP), 87
BidiTextArea, 293
BidiTextField, 293
Binary-exchange services, 75–76
Binding
    actions in EGL JSF, 253
    data in EGL JSF, 252–253
    in EGL deployment descriptor, 137
BindingKey annotation field, 165
BindService annotation, 165

BIRT. *See* Business Intelligence
    and Reporting Tools
Blog, 9
BMP. *See* Batch Message Processing program
Box, 278
Brand image, 36
Brokerage revenue, 37
Build, 147
Build descriptor, 147
Build parts, 147
Build path, 178
Business Intelligence and Reporting Tools
    (BIRT)
    example, 239–243
    overview, 93–94
    Web site, 272
Button, 293–294

C

CA. *See* Certificate Authority
Call statement, 216
Callback function, 110
Called program, 161
Case statement, 212–213
Certificate Authority (CA), 54–55
Certificate. *See* Digital certificate
CheckBox, 294–295
CICS. *See*
    Customer Information Control System
Cipher, 50

Clean option, 147
Client-side
    security, 58–60
Close statement, 226
Cloud computing, 15
Cloudscape, 88
COBOL, generated, 84, 86, 87
Code injection, 56–57
Code integration, 94–95
Collaboration, 35–36
Column annotation, 231
Combo, 295–296
Commit, 225–226
Compatibility rules, 202
Compilation, 146
Compiler, 146
Complex types, 150
Component tree, 263–264
Conditional processing, 211–213
Console UI, 91
Constants, 181
Container
    server as, 61
Container widgets, 277–284
    Box, 278
    Div, 279
    FloatLeft, 280–281
    FloatRight, 281–283
    Grouping, 283–284
Container-managed authentication, 62
Continue statement, 214
Controller
    in EGL JSF, 262
    in Rich UI, 113–119
Creative Commons, 41
Cross-site integration, 10
Cross-site scripting (XSS), 58–59
Cryptosystem, 50–52
CSS Style, 273–275
Customer Information Control System
    (CICS), 86, 87
    file types, 89
    Web services, 131–133

D

Data access, 225–237
Data dictionary, 151
Data in transit, 47–55
Data items
   defined, 151
   overview, 152
Data Language/I (DL/I), 88
Data ownership, 39
Data packets, 47–50
Data parts, 151
Data tables
   compared to dictionaries, 159
   defined, 151
   overview, 158–159
Data types, 149–159
   complex, 150
   defined, 149
   instances of, 150
   primitive, 150, 151
   reference, 183
   value, 183
Databases
   hierarchical, 88
   relational, 87–88, 230–236
DB2 Universal Database (DB2 UDB), 87
Debugger, 84
Default package, 179
DefaultSelectCondition annotation field, 234, 235
Delegate parts, 167–169
Delete statement, 226
Denial of service, 47
Deployment descriptor
   EGL, 136–137, 164
Deployment wizard, 134
Dictionaries
   compared to data tables, 159
Dictionary parts, 151, 156–157
Digest, 53
Digital certificate, 54–55
Digital signature, 52–54
Direct sales, 37–39
DisplayName annotation, 171, 255

DisplayUse annotation, 255
Div, 279
DL/I. *See* Data Language/I
Document element, 101
Document Object Model (DOM), 99–103
Dojo, 90
DOM. *See* Document Object Model
Domains, 22
DREAD, 65–66
Drive-by download, 59
Dynamic
   access, 202–205
   arrays, 186–187, 235–236
Dynamic Web page, 250

E

Eclipse, 83, 272
EGL
   benefits of, 22–24, 25, 59–60, 83–85
   build, 147
   build path, 178
   Cafe, 271
   compilation, 146, 148
   customer experience, 27
   data types, 149–159
   defined, 83–85
   deployment descriptor, 136–137
   integration with existing code, 94–95
   JSF handler, 251–260
   logic parts, 159–165
   prototype parts, 165–169
   runtime environments, 85–87
   services
      EGL, 76, 92, 137
      EGL REST, 79, 92, 139
   supported technologies, 85–94
   text reporting
      example, 243–247
      overview, 94
   use in MDD, 154
   user interface parts, 169–170
Eglpath, 179
Elevation of privilege, 47
Else statement, 212

Embedded handlers, 109–110
Encryption, 50–55
End-to-end processing, 133–136
Enterprise language, 22–24
    disruptiveness, 26
    flaws of abstraction, 27
    inhibiting innovation, 26–27
    old news, 28
    overview, 22–24
Enterprise mashup, 40
Entry point, 133
Equality operator, 200
Escape character, 229–230
Exception handling, 218–224
Exceptions record stereotype, 153
Execute statement, 226
Exit statement, 215
Expressions
    name resolution, 200–202
    overview, 199–200
ExternalType parts, 167

F

Factory mode, 5
FastPath, 87
Field-level annotations, 171
File access, 227–230
FileName annotation, 228
Firewall, 59
FloatLeft, 280–281
FloatRight, 281–283
For statement, 213–214
ForEach statement, 226, 233–235
Form
    print, 94
    text, 91
Form parts, 169
Form processing
    in Rich UI, 113–119
Form-based authentication, 62
Forward statement, 216
Framework, 261–262
Freemium, 37
Functions

callback, 110
in logic parts, 159
invocation of, 214–215
onException, 110
parameter modifiers, 160–161

G

Generalized Sequential Access Method
    (GSAM), 89
Generatable
    defined, 159
    logic parts, 160
Generation
    COBOL, 84
    defined, 84–85
    Java, 84
    overview, 145–148
Get statement, 226, 227, 231
Greater-than operator, 200
Grid, 284–286
GridTooltip, 305–307
Grouping, 283–284
GSAM. *See* Generalized Sequential Access
    Method

H

Handlers, 161
History of software, 18–21
Host variables, 57
Hover widgets, 305–310
    GridTooltip, 305–307
    Tooltip, 307–309
    TreeTooltip, 309–310
HTML. *See* Hypertext Markup Language
HTTP, 49–50
    port, 141
Hyperlink, 296
Hypertext Markup Language (HTML)
    generated, 84
    widget, 287–288

I

I/O object, 227

IBM i, 86
    access of programs as Web services, 133
    logical files, 89
    physical files, 89
IBM Toolbox for Java, 93
Identifiers
    local, 159
    private, 162
    program global, 159
    run-unit global, 162
If statement, 212
Image, 288–289
Import statement, 177
IMS Connector for Java, 93
IMS. *See* Information Management System
In operator, 200
Indexed files, 88
Inequality operator, 200
Infobus, 127–130
Information disclosure, 46
Information Management System (IMS), 86
    BMP, 87
    FastPath, 87
    Message Processing Program (MPP), 87
    message queues, 89
Information widgets, 284–293
    Grid, 284–286
    HTML, 287–288
    Image, 288–289
    Shadow, 289–290
    Span, 290
    TextLabel, 291
    Tree, 291–293
Informix, 88
InputRequired annotation, 171
InsertElement, 186, 199
Instance, 150
Instant messaging, 9
Integrating code, 94–95
Interactive Web sites
    benefits, 35–39
    overview, 9–10
Interactive widgets, 293–304
    BidiTextArea, 293

BidiTextField, 293
Button, 293–294
CheckBox, 294–295
Combo, 295–296
Hyperlink, 296
List, 297
ListMulti, 297–298
Menu, 299–301
PasswordTextField, 302
RadioGroup, 302–303
TextArea, 303–304
TextField, 304
Interface code, 93
Interface parts
    overview, 166–167
Internationalization, 119–120
IR files, 147
Isa operator, 157
IT as a commodity, 6–7

J
Java Database Connectivity (JDBC), 88
Java Enterprise Edition (JEE), 61
Java Platform, Enterprise Edition (JEE)
    application client, 86
    defined, 86
    Enterprise JavaBean stateful session bean, 86
    platforms, 86
    Web application, 86
Java Platform, Standard Edition (JSE)
    defined, 85
    platforms, 85
Java wrapper, 94–95
JavaScript
    defined, 90
JavaServer Faces (JSF), 249–269
    and Rich UI, 251
    component tree, 263–264
    defined, 90–91
    life cycle, 265–269
    overview, 249–269
    specification, 272
    tags, 262–263
    weaknesses, 251

JavaServer Faces (JSF), *continued*
    Web site, 262
JSF handler, 251–260
JSF. *See* JavaServer Faces

K

Key fields, 231
KeyItems annotation field, 231, 234

L

LDAP-compliant server, 60
Less-than operator, 200
Libraries
    system, 217
Libraries, *continued*
    use in Rich UI, 112
Library parts, 161, 162–163
List, 297
ListMulti, 297–298
Local identifiers, 159
Locale, 120
Logic parts, 159–165
Logical files, 89, 228
Logical unit of work, 225–226
Long Tail, 37–39
Loop control, 213–214
Loose coupling, 72–73

M

Main program, 161
Man in the middle (MITM), 48, 57
Mashups, 40–41
MatchInvalidTable stereotype, 158
MatchValidTable stereotype, 158
MaxSize annotation, 187
MDD. *See* Model Driven Development
Menu, 299–301
Message Processing program (MPP), 87
Message queues
    IMS, 89
    WebSphere MQ, 88
Microsoft SQL Server, 88
MITM. *See* Man in the middle

Model
    in EGL JSF, 264–265
    in Rich UI, 113–119
Model Driven Development (MDD), 154
Model of format, 161
Model, View, Controller (MVC)
    in EGL JSF, 261
    in Rich UI, 113–119
    overview, 112–113
Modifiers, 160–161
Move statement, 193–194, 209–211
MPP. *See* Message Processing program
MsgTable stereotype, 158
Multilingual, 119–120
MVC. *See* Model, View, Controller

N

Name resolution, 200–202
Native programs, 94
Network
    defined, 29
    effect, 30–35
    social, 30–35
    technological, 29–30
Network communication, 93
New operator, 184
Non-structured records, 154
Not operator, 200

O

OnConstruction function, 256
OnException blocks, 218–220
OnException function, 110
OnPrerender function, 256
Open statement, 226, 233–235
Operators
    and, 200
    equality, 200
    greater than, 200
    in, 200
    inequality, 200
    isa, 157
    less than, 200

new, 184
not, 200
or, 200
Or operator, 200
Oracle, 88

P

Packages
    default, 179
    overview, 176–179
Packets, 47–50
Page Data view, 258–260
Page flow
    in Rich UI, 120–126, 130
Parameter modifiers, 160–161
Parsing, 57
Parts
    Build descriptor, 147
    DataItem, 151, 152
    DataTable, 151, 158–159
    Delegate, 167–169
    Dictionary, 151, 156–157
    ExternalType, 167
    Form, 169
    FormGroup, 170
    Handler, 161, 239–247, 251–253
    Interface, 166–167
    Library, 161, 162–163
    Program, 161
    Record, 151, 153–156
    Resource associations, 228–229
    Service, 161, 163–165
    static, 151
PasswordTextField, 302
Physical files, 89, 228
PKI. *See* Public Key Infrastructure
Precedence rules, 200
Prepare statement, 226
Primitive types, 150, 151
Print form, 94, 170
Private identifiers, 162
Profiles, 10
Program
    called, 161

main, 161
    parts, 161
Program-global identifiers, 159
programmableWeb.com, 40
Programming models, 98–99
Projects, 134
Propagation, 221–222
Property field, 171
Protocol
    analyzer, 48
    defined, 164
    HTTPS, 49–52
    TCP/IP, 48–50
Protocols
    HTTP, 141
Prototype parts, 165–169
Public key cryptography, 52
Public Key Infrastructure (PKI), 54–55

Q

Quality interfaces, 41–43
Quality of service
    defined, 72

R

RA. *See* Registration Authority
RadioGroup, 302–303
RangeChkTable stereotype, 158
Rational products, 95
Really Simple Syndication (RSS), 9
Record parts, 151, 153–156
Record stereotypes, 153–154
Reference
    compatibility, 202
    types, 183
    variables, 182
Relational databases, 230–236
Relative files, 88
Reliance on IT, 3–6
RemoveElement, 186
Replace statement, 226
Report production, 93–94
Reporting, 239–247

Repudiation, 46
Request scope, 265
Resource associations, 228–230
REST services, 76–77, 78–79, 92, 139–141
REST-RPC services, 77, 79
Return statement, 215
Revenue from Web sites, 37–39
Reverse cipher, 51
RIA. *See* Rich Internet Application (RIA)
Rich Internet Application (RIA)
  benefits, 39–44
  deployment, 44
  overview, 10–12
Rich UI
  and EGL JSF, 251
  deployment wizard, 134
  editor, 107–109
  handler, 104–106
    embedded, 109–110
  proxy, 61
  security, 63–65
  service access, 110–111
  use of JavaScript libraries, 90
  widgets, 273–312
Risk, 65–67
Rollback, 225–226
Root CA, 55
RSS. *See* Really Simple Syndication
Run unit
  global identifiers, 162
  overview, 161–162

S

Scope
  application, 265
  request, 265
  session, 265
Secure Sockets Layer (SSL) *See* Transport
  Layer Security
Security, 45–67
  client, 58–60
  data in transit, 47–55
  for Rich UI, 63–65
  risk, 65–67

  server, 55–57
  threats, 46–47
  trends, 45–46
Sequential files, 88
Server-side
  security, 55–57
Service client bindings, 137
Service Level Agreement (SLA), 74
Service parts, 161, 163–165
Service registry, 74
ServiceLib.serviceExceptionHandler, 110
Service-oriented application, 69–70
Service-oriented architecture (SOA)
  architectural styles, 76–77
  aspects of services
    contract, 71–72
    elementary access details, 71, 137–141
    implementation, 70
  loose coupling, 72–73
  overview, 12–15
  Service Level Agreement (SLA), 74
  service registry, 74
  support for, 91–92, 131–142
Services
  access from Rich UI, 110–111
  deployment of EGL-generated, 134, 141–142
  EGL, 76, 92, 137
  EGL REST, 92, 139
  on CICS, 131–133
  REST, 76–77, 78–79, 92, 139–141
  REST-RPC, 77, 79
  SOAP, 77–78, 91–92, 138–139
  Web and binary-exchange, 75–76
Session scope, 265
Set statement, 211
SetError, 258
Set-value blocks
  nested, 175–176
  with annotations, 171
  with reference variables, 185
  with runtime values, 174–176
Shadow, 289–290
Silverlight, 90
Simple property, 171

SLA. *See* Service Level Agreement
SOA. *See* Service-oriented architecture
SOAP services, 77–78, 91, 92, 138–139
Social bookmarking, 10
Social network, 30–35
Social site, 9
Software Development Kit (SDK)
   defined, 85
   eglpath, 178
   example, 85
Sources of information, 271–272
Span, 290
Spoofing identity, 46
SQL
   defined, 87
   statements, 231–233
SQLRecord stereotype, 153, 230–236
Standalone Web server. *See* Web server
Standard output, 160
StartTransaction, 161
Statements
   add, 226, 227, 231
   call, 216
   case, 212–213
   close, 226
   continue, 214
   delete, 226
   else, 212
   execute, 226
   exit, 215
   for, 213–214
   forEach, 226, 233–235
   forward, 216
   get, 226, 227, 231
   if, 212
   import, 177
   move, 193–194, 209–211
   open, 226, 233–235
   prepare, 226
   replace, 226
   return, 215
   set, 211
   throw, 224
   transfer, 216

   try, 218–220
   use, 179–180
   while, 214
Static access, 202–205
Static part, 151
Stereotypes
   data table, 158
   defined, 154, 173
   record, 153–154
   syntax, 173–174
Strategic mode, 6
STRIDE, 46–47
Structured Query Language (SQL)
   security, 56, 57
Structured records, 154–156
Structure-field arrays, 188
Styles, 273–275
Support mode, 4
Symmetric cryptosystem, 51–52
SysLib.commit, 226
SysLib.rollback, 226
SysLib.setError, 258
System libraries, 217

T
TableNames annotation field, 231
Tagging, 9
Tampering with data, 46
TCP/IP, 48–50
Technical domains, 22
Technological network, 29–30
Technology domains, 22
Text form, 91, 170
Text reporting
   example, 243–247
   overview, 94
Text UI
   overview, 91
TextArea, 303–304
TextField, 304
TextLabel, 291
Threats, 46–47
Throw statement, 224
ThrowNrfEofExceptions, 237

Tiers, 97–98
TLS. *See* Transport Layer Security
Tooltip, 307–309
Transfer of control
    out of a program, 216
    within a program, 214–215
Transfer statement, 216
Transport Layer Security (TLS), 49–52, 62
Tree, 291–293
TreeTooltip, 309–310
Try statement, 218–220
Turnaround mode, 5

U

UML. *See* Unified Modeling Language
Unified Modeling Language (UML), 154
URI template, 140–141
Use statement, 179–180
User interface parts, 169–170

V

Validation
    in EGL JSF, 267–268
    in Rich UI, 116–119
ValidationOrder annotation, 256, 258
ValidatorFunction annotation, 256
Value types, 183
Value variables, 182
Value-binding expression, 263
Variables
    arrays, 186–188
    assignment, 189–199
    dynamic access, 202–205
    initialization, 183–184
    local, 159
    overview, 182–184
    private, 162
    program global, 159
    reference, 182
    run-unit global, 162
    static access, 202–205
    value, 182
VgLib.startTransaction, 161

View
    in EGL JSF, 262–264
    in Rich UI, 113–119
Virtual Storage Access Method (VSAM), 89
Virtual world, 9

W

Web 2.0
    overview, 8–12
Web page
    dynamic, 250
    static, 250
Web security, 45–67
Web server
    defined, 61
Web service deployment, 137, 142
Web services
    and binary-exchange services, 75–76
    on CICS, 131–133
Web Services Description Language (WSDL),
    77–78
Web transaction, 91
WebSphere MQ, 88
WebSphere Unit Test Environment, 85
While statement, 214
Widgets, 276–312
    container widgets, 277–284
        Box, 278
        Div, 279
        FloatLeft, 280–281
        FloatRight, 281–283
        Grouping, 283–284
    hover widgets, 305–310
        GridTooltip, 305–307
        Tooltip, 307–309
        TreeTooltip, 309–310
    information widgets, 284–293
        Grid, 284–286
        HTML, 287–288
        Image, 288–289
        Shadow, 289–290
        Span, 290
        TextLabel, 291
        Tree, 291–293

interactive widgets, 293–304
    BidiTextArea, 293
    BidiTextField, 293
    Button, 293–294
    CheckBox, 294–295
    Combo, 295–296
    Hyperlink, 296
    List, 297
    ListMulti, 297–298
    Menu, 299–301
    PasswordTextField, 302
    RadioGroup, 302–303
    TextArea, 303–304
    TextField, 304
Wiki, 9
Wizard, 83
Workbench, 85
WriteStdOut, 160
WSDL. *See* Web Services Description Language

X

XSS. *See* Cross-site scripting

Z

z/OS, 86–87
    batch, 86
z/VSE, 87
    batch, 87